PRAISE FOR

INSIDE DELTA FORCE

THE STORY OF AMERICA'S ELITE COUNTERTERRORIST UNIT

"A vivid portrait of the first decade of the elite U.S. counterterrorist unit . . . Adding considerably to public knowledge about basic and sophisticated security and antiterrorism issues, his valuable book is also, after 9-11, a compellingly timely one." —*Booklist*

"A BOOK THAT YOU WON'T WANT TO PUT DOWN."
—*Playboy*

"Developed in the late 1970s, the Delta Force is so secretive that it's surprising retired Sergeant Major Haney was permitted to write this account. . . . Perfect for military enthusiasts."
—*Kirkus Reviews*

"A book that could not be more timely, written by a warrior who knows what he's talking about. Enthusiastically recommended."
—James Webb, author of *Fields of Fire* and *Lost Soldiers*

"Fascinating . . . timely . . . well-written story of the U.S. military's elite counterterrorism warriors."
—*Atlanta Journal-Constitution*

"Readers will be struck by Haney's sensitivity, depth and skepticism. . . . Eminently readable." —*Sunday Oregonian*

"Both thrilling and disturbing . . . *Inside Delta Force* gives us the hope that, if deployed properly, this is the type of force and the kind of men of which we will all be proud." —*Tampa Tribune*

A FEATURED ALTERNATE SELECTION OF MILITARY BOOK CLUB

INSIDE DELTA FORCE

INSIDE DELTA FORCE

THE STORY OF AMERICA'S ELITE COUNTERTERRORIST UNIT

FOUNDING MEMBER
ERIC L. HANEY
COMMAND SERGEANT MAJOR, USA (RET.)

DELTA TRADE PAPERBACKS

INSIDE DELTA FORCE
A Delta Book

PUBLISHING HISTORY
Delacorte Press hardcover edition published May 2002
Dell mass market edition published August 2003
Delta trade paperback edition / September 2005

Published by
Bantam Dell
A Division of Random House, Inc.
New York, New York

Book design by Glen M. Edelstein

Library of Congress Catalog Card Number: 2001058408

Delta is a registered trademark of Random House, Inc., and the colophon is a
trademark of Random House, Inc.

ISBN 0-385-33936-4

Printed in the United States of America
Published simultaneously in Canada

www.bantamdell.com

BVG   10   9   8   7

INTRODUCTION

I am a nomad, son of an ancient line of nomads. The larger part of my family line is made up of the Scots-Irish, a people descended from that peculiar mixture of the Celts of the northern British Isles and the invading Danes and Norsemen. The result was a landless, illiterate, anarchic, and warlike people who were always difficult, if not downright impossible, to govern. They were a race the British Crown rightfully viewed as dangerous rebels, and consequently exiled to the New World by the tens of thousands.

On arrival in the American colonies, these people fled as far as possible from government control, many of them crossing the Blue Ridge Mountains, and migrating from there throughout what eventually became the highlands of the southern United States. They were the original "backwoodsmen" of American history. In their new home these renegade peoples tended to travel together in inter-related clans that also married and bred quite readily with the Cherokee and Creek Indians of the region.

Both sides of my family were landless sharecroppers and mountain people as far back as I can determine. There is no written record of ancestry, for my parents were the first of our people to read and write and to own a little property. Inherited wealth may be something easily squandered, but inherited poverty is a legacy almost impossible to lose.

What did I receive from this lineage? Things I consider to be very valuable: a good raw intellect and a good tough body. A sense of independence and a realization that wherever I am is my home.

A sense of humor. A sense of personal honor that results in a touchiness common to our people. We are easily offended and prone to violence when offended. When the only thing you own is your sense of honor, you tend to protect it at all costs.

I inherited a sense of wanderlust and a curiosity about the world. I inherited a warlike attitude; we have always been good soldierly material if properly disciplined and broken in. I inherited a sense of spirituality rather than "religion," which has served me well, especially in trying times. I am self-confident and resilient. My psyche is self-cleansing. I love life.

I grew up in the mountains of north Georgia during the fifties and sixties. It was then part of the "third world," and some say it still is. Electricity came to our home when I was a young boy. Indoor plumbing followed some years later.

Though I have some fair native intelligence, I never received any direction in school and was often an indifferent student. But I loved to read and would consume all my textbooks at the start of the year and then coast after that. I preferred roaming the mountains, hunting, fishing, and exploring.

I would become the first of my family to graduate high school, and for us that was considered a pretty good achievement, as our expectations weren't very high. It isn't that my parents were against education, it's that neither of them had gone further than elementary school and they just didn't have the ability or the understanding to help.

Though we may not have been scholars, we did know how to go into the military. I had grown up listening to the war stories and tales of my family and friends and I was determined to join up just as soon as I was able. I enlisted in the Army in the spring of 1970, while still in high school, with a reporting date immediately after graduation. I fell in love with the Army as soon as I met her.

I became a professional soldier, and that is what I will be until I die. The military is a profession that brands itself on the soul and causes you forever after to view the world and all human endeavor through a unique set of mental filters. The more profound and intense the experience, the hotter the brand, and the deeper it is plunged into you. I was seared to the core of my being.

For twenty years, I served America in the most demanding and dangerous units in the United States Army. As a combat infantryman, as a Ranger, and ultimately, as a founding member and eight-year veteran of the Army's supersecret counterterrorist arm, Delta Force.

Close brutal combat puts a callous layer on each individual who undergoes the experience. With some men, their souls become trapped inside those accrued layers and they stay tightly bound up within themselves, unable or unwilling to reach outside that hard protective shell.

For others, the effect is just the opposite. That coating becomes like a looking glass, highlighting and magnifying the things that are really important in life. Every sensation becomes precious and delicious. Even the painful ones. Sometimes especially the painful ones. I feel that's what my experiences have done for me.

I hate the destructiveness and waste of warfare, but I love the sensation of it. In combat, mankind is seen in absolutes—at his very best or his very worst. There are no in-betweens. No one has a place to hide.

War has also taught me that each one of us contains every ingredient of the human recipe. By varying measure we are all cowards and brave men, thieves and honest men, selfish and selfless men, malingerers and champions, weasels and lions. The only question is how much of each attribute we allow—or force—to dominate our being.

In combat, there are no winners. The victors just happen to lose less than the vanquished. One side may impose its will on the other, but there is nothing noble or virtuous about the process. People are killed and maimed, homes and communities are destroyed, lives are shattered, families are broken apart and scattered to the wind—and just a few years later, we can barely remember why.

Above my desk is a picture taken in 1982 of B Squadron, my old Delta unit. It is one of the very few group photos ever taken within our organization. It shows a group of hardened Special Operations combat veterans. In the course of the next decade, nearly every man in that photo would be wounded at least once, some multiple times. Many were maimed or crippled for life. A number would be killed in action. All of us are freighted with the memories of those times and events, and all of us are better men for the experience.

This is my story of that perilous yet fascinating world, as seen through my eyes and lived in my skin, told as honestly and faithfully as I can. I can do no more than that.

And in honor of my fallen comrades, I can do no less.

INSIDE DELTA FORCE

During the 1970s, the United States became the favorite whipping boy for any terrorist group worthy of the name. They had come to realize that American interests could be struck with practical impunity throughout the world, and as the decade unfolded, the pace and severity of those assaults quickened. America, the Gulliver-like giant, had sickened of warfare in Vietnam and was both unable and unwilling to slap at the mosquitoes of terrorism.

For years, famed Special Forces officer Colonel Charlie Beckwith had been the lone voice crying in the wilderness about the terrorist threat facing the nation, and what it would take to effectively confront that threat. He had seen the need within the U.S. military for a compact, highly skilled, and versatile unit able to undertake and execute difficult and unusual "special" missions.

Modeled along the lines of the British commando organization, the Special Air Service (SAS), such an element would be the surgical instrument that could be employed at a moment's notice to execute those tasks outside the realm of normal military capability.

It was Charlie's tenacity that finally won the day and set the wheels in motion that would ultimately bring such a unit into existence. But creating that organization and bringing it to life within the hidebound hierarchy of the Army was a task not dissimilar to electing a pope.

As a rule, armies hate change—and no one hates change more than the ones who have benefited most by the status quo: the general officers. Now and then, innovative thinkers do happen to wear stars on their collars, and Colonel Beckwith's loud and persistent calls for a national counterterrorism force had found the ears of two such men: Generals Bob Kingston and Edwin "Shy" Meyer.

Kingston was stationed at Fort Bragg, North Carolina, and he readily saw the possibilities of the type of force Beckwith was proposing. But he knew that presenting the idea through Army bureaucracy was like walking in a minefield—it could be killed in a thousand different ways. To make headway would require someone with horsepower and a mastery of the military political system, and Shy Meyer was that man.

General Meyer was serving as the Deputy Chief of Staff of the Army, and rumor had it that he would soon become the Chief. Beckwith and Kingston floated their idea of a counterterrorism force to Meyer and immediately realized they were preaching to the choir. Meyer, too, had entertained ideas along that same line, and now the three men enthusiastically shared their thoughts on the subject. The need was evident, but creating a force from whole cloth was going to be extremely difficult.

First they had to determine what types of missions their fictional unit would be tasked with, because the mission dictates a unit's size. With that they were able to build a Table of Organization and Equipment (TO&E), which outlines unit configuration, rank structure, and arms and equipment. The completed TO&E allowed them to forecast a budget for both start-up and annual costs.

Once their "straw man" was complete, from his position in the Pentagon, Meyer started digging, looking for the places to extract the money and the men for the outfit. It may come as a surprise, but the Army does not just have men hanging around and unemployed. Every unit has a manpower quota, and every soldier is assigned to a unit, even if he doesn't work there. But sometimes there are units that are alive on paper but not actually in existence at the time, with the men allocated to those paper units being used elsewhere. Meyer found enough of those slots to man their dream organization, and he uncovered a source of untapped money to breathe life into it.

Next they spent months "what-iffing" their paper unit. They had to be able to anticipate every objection to their creation in advance and have a sound, well-thought-out response to every question. Allies were sought. Powerful and influential generals who could block the formation of the unit were sounded out as to their feelings on the idea. Nothing was ever presented to anyone as a proposal; it was much too early for that. For the time being they just wanted to know who were the friends and who were foes.

But when the more powerful generals realized that a new unit wouldn't intrude on their turf or siphon money from their budgets, they gave their nods of acceptance, if not approval. With that, the trio of Kingston, Meyer, and Beckwith were ready to present their plan. The formal proposal for a national counterterrorism force was presented at the Fort Benning Infantry Conference in the summer of 1977. With all the details and political machinations completed in advance, the proposal was duly approved, and it was recommended to the Chief of Staff of the Army that such an organization be formed immediately. By that time General Meyer *was* the Chief.

1st Special Forces Operational Detachment—Delta was given official life on 21 November 1977 by order of Headquarters, Department of the Army. When Beckwith was chosen to command the new outfit, he immediately set to work. He handpicked a few staff members, found an old derelict building in an out-of-the-way spot on Fort Bragg, North Carolina, and started the struggle to midwife his baby.

It would not be an easy birth.

IN THE BEGINNING

"C-One-Thirty rollin' down the strip,
Airborne Ranger on a one-way trip.
Mission unspoken, destination unknown,
Airborne Ranger ain't never comin' home!"

—Ranger Running Cadence

THE C-130 TRANSPORT PLANE BUCKED AND SHOOK SIDE TO SIDE like a malevolent rodeo bull. *It's going to be a helluva ride till we can get out of this baby,* I thought as the big iron bird descended to jump altitude. Then the plane leveled out, and the bouncing and shivering, though still severe, took on a slightly more predictable tempo.

Now it was time. Barely able to move, encased in the weight of parachute, rucksack, equipment harness, and rifle, I lurched to my feet, hooked the parachute's static line to the overhead steel cable, and turned to face the forty other Rangers still seated on the red nylon benches that ran down the sides and center of the aircraft.

I looked at the Air Force loadmaster as he spoke into his microphone and watched for the red jump light to come on. Then, with a sudden whoosh followed by a deafening roar, he and his assistant slid the jump doors into the opened and ready position. Wind howled through the plane and whipped at my legs as I glanced across the plane to my assistant jump master, Sergeant Allie Jones. He nodded that he was ready, and it began.

I looked back down the line of expectant men seated in front of me, gave the fuselage floor a powerful stamp with my left foot, threw my hands and arms into the air with my palms facing the men, and yelled at the top of my lungs, *"Get ready!"*

The men unbuckled their seat belts, focused their attention on my assistant and me on the other side of the plane, and sat upright in their seats, ready for the next command.

"Outboard personnel. Stand up!" I shouted, as I pointed to the men seated against the skin of the aircraft. They struggled to their feet in spite of the plane's wild lurching, and when they were in line facing me, I continued the jump commands.

"Inboard personnel. Stand up!" I pointed with extended arms and hands to the men still seated on the centerline seats. With help from their standing comrades, they got to their feet, and the two groups formed into a continuous line.

The plane was bouncing and rattling now like an old truck hurtling over a washboarded dirt road, and it was all the men could do to keep their balance. *I hope no one starts throwing up. If they do it'll spread like wildfire, and the floors will become slippery and dangerous.* But this was a veteran bunch of jumpers and no one became airsick, even though the ride was getting worse now that we were on the jump run.

"Hook up!" I called, extending my arms high overhead and making crooks of my index fingers.

Only the first few men in line could hear the commands and understand my voice over the roaring blast coming in the open doors, but everyone could see the hand and arm signals of the jump commands, and it was a code they knew by heart. In unison the jumpers detached their static line clips from the top of their reserve parachutes, snapped them in place on the overhead steel cable running the length of the fuselage, and inserted the safety wire though the sliding lock.

I slid my fingers back and forth over imaginary steel cables. "Check static lines!"

Every man checked his own static line and then the line of the man in front of him. This was the crucial check; a fouled static line could kill you.

With exaggerated movements I patted the front of my chest with both hands. "Check equipment!"

Each Ranger checked his helmet, his reserve parachute, his rucksack and lowering line, and his weapon, making sure everything was securely and properly fastened.

I placed cupped hands behind my ears and shouted, "Sound off for equipment check!"

Beginning with the last man in the rear of the plane, the response came up the line, each Ranger slapping the ass of the man in front of him and yelling into his ear, "Okay!" I heard the muffled reply faintly at first, but it gathered power and speed as the call rippled up the line, until the man directly in front of me threw out his hand with the circled fingers of the "okay" signal, stamped his foot on the aluminum floor, and shouted, "All okay!"

Now I turned to the open jump door. I checked to make sure my rucksack was securely tied to my upwind leg. Then I took a firm hold of the door frame with my right hand and ran my left hand down the other edge of the door, making sure there was no sharp edge that might cut a static line. Next I kicked the side locks of the jump platform and gave it a stomp with one foot to make sure it was secure.

Satisfied that all was well with the door, I slid my legs forward, hooked my toes over the outer edge of the platform, and with a white-knuckled grip on the frame of the door, arched my back and shoved my entire body outside the plane to perform the first air safety check.

The 120-mile-per-hour wind tore at my clothes and equipment and tried to wrest the plane from my tenuous grasp, but I hung on with determination. I still had a job to perform, and we were miles short of the drop zone.

First I looked forward to orient myself and then I checked for the position of the other planes. Then I looked up to make sure no one was above us, and toward the rear to make certain no one was back there. We were the last plane in the flight, and I was glad to see the other birds all in their proper position. I tilted my head down just a bit so the brim of my helmet helped cut the wind from my eyes and then concentrated on the ground ahead as I looked for the checkpoints that told me we were approaching Fort Stewart, Georgia, and Taylor's Creek Drop Zone.

In the distance ahead, I caught sight of the huge DZ, showing as a rectangular slab of white sand and scrub brush in an endless green forest. I watched its steady approach, and when it was just in front of the plane's nose, I wrenched myself back inside, pointed to the open doorway, and shouted to the first man in line the phrase that thrills every paratrooper, "Stand in the door!"

The human energy in the plane crackled as the soldier threw his static line into my waiting hand, put his feet on the jump platform, and grasped the outside of the shuddering door frame. Knees cocked like levers, arms tensed, he looked with steady eyes straight out the wind-blasted and howling door, waiting for the ultimate command. An eighteen-year-old private first class, Ricky Magee was the youngest jumper in the plane, but he was showing the steady courage of an old hand.

I held him by his parachute harness and looked around the front of his chest as the drop zone slid under the belly of the plane, then I looked back inside just in time to see the red light extinguished and the green light come on in its place.

It was as if a switch had been thrown. My right arm felt electric as I swung it sharply forward, gave the jumper a stinging slap low on the back of his thigh, and yelled into his ear, "Go!"

He sprang out the door like he'd been shot from an automatic cannon, while behind him a human conveyor belt of fresh ammo rushed for the breach of the exit door.

Slap, "Go!" Slap, "Go!" Slap, "Go!"

The rapidly shortening line of men disappeared from sight as the wildly lunging plane, a thousand feet above the ground, disgorged its human cargo into the ether. *Like Jonahs from the belly of the whale.* As the last man hurled himself into space, I looked out the plane and back down at the descending jumpers to make sure no one was hung up on the plane and being dragged to his death.

Satisfied that all was okay, I looked to my assistant in the other doorway who had been doing the same thing. He shouted across to me, "Clear to the rear!"

I gave him a thumbs-up and answered "Clear!" then pointed a finger at him and yelled, "Go!"

He turned to the door, hesitated the split second he needed to take a good door position, and then launched himself from view. I quickly checked outside and below to see that he had a chute over his head, glanced at the still-green jump light, and rocketed myself out the door into the full blast of the air.

Tight body position. Feet and knees pressed together, hands grasping the ends of the reserve chute, head down with my chin tucked into my chest, I counted.

One thousand! Two thousand! A hard tug at my back as the parachute was jerked from its pack. *Three thousand!* The drag of the elongated but still unopened chute acted as an air brake, immediately slowing my forward movement, tilting my back toward the earth, and I watched as the tail of the plane sailed past over the tips of my boots.

Four thousand! A full parachute. Feet once again pointed toward the ground, I checked the canopy. It looked good. No tears in the green fabric and no lines out of place. *And after the overwhelming noise inside the airplane, the world is suddenly silent.*

I grabbed the handles of the control lines and pulled them down to the level of my helmet as I quickly looked all around for other jumpers. *Ah, plenty of clear air.* I checked for the direction of smoke on the drop zone and then let the parachute fly so that I could also gauge the direction of the wind up here. I let the canopy run with the wind; I was a long way from the assembly point and I wanted the parachute to take me as close as it possibly could.

Two hundred feet above the ground I bent my knees so my rucksack would have a ramp to slide off. I reached down and pulled the quick-release tabs to the rucksack and felt it drop free until it hit the end of the twenty-foot lowering line with a yank. The tall Georgia pines at the side of the drop zone drifted lazily upward, and when I was level with their tops, I faced the canopy into the wind and prepared to land.

Shove the rifle over so that it's not under my armpit or it'll bend the barrel and dislocate my shoulder when I hit the ground. Legs slightly bent, feet and knees together, elbows in front of the face, hands even with the top of the helmet…and relax. Now the ground came hurtling upward with amazing speed and the rucksack hit with a solid *thunk. Relax, relax, relax…*

At a speed of twenty-two feet per second, I made jolting impact with the earth. Balls of the feet, calves, sides of the thighs, ass, and backs of the shoulders making contact in a practiced rolling sequence that spread the energy of the controlled crash across the length of my body. I heard, as from a distance, the thump and jangle of equipment as my load and I completed our short flight and sudden landing. And then it was over.

Everything still works. And any parachute landing is a good one if you can get up and walk away. I came to rest, shucked myself out of the harness, and ran to the canopy to fold and stow it away before a puff of wind could inflate it again. I quickly stuffed my chute into its kit bag, donned my gear, and set out at a fast trot to rejoin my company.

Today we had a rare and unexpected treat. Following an exercise, we usually road-marched the twenty miles from the drop zone back to the barracks. But we were returning from a long and arduous month in the jungles of Panama. And we had a lot of work ahead of us cleaning and turning in weapons and equipment, so the colonel had us trucked back to camp instead.

Four hours later everything was accounted for and back in its proper place. The formation came to attention, the first sergeant called, "Dismissed!" and with a thundering *"Hoo-ah!"* the 158 men of Charlie Company, 1st Ranger Battalion, were released for a well-deserved three-day weekend.

I watched my platoon as it immediately disintegrated into individuals and small groups of buddies. I was about to walk away when Glenn Morrell, the battalion command sergeant major, called me to his side.

"Sergeant Haney, I want you to report to the battalion conference room and meet someone who'd like to speak with you."

"Certainly, Sergeant Major," I said. "Who is it?"

"He's an old friend of mine, and I think you'll find what he has to say pretty interesting," he replied with the lopsided smile that habitually adorned his rugged face. "He's waiting for you now."

"Wilco, Sergeant Major. I'm on my way." And with a salute I moved out sharply in the direction of battalion headquarters.

I thought the world of Sergeant Major Morrell. A practical yet deeply thoughtful man, he is that very rare combination of action and intellect.

Morrell had come to us the previous year after our former sergeant major, Henry Caro, had been killed on a parachute jump. With the battalion's reputation as a hardship posting, no other sergeant major in the Army would come to join us. When Morrell heard that no Ranger-qualified sergeant major would accept the assignment, he volunteered and at age forty-two attended Ranger School so he could accept the posting as command sergeant major. He was as hard as woodpecker lips and he had my utter respect. If he wanted me to meet Beelzebub himself, I was confident it was all for the best.

The meeting in the conference room turned out to be an interview to attend tryouts for a secretive new unit that was forming at Fort Bragg, the one we had been hearing rumors about. The man I spoke with was tall and broad-shouldered, with dark, well-combed hair, penetrating brown eyes, and a hint of tin-roof twang in his voice. He was dressed in civvies, never gave his name, and told me damn little about his organization. I later came to know him as Sergeant Major William "Country" Grimes, the man handpicked by Colonel Charlie Beckwith to be his sergeant major.

He had my personnel records open on the table in front of him and he glanced at them occasionally as we talked about my career, about the units I had been in and the assignments I had held to that point. He told me this was a chance to be a charter member of a unit that would be unique in the American military—the nation's first unit dedicated to fighting international terrorism.

The prerequisites to try out were:

Minimum age of twenty-two. Minimum time in service of four years and two months. Minimum rank of staff sergeant. Pass a 100-meter swim test while wearing boots and fatigues, and pass the Ranger/Special Forces PT test. Have a minimum score of 110 on the Army general aptitude test, no court-martial convictions, and no record of recurring disciplinary problems.

About the only other thing Grimes told me was that if I was accepted, I could expect hard work, plenty of danger, and no recognition.

I had been thinking a great deal lately about what I wanted to do after my assignment with the Rangers. I didn't know if I wanted to go back overseas again or into Special Forces. I was positive of one thing: I didn't want to be detailed as an instructor at a school somewhere. But since I had just been picked up for promotion to sergeant first class, and had never had a nontactical assignment, that was a distinct possibility. I had a fair number of options, but none sounded as good as what I had just heard. Given all this, I signed up on the spot.

Grimes told me to expect orders soon to come to Bragg for about a month. He gave me a phone number to call if I had any questions or changed my mind about coming. And that was it. Just a few weeks later, I received orders directing me to report to Moon Hall at Fort Bragg on or about noon, 13 September 1978.

Forming a brand-new outfit and creating new operating methods is an NCO's dream come true, but still, I was apprehensive. There was a lot of unknown here, not the least of which was what I would do if I failed to make it through the selection program. I had turned my platoon over to Tom Duke, the new platoon sergeant. Duke was a solid, experienced leader who had been with us for a year. I had come to know and respect him in that time, so I knew the men would be in good hands no matter what. As it became known I was going to Fort Bragg, my troops wished me well and told me, "If anyone can make it into that new unit, you can, Sergeant Haney." Man, they were going to be a hard bunch to face if I came back a failure.

In my favor, I had been in the Army eight years. I was a seasoned and experienced infantryman. I had successfully attended two of the hardest courses in the military—Ranger School and the Jump Master Course. I had been a platoon sergeant for more than four years, with the last two of those years in the Rangers.

Life in the Rangers was austere. In fact, it was downright severe. If there were two ways of accomplishing a given task, we always took the hard way. We never took shortcuts and we never spared any effort. We spent at least three weeks of every month in the field, and deployed on extended training to the Arctic, the desert, and the jungle, three times a year. We were also subject to two "no-notice" exercises annually and participated in major Army or NATO programs every year.

Life in the Rangers was so difficult that most men failed to complete a full two-year tour with the unit, and numerous injuries also winnowed the ranks. But it was good preparation for accomplishing other, still more difficult tasks. I was determined to give this new challenge my utmost effort, and if that wasn't good enough, I would at least have the satisfaction of knowing I had tried. Small satisfaction, but some.

I had almost no idea of what to expect on the morning of 13 September 1978, when I loaded my pickup, kissed my family goodbye, and set out on the five-hour drive up I-95 from Hunter Army Airfield in Savannah, Georgia, for Fort Bragg, North Carolina—and points unknown. I merely reminded myself that the future is always perfect. And wished it to be so.

Some Army posts have a real beauty about them. The Presidio of Monterey and the main post areas of Forts McClellan and Benning are a few that come to mind, principally because of the Spanish Colonial architecture of the old buildings. Fort Stewart has magnificent live oaks and cypresses draped in Spanish moss.

But I can't think of a single aesthetic recommendation for Fort Bragg. It is about as drab and unappealing a spot as you can find in North America.

The post sprawls over the Sand Hills of North Carolina. It was established on near worthless land as an artillery-training center during World War One. The land is sparsely covered with straggly pines and stunted scrub oak trees. The layout of the cantonment areas, the places where people live, seems haphazard. The whole place has a temporary, transient feel about it.

But it is the "Home of the Airborne," and as such, contains the 82nd Airborne Division, the Special Forces Center and Schools, 5th and 7th Special Forces Groups, 18th Airborne Corps Headquarters, and the 1st Corps Support Command. There were also some smaller miscellaneous organizations scattered in odd, hidden corners around post.

One of these was 1st Special Forces Operational Detachment—Delta.

I pulled into the parking lot of Moon Hall on the main post of Fort Bragg shortly before noon. I made my way into the lobby and saw a sign directing me to "1st SFOD—D." I followed the arrow to the left and saw a man wearing unmarked fatigues sitting at a desk in a small room.

"Here for Selection, Sarge?" he asked.

"Yes, I am."

"Well, find your name and sign in here," he said as he indicated a roster on the desk and handed me a pen.

I eyed him surreptitiously while I found my name and wrote my signature next to it. He was about forty years old, soft-spoken, and good-looking. He wasn't exactly what I had expected to meet. The first person you usually encounter when signing in to a new unit is some foul-tempered clerk. A person who, with all the power of a petty czar, seems to believe he has been ordained by God almighty to spread irritation to every man he meets. This man was not that at all.

"You won't be staying here; you'll be going to Aberdeen Camp. Have you ever been there before?" he asked as he looked me directly in the eyes.

When I told him that I had not, he handed me a strip map and explained how to find the place. It was on the western edge of post, about thirty miles away.

"Do you have a POV [privately owned vehicle] or do you need transportation?"

"No, I have my own vehicle."

He detached one sheet from the ream of orders I had given him.

"Okay, Ranger. When you arrive at Aberdeen, park out front and report to the man at the gate. He'll square you away." And as he handed me the rest of the orders, he said with a slight smile in his voice and on his face, "You have a good one, and I hope to see you later."

"Thanks," I replied, "I hope so too."

I took my time driving out to the camp. Aberdeen was what I expected it to be—an isolation camp. These are small, out-of-the-way places a unit can stay while planning for a deployment or mission—a secure spot offering refuge from the normal distractions of life. They will have rustic barracks, a mess hall, orderly room, and offices for staff sections, a supply building and warehousing, a small motor pool, a landing zone for a few helicopters, and maybe a range for zeroing and test-firing weapons.

I was waved inside the gate and parked in the lot nearby. The guy at the gate walked over as I was getting out of my truck.

He was in fatigues without a name tag or insignia of any kind. He stuck out his hand as we approached.

"Hello, Sergeant Haney, glad to have you here. Take your gear down to Barracks A and grab a bunk. Then find Sergeant Major Shumate. He'll get your equipment issued to you. Chow is at 1730. Instructions for tomorrow will be posted on the board outside the mess hall. See you later. Have a good one."

"Okay, thanks," I replied, as I shouldered my kit bag and rucksack and turned in the direction of the barracks.

The barracks were the standard "tropical hooches." Low frame buildings twenty-four feet wide and seventy-two feet long. Concrete floors and tin roofs with wide overhanging eaves. The upper halves of the walls were hinged on top and propped open at a forty-five-degree angle to serve as windows. The open "windows" were screened. A row of GI cots ran down each side of the building and a string of bare lightbulbs hung from the centerline of the exposed rafters. Not a bad home at all.

I went about halfway down the building, found a bunk on the left side, and dropped my bags. My idea was to get away from the door and avoid as much traffic and stirred-up dust as I could.

There were eight or ten other men in the hooch. Their shoulder patches showed them to be from overseas units or from some of the forts out West. I nodded to the ones who looked up as I went out to find the sergeant major.

I stepped out the door and took my bearings. There was a warehouse-looking building near the motor pool. Probably a good place to start. About halfway there I met a guy hurrying up the sidewalk.

"Hey, Bud, do you know where I can find Sergeant Major Shumate?" I asked.

"Yeah, that's him over by the deuce-and-a-half." He pointed to a man with his shirt open and his hat on the back of his head, standing next to an Army two-and-one-half-ton truck.

"Okay, if you say so." I started over to see this alleged "sergeant major."

Sergeants Major are the walking, breathing embodiment of Everything That's Right in the U.S. Army. This guy looked like Joe Shit the RagMan. His shirt was wide open and he wore no T-shirt. His dog tags were gold-plated. His hat was tipped up on the back of his head, and he wore a huge, elaborately curled and waxed handlebar mustache.

There was trickery of some kind here. The only thing I expected on this trip was the unexpected. So if this was a game, I figured I'd play along and see what happened.

I stepped three paces in front of the man, slammed to a halt, and from the rigid position of parade rest barked, "Sergeant Major, I was told to see you and draw some equipment!"

He eyed me for a second or so as the wrinkles of a grin crawled from beneath his mustache to settle around his eyes.

"God damn, Ranger, relax a little bit, will you. This ain't no promotion board. You keep that shit up, you're gonna wear me out." His voice was rumbling and rich with a tinge of the hills deep within.

It was force of habit. In the Rangers, when you addressed a more senior NCO, you stood at parade rest. I relaxed slightly to the position of "at ease."

"That's a little better," he said. His grin widened. He didn't seem to be making fun of me, just surprised at being addressed in such a formal manner.

"Go over to the supply shack, get yourself a bag of junk, and sign your name on the roster at the door. Don't worry about getting it too clean when you turn it in. Everybody knows my standards ain't very high."

Christ almighty. This was shaping up to be a strange place. I hustled down to the supply shack, signed for a bag of equipment, and talked to the guy on duty while I checked the contents of the bag against the equipment list.

"Is that guy up there really a sergeant major?"

"Shumate? Yeah, he really is. He's the sergeant major in charge of Selection."

"Well, he's certainly different from any sergeant major I've ever met before."

"He's different from any *human being* you've ever met before."

Sergeant Major Walter J. Shumate was a living legend in Special Forces. An old veteran who had entered the Army during the Korean War, he had seen and done it all. At forty-four he was the oldest man to ever make it through Delta Force Selection. And he was invaluable to the formation of the unit. Shumate added an element of humanity that could have very well eluded the organization in those critical early years. Without his special touch and unique influence, the outfit could have easily taken on an apparatchik-like attitude. But with Shumate around, no matter how special you thought you were, he could always convince you that you were still just a human being. Walt was serious about soldiering, but he was the antithesis of an automaton.

Barracks A was starting to fill up when I returned. So far, everyone was from somewhere other than Fort Bragg. There were a few guys I knew from various courses we had attended together, and two I had served with in other units. As large as the Army was in those days, I had been around long enough that I knew someone no matter where I went. A few guys were loudly expounding their expertise on special operations and counterterrorism (CT) as I walked down the aisle to my bunk.

Trying to impress each other and playing to the crowd. Very little knowledge and a lot of talk.

1st Ranger Battalion had been working for almost a year with the Army's interim CT force, Blue Light, trying to develop techniques for combating terrorist action. Both units had worked pretty hard at the tasking, but after a couple of joint exercises and thorough after-action analysis, it was apparent we weren't making much headway. In fact, the last exercise had gone so badly that our battalion commander had been relieved of command. So far, no one was very expert at what it would take to engage and defeat terrorism.

A guy was sitting on the bunk next to mine unpacking his kit bag. He looked up as I put my equipment down. Our eyes met and we both put out a hand.

"Keekee Saenz, Three/Seven Special Forces—Panama," he told me, with a slight Hispanic accent.

We shook hands. "Eric Haney, First Ranger. *Mucho gusto en conocerle,* Keekee," I replied.

"El gusto es mío," he returned with a smile.

Keekee was a medium-sized guy, with the wiry muscled build of a runner. His hair was thick but short, and he wore a pencil-thin Puerto Rican bandleader mustache. He looked to be about my age, twenty-six or so. He had the air of a tough, competent soldier.

"Keekee, y'all heard much about this outfit down in Panama?" I asked as I sorted my equipment.

"Probably not much more than you have," he said. "My company was tasked by CINC SouthCom [Commander in Chief,

Southern Command] with working up a CT program for the Latin American theater, but we haven't had any more success than you guys and Blue Light. And everything about this group has been very close hold. One of our guys made it here in the spring, but no one's heard anything from him since."

"We had one tryout, too, last spring," I said. "But he was back after the first week and he won't say a word. So far information has been pretty tight. I guess we'll find out what we need to know as we go along."

"*Ojalá,*" he said, turning back to his gear.

"*Si, Ojalá.*" *Yes, God willing indeed.*

I finished unpacking and then changed into running shoes and shorts and went out for a run. The afternoon was too beautiful to waste sitting around the barracks, gossiping like a bunch of old women. Summers in the Southeast are pretty rugged affairs, but fall is usually a long season of glorious weather. And today was a perfect example: bright, sunny, and dry.

As I went out the gate, the guy on duty nodded and said, "Have a good 'un."

"Have a good one" must be the unit mantra, I thought as I trotted away from the camp. The atmosphere of this place was so relaxed, I felt slightly uneasy. All could not be what it seemed.

As I ran along and worked up a good sweat, I tried to imagine what this "Selection course" would be like. But I had no frame of reference to make a determination. This was unlike anything I had seen in the Army. So far, it was just a bunch of guys gathering at an out-of-the-way camp, administered by what looked like a bunch of military hobos. I would just keep my mouth shut, my eyes and ears open, and respond to whatever came up. It's the system I'd always used in new situations, and so far it had served me well.

Lost in the privacy of my thoughts, I trotted a few miles over the swelling pine-clad hills, listening to the rhythm of my feet on the ground and the sound of air rushing in and out of my chest. Happily soaked in sweat, I turned about and made my way back to camp, where I waved to the guy at the gate, who replied with a nod and a smile. I headed for the showers, took my time cleaning up, and went to supper.

The mess hall was full and noisy. I sat at a table with several guys from units in Germany. We had a few friends in common. They said about fifty guys had come over from Europe to attend Selection. Looked like there was going to be quite a crowd.

Chow was remarkably good for a field camp. I finished, turned in my tray and utensils, and went outside to read the bulletin board. It said:

14 September 1978.
Formation: 0600 hrs.
Uniform: Boots, fatigues, soft caps (no berets)
ID Cards and Dog Tags

Well, that was clear enough, no overload of information there. But some people would be pissed about the "no berets" part.

I heard someone from the 101st Airborne Division ask a cadre member if we were restricted to camp. He was told there was no restriction, just take your information from the bulletin board, no more and no less.

A lot of guys won't be able to handle that. They'll be in the NCO Club tonight and hungover or still drunk in the morning. Should be interesting.

I lounged around outside for a while and talked with a few acquaintances. Then I returned to the barracks, finished arranging and putting away my gear, and read for a while.

At 2030 I rolled up in my poncho liner and enjoyed the feeling of stretching out on a bunk. Not bad at all. As a Ranger, I was more accustomed to sleeping on the ground than in a bed. This was nearly luxurious. I rolled onto my side, pulled a corner of the poncho liner over my head, and went to sleep.

Seasoned soldiers have the ability to fall asleep almost immediately. Like food and water, sleep is a commodity you take whenever you can get it. I wasn't buying this laid-back routine at all. If this was like Ranger School, someone would come screaming into the barracks after midnight, to destroy our rest and play mind games. Barring any middle-of-the-night disturbances, I would wake myself at 0515.

I awoke at 0512. I've never had to use an alarm clock; I tell myself what time to wake up and that's it. I lay there for a few minutes, listening to the sound of the sleeping barracks.

The extra sleep this morning felt good. Back at Battalion, I was always up at 0430 and in the barracks by 0500 for a cup of coffee with my squad leaders before they got the troops up at 0530.

I slid out of the bunk, put on shorts and shower shoes, grabbed my shaving kit, and went to the latrine to get squared away. The air was chill and crisp. There was no moon, and the stars were still very bright. I like this time of the day. It's one of those "in-between" times. The world is silent and still, the night creatures are back in their hideaways, and the day animals aren't stirring yet.

When I came out of the latrine, other men were up and moving about, and vehicle lights were coming through the gate. Half the guys in the barracks were still in their bunks as I dressed and laced on my jungle boots. I put on my oldest pair of field boots, a pair that had been oiled with Neat's Foot until they were as soft as moccasins. A soldier doesn't need much in the way of uniforms, but good boots are indispensable. I checked to make sure I had a notebook and pen in my breast pocket and then made my way outside.

The parking lot was rapidly filling up, and a number of guys were ambling to the center of the compound. Glowing cigarette tips illuminated faces, and quiet voices drifted about the area.

"God damn, Haney! What the fuck you doin' here?" a voice brayed at me from out of the darkness.

There was only one person with a voice like that. I turned around and said, "Hello, Parks. How did you ever find your way here?"

Virgil Parks was a bona fide, twenty-four-carat, dyed-in-the-wool curmudgeon. Virg had joined the U.S. Army in 1968 specifically to go to Vietnam, and he had been a Ranger ever since. We had been platoon sergeants in the same company until late last year, when he transferred to Fort Benning to be an instructor at Ranger School.

I could only imagine he was here because he had worn out his welcome with the Ranger Department. He had a habit of doing that wherever he went. He was eccentric to the point of lunacy—and that takes some doing in the Ranger world. Parks went full blast and unaimed at all times. He was utterly unable to modulate his output of energy to the task at hand. And even in the politically conservative military society, he was known as being well to the right of Attila the Hun.

He closed his eyes, tilted his admirable nose up in that peculiar fashion of his, and took a long drag off the cigarette he held between his thumb and forefinger. As always, I watched him in fascination. Nobody could make love to a cigarette like Staff Sergeant Virgil Parks.

"Just thought I'd come and see what these yahoos are up to around here. 'Sides, the Ranger Department's turning into a bunch of pussies. They're even going to issue a candy bar every day to the little troopies in Florida Phase during the winter classes, just 'cause those assholes froze to death last year."

There was nothing "pussy" about that tragedy. During the Florida phase of Ranger School, students received only one C ration a day. They were expending calories at a much higher rate than they were taking them in and were already in a weakened state from the previous phases of the course. If the temperature of the swamp water they were constantly in fell too low, they were in real danger of hypothermia.

It had happened during a particularly cold night on a patrol the previous winter. Twenty-three men had gone into hypothermia on a night crossing of the Yellow River. Four died in the swamps. The Ranger cadre had crossed that fine line between hard-ass and dumb-ass, and men had died as a result. I was surprised no one had been court-martialed over that affair.

"Yeah, I've heard that." There was no use reasoning with Parks—he was impervious to logic.

A line of deuce-and-a-halves pulled up and parked while we were BS'ing. At two minutes until six a guy with a clipboard in his hand walked out of the HQ shack. He was dressed in jeans and a T-shirt and wore a baseball cap. He stood at the edge of the crowd and looked at us dispassionately until everyone became quiet.

"Fall in, in four ranks," he called. We shuffled into formation in about a minute. The 163 men gathered there stood at attention.

"At ease! Listen up! Sound off when I call your name and get on the truck I've indicated. If your name's not called, stand fast and I'll get to you. Truck number one—_____." He started calling names in alphabetical order.

Each truck had a big chalk numeral on its tailgate. When my name was called, I shouted "Here!" and climbed aboard. Soon the trucks got under way, and we rumbled out the gate just as the sun splashed its rays over the eastern horizon.

"Join the Army and see the world," the recruiting posters said. I've seen at least half of it from the back of a truck.

Fifteen minutes later, we halted along the edge of what looked like a drop zone. "Holland DZ," I heard some of the Fort Bragg troops say as we dismounted.

Sergeant Major Shumate was standing nearby wearing khaki pants, a Hawaiian shirt, and a Panama hat. "Fall in on me, ladies!" he called. "Make it six ranks, I want a tight formation."

As we were forming up, somebody walked up with a camera and tripod and prepared to take a photograph of the formation.

"What the hell's this about, Walt?" an anonymous voice squawked from somewhere in the crowd.

"This is going to be the 'before picture' of this group, my young darlings, and we'll take a second shot in a few weeks," Shumate replied.

I was aghast that someone had called a sergeant major by his first name, but Shumate seemed to take no offense. But when a small cluster of the men started laughing and yahooing from within the group, like this was some sort of stupid joke, Shumate became steely. The jocularity in his voice came to a screeching halt and he growled in a volcanic tone, "Yeah, well, we'll see who's laughing when you motherfuckers are finished, and the next picture I take is about half the size of this front rank standing here. The serious ones will be in that photo and the rest of you shitbirds will be back home, lying to your teammates about why you didn't make it. So since you loudmouths—and a bunch more of you besides—won't be here for the 'after photo,' I'll just have my laugh at you dickheads right now—ha-fucking-ha!"

It was a sober group he addressed now as he called us to attention. The photographer took the shot and departed.

Shumate continued as though nothing had happened, "This is the Ranger/Special Forces PT test. Your graders for events one through four are arranged behind me, from left to right. When I call your name, go to the grader indicated. Have a good one. Event number one!" and he started calling off names. I fell in on my grader.

The Army had four PT tests in those days. There was a test for staff and support troops, a more strenuous test for the combat arms, a test for Jump School, and the Ranger/Special Forces test.

The first three tests had a descending grade scale based on age. The older you were, the less you had to perform for a given score. For the Ranger/SF test, age received no breaks—everyone was graded at the seventeen-year-old level. The test consisted of push-ups, sit-ups, the run-dodge-jump, the inverted crawl (known as the perverted crawl), and the two-mile run. The uniform for the test was fatigues and combat boots—running shoes were not yet in style in the Army. Shirts could be removed in warm weather.

My first event was the run-dodge-jump. This was an agility and quickness drill. You took off from the starting line, sprinted forward to a set of gates perpendicular to your path, ran through them and then jumped a ditch, continued sprinting to a second set of gates, went through these, then around and back through them again, over the ditch, back through the first set of gates, repeated the whole process once more, and finished at the starting point. I usually completed this event in about thirteen seconds. A time of fifteen seconds gave a score of one hundred. Minimum passing time was nineteen seconds.

I ran through the event in my normal time. A grader handed me my scorecard and directed me to the push-up station. I fell into line and had barely recovered my breath when I was called forward and told to assume the starting position.

I had just gotten into the starting position and asked my grader to count out loud for me when the "go" command was given. When the grader had counted "fifty-three," I stopped and came to rest on my hands and knees with a few seconds to spare. I had found that the easiest way to do this was to breathe like a runaway steam engine and do the push-ups as fast as possible. You just had to make sure you did them all correctly or the grader would not count them.

Time was called. I was given my card and sent to the inverted crawl—an event that ranks as one of the stupidest things ever imagined in an institution that seldom shunned the stupid. Whereas other events on the PT test measured things like agility or upper body strength, the inverted crawl measured, well... no one has the faintest idea what it measures.

On the command "go" you lift your butt off the ground and crawl, crablike, with your back to the ground and torso facing skyward. In this position you "sprint" forward, feetfirst, for twenty meters; then straight back, hands first, unable to see where you're going, all the way back to the starting point.

I executed the event, received a max score, picked the sandspurs from my hands and went to the sit-up station. It was obvious to me now that there was no rest between events. As soon as I finished one station, I went directly to another without waiting around. Everything was organized and businesslike. There was no shouting or any other form of normal military histrionics—and there was no way to slip to the back of a line and catch any rest between events.

I was motioned forward for the sit-ups. On my back, fingers interlaced behind the head, knees bent, and the grader holding my feet. The cool sand felt good on my back as I waited for the command to start. Then the command "go." I was knocking them out as fast as I could, while in my peripheral vision I could see other bodies slamming up and down in a discordant cadence. *We look like pistons in an engine,* I thought as I finished the exercise and fell back on the ground to take a breath before getting to my feet and retrieving my scorecard.

Within a minute or two, all the events were finished and we were called over to the trucks for a loose formation.

"Make sure your fatigue jackets are on the truck you arrived in," announced Shumate. "Then fall in on the grader you had for your last event." He motioned to the graders standing on the dirt road to our right.

"Okay. Do it," he barked.

I folded my shirt and put it under the bench of my truck, then made my way down to my grader for the start of the two-mile run. The grader took our scorecards and gave each of us a red cloth bib to hang around our necks. As he gave us the bibs, he also assigned each of us a different number. My number was six. The other groups had other colors.

Then Shumate called us to the start line.

"Okay, ladies, we've all done this once or twice before in our lives. On the command 'go,' take off. Stay on this road for two miles to the finish point. As you come into the finish, look for your grader, he will be holding up a panel with the same color you're wearing. Everyone ready . . . *go!*"

And off we went. At first it was the same cluster as the start of any race. Some guys sprinted off; others hung back and let the crowd thin down a bit. I took the middle course. I'm a good runner but not a great one. Within a couple of hundred meters I was able to settle into my pace and hold the speed I liked.

It was a good morning for running. It was warm enough to be comfortable, but the cool air felt good on my face. The sand underfoot was firm and the sun was to my back. I had my breathing in sync with my legs and decided to take a few seconds off my normal time. I usually ran the test in about thirteen and a half minutes. That gave a score of 90 on the test. A time of twelve minutes and something gave a score of one hundred, but that wasn't in my reach. So I settled in, stretched my stride a little, and galloped down the road.

This beat the hell out of running around a track, the usual setting for a PT test. Sooner than I expected, I could see the finish point. The gazelles were already crossing the line.

I stretched out my stride a little more and concentrated on blowing the spent air from my lungs in order to breathe more deeply. I was running beside someone and we were matched pace for pace. As I tried to pull ahead he stayed with me. I glanced over at the man: it was Keekee Saenz. Soon we were running flat out with neither of us able to outpace the other.

Up ahead I saw my grader and then heard the timekeeper calling out the minutes and seconds, "Twelve minutes, fifty seconds—fifty-one, fifty-two, fifty-three, fifty-four—" he shouted, as I crossed the finish line, made eye contact, and yelled "Red six!" to my grader.

"Roger, red six," he replied as he marked down the time.

I slowed my pace to a trot and continued down the road for a hundred meters or so before coming to a walk. I put my hands on my hips and walked back to the finish point as my breathing returned to normal. When I got near the finish line, one of the cadre members told me to go down the road to where the trucks were now parked, retrieve my shirt, and stand by for instructions. Back down the road I went.

The trucks must have gone around us by another route, because there they were, lined up in order, about three hundred meters down the dirt track.

As I neared the trucks, I saw Sergeant Major Shumate talking to someone. He looked up as I got my shirt from the truck.

"Having fun, Ranger?" he asked as I buttoned up my fatigue shirt.

"I sure am, Sergeant Major. Where to next?"

He eyed me from under lowered brows. "You look a little heated. Why don't you go down to the lake and have yourself a dip? Someone down there will give you instructions. And..." He paused deliberately, so I stopped to look at him. "Have a good 'un."

Damn, I thought as I walked away. *Is everything funny to that man?*

I walked to the edge of the lake where a small group was gathering. A short, sandy-haired guy motioned me to come and join them.

"This is the swim test, men. From the buoys on this side to the buoys on the other side is one hundred meters. Uniform for the swim is combat boots and fatigues. This is not a timed exercise. You may use any stroke you desire, but you may not stop until you have reached the buoys on the other side. Wade out to the first set of buoys and start swimming. Don't put your feet down until you have reached the other set of buoys. At that time, you will be instructed to stand up and wade out. No questions? Okay, have a good 'un."

The dozen or so of us in the group waded out into the water. It was coffee-colored tannic water and as warm as a bath. The water was to the middle of my chest when I reached the line of buoys. I sank down to my neck to let the air out of my clothes and then started to swim. First I did a sidestroke on my left side and then rolled over to my right. About two thirds of the way across, I rolled onto my back and backstroked the rest of the way. If there is any secret to swimming while clothed, it is that you have to relax and not get in a hurry. You're still buoyant; you just have more drag to contend with.

This swim wasn't bad at all. For the Ranger swim test, you were blindfolded and walked off a high dive, fully dressed and armed, carrying an M-16 and load-bearing equipment with magazine pouches and two canteens. After hitting the water, you swam to the side of the pool and climbed out. The point of the test was to simulate walking off a stream bank at night. If you could successfully perform the test, you weren't likely to panic if you suddenly and unexpectedly found yourself in deep water and unable to see. I was sure this test was just to see if you were confident and comfortable in the water.

I climbed out of the lake and moved up the bank to a stand of large pine trees. Then I took my uniform off, wrung the water out, and redressed. I didn't have to empty my boots, because the jungle boots I was wearing drain themselves. Drying my hair wasn't a problem either. I was wearing the Ranger standard 'do—a quarter inch on top and white-side walls.

I walked down to a cadre member who was watching the people still in the water. Men were in the lake from one side to the other now, with some crawling out and others getting in. Two safety boats flanked either side and moved back and forth as the lifeguards aboard kept an eye on the weaker swimmers. I saw one guy on the other side of the lake walk out to his waist, shake his head, and then walk back to shore. I guess he knew his limitations.

About halfway across the lake, one of the boats moved to a man floundering at the edge of the pack. They waited nearby until it looked like he was in serious trouble, and then extended a pole to him. He grabbed it in desperation and was pulled to the side of the boat, where he clung like a tick on a dog's ear. Another one down.

A small group of us had now made it across the lake, and a steady trickle of men was coming up the bank. The cadre member pointed to a truck and told us that when we had a full load, to mount up for the ride back to camp. We were to follow the new instructions posted on the bulletin board.

We arrived back at camp and checked the board.

Lunch: C Ration
Supper: 1700
Formation: 1830
Uniform: Fatigues with soft cap, rucksack weighing 40 lbs., two
    canteens of water

A set of scales hung from the chin-up bar in front of the mess hall. A stack of C ration cases stood next to the bulletin board. I fished out two (one for lunch, one to stash—just in case) and went to the hooch to change into a dry uniform. It was still only 1030, so there was a lot of time to kill.

I changed into dry clothes and then walked around camp just to pass the time. There was a long line of men at the Orderly Room, out-processing. They were the ones who had failed the PT test or the swim test. I wondered what the hell they had even come here for if they couldn't pass a simple PT test. Some of these guys had come over from units in Europe—which was a pretty expensive trip just to flunk out within the first few hours.

I overheard a couple of guys from SF grousing that it wasn't fair and they should be allowed a retest. I recognized one of the men in the "go home" line as a sergeant first class I knew from the 25th Division in Hawaii. We had attended the Infantry Noncommissioned Officers Advanced Course together last year. We nodded to each other in mutual recognition, but he didn't look as if he wanted to talk.

My rucksack registered forty-two pounds when I hung it on the scales just before supper. I took it back to the hooch and added what seemed about three pounds, then fastened two canteens of water to the lower sides of the ruck. I wanted to be able to get at them without taking my rucksack off. And I wanted my load to weigh just a bit more than prescribed, just in case these scales were a little off.

Normally I would also be wearing my LBE—load bearing equipment. This consists of a pistol belt and its shoulder harness, to which are attached magazine and first-aid pouches, compass, strobe light, knife or bayonet, canteens, and other odds and ends. The LBE is your fighting load; it is how you carry your ammunition and the items you need to fight and survive in combat. Loaded for combat, it weighs about forty pounds. The rucksack is then worn over the top of the LBE. But the bulletin board instructions said nothing about LBE, and I intended to follow instructions to the letter.

At 1830 we boarded trucks for a trip across Fort Bragg. Some of the local guys said we were on Chicken Road, a wide sandy tank trail leading straight as an arrow through the sparse pines and scrub oaks of the monotonous Sand Hills. I've never seen a more ugly place. We bumped and swayed along, shrouded within a fog bank of gritty, truck-churned dust.

After about thirty minutes, we came to a stop at a crossroads, where we dismounted. Sergeant Major Shumate stood nearby, watching us with a challenging grin.

"All right, y'all, gather round, we don't need a formation...a cluster-fuck will do," he said as we grabbed our rucksacks and formed a semicircle around him.

"Well, our happy little band is slightly smaller than it was this morning, isn't it?" Shumate asked. "What, no comments? Then let us proceed. This event is the eighteen-mile rucksack march. We call it that because from here to the finish point is eighteen miles, and you will be carrying a rucksack while you march.

"Complete the march as fast as you can. Stay on this road. Don't accept rides from strangers. Don't give piggyback rides to one another. Cadre members will be posted along the way. They will be holding green chem lights. As you go past, give them your color and number. The finish point is where this road hits the pavement of King Road. A cadre member will be there to mark your finish time. Water is available along the route. You may quit at any time; to do so, merely give your color and number to any cadre member and tell him, 'I voluntarily withdraw.' He will ask you no questions. If you wish to withdraw now, just stand fast when the others depart."

No one moved or spoke.

"Since there are no questions," he looked at his watch, "time will start in two minutes. Direction of march is north." He pointed in the direction we had come.

"I won't fire a gun or anything. Put your rucks on and depart when I call go. And...have a good 'un." I mumbled the last part along with him under my breath.

Eighteen miles. I wondered how they came up with that distance. It seemed a little odd. The Ranger Battalion standard for a twenty-miler was six hours, and that was with weapon, full combat equipment, and steel pot locked on your head. I was much lighter than that, and this would be a night march on a cool, dry evening. I would try for four and a half hours. That would equal four miles an hour or a mile every fifteen minutes. No, that's too fast. I can't do that without running, and I'm not gonna run. Five hours would be a good time. I was certain no one in the Army had a faster standard for road marching than the Rangers.

Shumate called "Go," and off we went. A dozen or so guys took off running, most of them in pairs. Another wad of perhaps thirty men tore off at a furious walking pace. To each his own, I figured, and concentrated on settling into my stride and getting my rucksack situated on my back. Within a few minutes, the crowd at the starting point had spread out and I had room to establish my pace.

Eighteen miles is a long way, and you can't do it at a sprint. That had been the distance of the graduation swim when I had attended the Special Forces/Scout Swimmer course in Greece back in 1972. Then I remembered something. Country Grimes, the man who had recruited me for Selection, had been the senior instructor when I attended that course.

After about two miles I was warmed up and moving well. I like to walk. Breathing in sync with the movement of arms and legs; shirt and fly unbuttoned to let the air circulate—it all feels good. On a long, hard march my mind slips off to a place of its own and my body switches to autopilot. It makes for a private and interior time in an otherwise highly socialized military existence. It's also when I hatch some of my better plots and schemes.

Within four miles I was catching and passing some of the runners. I planned to march for two hours before I took a breather and thereafter take a few minutes' break every hour. It was full dark now, but the ambient light was pretty good and the white sand of the road showed all the holes and furrows to be avoided. All in all, a pretty good route.

When I was about seven miles into the march, I saw a cluster of lights up ahead on the side of the road with shadowy figures moving around within. As I got closer, I saw several trucks circled around a group of trees with their lights illuminating some kind of activity.

As I approached, a cadre member beckoned me over. I gave him my color and number and he told me to drop my rucksack under any one of a set of scales that were dangling from a pole tied between two trees, and to fill my canteens from the water cans on the back of one of the trucks. I dropped my rucksack, grabbed my canteens, and drained one straight down as I walked over to find the water cans. Without my rucksack I felt light enough to fly. But that would change in a few more hours. I watched the activity in the circle of light as I took another drink and filled my canteens.

When I walked back over to the scales, I saw an interesting exchange between one of the walkers and a man who seemed to be the cadre member in charge of the site.

The cadre was saying, "Sarge, your rucksack is light. It doesn't meet the forty-pound requirement."

Before he could continue, the walker interrupted, saying, "Well, it's got to be close. How much *does* it weigh?"

"I really can't tell you," the cadre replied in a monotone. "If you look at the scales, you'll see they don't register anything less than forty pounds. So as far as we're concerned your rucksack weighs nothing."

I looked up at the set of scales above my rucksack, and he was correct. The face was painted a solid white until it reached the forty-pound mark.

The cadre continued. "And since you're carrying nothing, the only way you can meet the weight requirement is to take this." He reached behind him and handed the guy a big, ragged piece of concrete that looked like it came from a roadbed that had been dug up. "I weighed this myself," he went on, "and certify it as weighing exactly forty pounds. Now, for you to continue the march, you will sign for this item, strap it to your rucksack, and turn it in at the finish point when you complete the march. Any questions?"

The walker stood there holding the chunk of concrete against his chest while a half smirk, half-incredulous look materialized on his face. I recognized him as one of the loudmouths who had been ready with a comment all day, but he was quiet now.

He looked up at the cadre in front of him and asked in a pleading voice, "Marvin, are you serious?"

So they knew each other. This was getting better.

"Completely" was the reply.

The guy thought a few more seconds and then said, "No, I can't do that." Dropping the concrete, he stood with his arms hanging down by his side.

"Are you voluntarily withdrawing from the course?"

A pause. "Yes, I guess I am."

"Take your ruck and get on the back of that truck." The cadre chief indicated a vehicle off to the side of the rest.

The guy stood there a beat or two longer, looking like he couldn't believe what had happened. Our eyes met, and he gave a slight shrug of acceptance, then picked up his rucksack and moved away. That little exchange sure got my attention—and the attention of everyone else who witnessed it.

I grabbed my rucksack and asked the cadre who had weighed it. "Good to go?" as I put my arms through the straps.

"Yep, you can roll," he said as he scribbled something on a clipboard. Then he looked up and said to me as I got the rucksack settled on my back, "Have a good 'un."

I was out of the circle of light and back onto the road in a few steps. I was glad to be away from there. That had been some little scene. The cadre chief had never been loud or threatening, and he never spoke in a demeaning or insulting manner, but it had been clear he would neither listen to nor tolerate any bullshit. I liked that style. The seriousness of this was starting to feel genuine.

The rest of the march was, well—just a night rucksack march. After twelve miles I was tired, my feet hurt, my shoulders ached, and I was soaked in sweat.

I hit the finish point on King Road at a few minutes under five hours of march time. The cadre member logged me in on his clipboard, told me it was only two miles back to camp, that there was soup in the mess hall, that new instructions were on the bulletin board, and to have a good 'un.

I took my time on the walk back to camp. I dropped my ruck by my cot and went to the mess hall for a canteen cup of soup. There were about a dozen other footsore and tired guys in the mess hall, but every one of them wore a look of contentment. It comes from completing a strenuous task and knowing you've acquitted yourself well. Completing a road march is no huge triumph, but it's one of those many small things in life by which you measure yourself.

Also, the soup was pretty darn good. One of the things the Army always does right is soup. It's prepackaged, and the cooks make it in fifteen-gallon pots, but you can always count on it to be steaming hot and it's just the ticket when you're footsore and tired, and the sweat you're soaked in is starting to chill. It's a simple thing, but one that makes a difference.

I said goodnight to the guys in the mess hall and headed for the shower. It was a little after 0100 hours when I checked the bulletin board. It said:

1000 hours
Classroom

I hit my cot, wrapped up in my poncho liner, and slept the sleep of the righteous.

1000 hours. Sore feet, stiff leg, back, and shoulder muscles. Seated in the classroom. A closed folder and a couple of sharp pencils on the desk in front of me and a smiling guy up front giving instructions.

"Just a questionnaire about yourself, men," he smiled. "It's not timed. Answer every question and give each question your best answer. If something is unclear or confusing, give it your best guess. If something completely stumps you, I'll be at the back of the room. This is strictly an individual effort, no collaboration. Okay, open your booklets and begin."

I opened the cover. Psychological test. This would be just the first of many. Throughout Selection we took these tests over and over again. Each was worded a bit differently than the others. The questions were crafted differently, but they were essentially the same questions. Just mixed about and phrased in a different manner every time. We always took the tests when we were tired—but not while we were exhausted.

By answering the same questions again and again, at seemingly random times, an individual was less likely to be able to sustain duplicity or deception. The same held for testing fatigued men. The person who may be trying to craft a lie has less energy to put into the effort. It becomes easier to tell the truth when you can't remember what you might have said last time.

But this was the first test of its kind I had ever taken. Most of the questions seemed to have an obvious point: "Do you hear voices? Are you an agent of God? Are people following you? Are you often misunderstood? Do you have thoughts too terrible to speak about?"

The only ones I really wondered about were the several variations of "Is your stool black and tarry?" That question was in every exam throughout Selection. Years later, during the annual mental evaluation in the unit, I asked the shrink about that question and why it had been asked so often. The answer was straightforward and made a lot of sense.

"Oh," he said, "black and tarry stool is an indication of blood in the digestive system, which could mean ulcers or indicate someone with a drinking problem."

Very sensible.

An hour later I finished the questionnaire, closed the folder, and carried the material to the cadre member at the back of the room. "Smiley" cautioned me not to speak about the test and told me that new instructions were on the bulletin board.

I stepped outside and blinked in the bright sunshine. The camp was quiet. A line of men was outside the orderly room for out-processing. Some looked a little sheepish, and some covered up their embarrassment with a display of bravado or unconcern.

I checked the bulletin board and saw there was nothing scheduled until PT formation the next morning. The whole rest of the day and night free.

I went over to B Barracks to see about a comrade. Joe McAdams was an old-timer from our Ranger company who had gone into Special Forces last year. I had not seen him, but I'd heard he was in the Selection course. This morning at chow, Parks told me Joe had been injured on last night's march and was in his cot waiting for his unit to send someone to pick him up.

Must have turned an ankle, I figured as I walked into the hooch and scanned the line of bunks for Mac.

"Hey, Haney. Down here," he called and gave a languid wave from a cot midway down the building.

"God a'mighty, Mac, what happened to you?" I asked as I came close enough to see the raw and bloody soles of his propped-up feet.

"Pads of my feet stayed in my boots when I took 'em off after the road march."

From toe to heel, the bottoms of his feet were completely devoid of skin. It looked as though some ancient Indian warrior with a perverted sense of humor had scalped his feet instead of his head. That raw, naked flesh must have hurt like hell exposed to the air.

"Yeah, it smarts a mite," he said, reading my mind. "You know what happened? All those old Ranger calluses were still on my feet, but they weren't very well anchored anymore. I haven't done any rucksack marching since I got out of Phase Training [Special Forces Qualification Training] a year ago. The medic said that during the march last night, I got blisters under the old calluses and eventually the whole mess just came loose. Now, ain't that some shit?"

"Yeah, Mac. It is," I said, wincing at the sight of his feet. "Looks like you'll be on your ass for a while."

"Reckon so," he replied, taking a drag from the cigarette he had just lit. "Guess I'll get a chance to catch up on my reading now."

"I guess you will. Are you squared away? Somebody coming to get you?"

"My team medic is coming out with an FLA [field litter ambulance] to pick me up, and the group surgeon is going to meet us at Womack Army Hospital. Probably spend a day at the hospital to clean 'em and treat for infection, and then go on convalescent leave until I can grow some new skin," he said, waggling his feet.

"You need anything?" I asked as I got up to leave.

"Nah, I'm okay. Medic'll be here soon and I got plenty of cigarettes, so I'll just take it easy until he gets here."

"Okay, partner, you hang in there. And tell any of the old gang you see that I said hello."

"Will do, man. You do the same—and come and see me when you finish here."

"Sure, Mac. Take care."

We shook hands and I left, walking away with the image of those obscenely skinned feet in my mind. I was left wondering again where that line was between hard-ass and dumb-ass. But I guess that's an individual determination. Mac found it last night, somewhere along those last eighteen miles.

Joe McAdams immediately went into Army legend as "The Guy Who Walked His Feet Off in Delta Force Selection." Everybody knew the myth, but few ever knew the man it happened to.

Next morning we fell in for PT at 0600. I maneuvered a spot on the right end of the front rank that would put me in the front of the formation for the run, because I hate running in the middle of a formation. It's always best to be the lead dog. The scenery's better.

As we were coalescing into formation and before a cadre member came out to take charge, I heard more than the usual laughter from back in the group. I looked back to see what kind of stuff was going on and saw a guy standing in formation wearing a gorilla mask that covered his entire head.

His rank insignia said he was a captain, his shoulder patch said he was in Special Forces, and the mask he wore said he was a nitwit. As the twittering died away, no-nonsense Marvin stepped out of the Orderly Room to take charge of the formation.

"Group! Aaaten-*shun*!" he called. "Stand at . . . *ease*!

"Just some light PT to loosen up before we start the day, men. And since my voice is a little hoarse this morning, I'm gonna need some help calling cadence. Let's see. Yeah you, Gorilla Man. Get up here and call cadence for me."

Gorilla Man made a move to take off his mask.

"No," Marvin snapped. "Leave the mask on. You'll take it off when I tell you to. This is my formation and you'll follow my instructions."

We then extended ranks for PT and Marvin put us through one helluva pace of calisthenics. Gorilla Man was shouting the cadence *and* exercising while Marvin shouted at him.

Side straddle hops, the high jumper, squat thrusts, push-ups, turn and bounce. We continued the furious pace until the Masked Moron finally went to his knees, hyperventilating inside his mask.

"Get back in the formation," Marvin told him. "Keep the mask. It suits you. Now, group! Aaaten-*shun*! Close ranks! *March!* Chow's on in the mess hall. Take your instructions from the bulletin board. Fall out!"

As the formation fell out with nervous laughter, I watched Gorilla Man pull the mask off his soaking wet head and blanched face. He walked away looking confused by what had happened. I could not fathom what he had expected. Applause?

The bulletin board announced another formation at 0800. Plenty of time to clean up and have breakfast.

We fell in at 0800 and, from there, filed through the warehouse where we each picked up a machine gun ammo canister. Once back in formation, the cadre member in charge had us open and inspect the contents of the emergency canisters we all now had.

I opened my can and took out the items it contained and checked them off against the list the cadre was reading out loud.

URC-68 emergency signaling radio
VS-17 aircraft signaling panel
Signal mirror

Red smoke grenade
Purple smoke grenade
Whistle
Waterproof match container with matches
Tourniquet
Cravat
Two pressure dressings

When we had checked all the items and repacked them in the canister, a new man appeared and took charge of the formation. He identified himself as Major Odessa, the commander of the Selection Detachment. He was medium-sized with sandy hair and a close-cropped mustache. His skin was the color of light rust. He had the unassuming appearance of a man who would not be singled out in a crowd. But there was an inner power to him that could be felt from a distance and could be seen in his eyes.

"Now that the preliminaries are out of the way and some of the less-determined individuals have departed for home, we can get down to business," he announced.

"For the next several weeks you will undergo the Selection process for acceptance into the 1st Special Forces Operational Detachment—Delta. Despite the name, this is not a Special Forces unit. It neither belongs to, nor reports to, the Special Forces Command. This is a new organization whose sole purpose is to perform counterterrorist and other special operations as directed by the National Command Authority.

"This is not a training course. It is a Selection course. Those who are accepted will be trained once they are assigned to the unit.

"Now, some ground rules. They are simple and few. Everything you see, hear, and do during this course is classified. You will keep it to yourself. Everything you will do is an individual effort. That means you will assist no other Selection candidate and you will accept assistance from no one whatsoever.

"You are all seasoned soldiers, and experienced NCOs, and officers. So we know that each of you can operate as a member, and as a leader, of a team. But that isn't our concern. We want to know how you operate as an individual. The vehicle we will use to assess that is cross-country navigation, or, as the civilians call it, orienteering.

"Each day you will receive the instructions necessary to get you started and as you go along, you will receive the instructions you need for the next event. Much as you have received to this point.

"You will carry a prescribed load between designated rendezvous points, or, as we call them, 'RVs.' Upon arrival at a new point you will receive new instructions from the cadre member manning that point. You will have finished the day when a cadre member tells you to take off your rucksack and sit down."

We were riveted to the sound and meaning of his voice. No one moved a muscle as he spoke.

"You will be operating against an unannounced time standard. However, at the start of every day you will be given an 'Overdue Time.' If you are not at an RV point at that time, you will move to the nearest road and sit down where you can be seen. The cadre will begin looking for you at the Overdue Time.

"If you become lost to the point that you cannot find a road at Overdue Time, or you become injured and can no longer go on, use your emergency signaling kit. If you have a life- or limb-threatening injury, use the radio. If night has arrived and you have not been found, build and maintain a small fire in the largest clearing or open area you can find. We will be searching for you, and you will be found.

"As you move from RV to RV, you will stay off all roads and trails. We define a road or trail as one currently capable of jeep traffic. If you find that your route is running parallel to a road or trail, you will stay at least fifteen meters away. You may walk on a road or trail for the fifteen meters approaching or departing an RV.

"If you become injured or sick and require medical attention, tell the nearest cadre member, 'I require medical attention.'

"If for any reason, at any time, you no longer desire to continue with the Selection course, tell any cadre member, 'I wish to voluntarily withdraw from the course.' No one will question your decision; you will be immediately withdrawn and returned to your parent unit.

"No course reports will be filed on you and sent back to your parent unit. Neither you nor we will talk about anything that takes place during this course. Is there anything I've said to this point that is unclear?"

Amazingly, there were no questions from anyone.

"Then we will begin," continued the major. "Remember, you are competing against an unannounced time standard; you are not competing against one another. You will receive the instructions you need to complete each event. Add nothing to the instructions; subtract nothing from the instructions; read nothing into the instructions that is not stated.

"The cadre will not assist you and you will not assist one another or accept any outside assistance. This is an individual effort. Willful failure to follow instructions will result in dismissal from the course. Failure to meet Selection standards will result in dismissal from the course.

"Do your utmost at all times, and you may find that to be sufficient." He finished his presentation and then looked us over once more before turning us over to a cadre member and silently departing.

We were then instructed to fall out in thirty minutes with a forty-pound rucksack, emergency kit packed inside, a compass, and one C ration meal. At formation, we were given a color and number as our individual identification codes and a map sheet of Fort Bragg.

We were assigned to trucks by color and number. I couldn't detect any pattern in the assignments. Normal Army method would be to put all "reds" on one truck, all "blues" on another, all "greens" on yet another. Or at least, if mixing color groups, the numbers would run in sequence. The arbitrariness of this was obviously purposeful. For a reason I couldn't explain, I liked it.

Our convoy of trucks moved out of the compound and scattered in all directions as soon as we hit the road. Some went left and some went right; one moved straight across the highway and stopped. As our group continued on, a truck would turn off here or there until we, too, pulled off onto a sand trail and eventually came to a stop in a choking miasma of dust.

The driver opened the tailgate and a cadre member told us to dismount but stay on the other side of the truck until he called us forward, four at a time, each with a different color.

I was in the first group called forward, and as we approached, he pointed out a spot for each color and told us we would find our instructions on a sheet of paper at our spot.

I moved to the place he indicated, a large persimmon tree about twenty meters away, and found an acetate-covered sheet of paper tacked to the base of the tree. The sheet was marked with my color and had a set of map coordinates for this location.

It also said: "Your next RV is located at..." and gave the eight-digit grid coordinates for that point. Below this was printed the Overdue Time for the day.

I sat on my rucksack and transposed both sets of coordinates, marked each location on the map, and wrote the Overdue Time in the green Army pocket notebook I habitually carried in my shirt pocket. I took out my compass, oriented the map, and was studying the possible routes and calculating distances when the cadre member called me to his location.

"Open your map, show me where you are, and show me where you're going," he instructed in a flat, matter-of-fact tone.

I picked up a twig from the ground, and using it as a pointer said, "I am here and am going there," pointing to each location in turn with the twig.

"Okay," he replied, and looked into my face with a deadpan stare. "Have a good 'un."

I made no reply, just nodded, shouldered my rucksack, took my initial compass bearing, and set out on the first steps into the unknown.

I picked a pace that, given the terrain and the offsets of my route, could move me to my destination at about five kilometers an hour. It was a pace that covered ground well enough but was also one I could maintain with the load I was carrying for a long, long time. I had to move fast but not burn myself out, because I didn't have any idea when I would finish.

That initial leg was about six kilometers. Along the way I saw one or two other guys scurrying along different routes. We studiously ignored each other and continued on our respective paths.

The day was warm, but not hot, and the air was dry. There was even a little bit of a breeze blowing as I crossed the tops of the broad, low hills. The ruck was settled on my back and I soon worked up a good sweat.

There were no land mines. No one was shooting artillery or machine guns at me. I had no one to worry about other than myself. I was healthy, strong, and moving well on a new adventure. All in all, a pretty damn good day.

I was getting close to the RV. I had marked the location at a slight bend of a sand trail that contoured about halfway up a small hill. I saw the point when I was about twenty-five meters out. As I closed with it, the RV sitter saw me and called, "Color and number."

I responded with my code for the day and the sitter replied, "Roger, Green Six. Your instructions are over there," and he pointed to one of the sheets posted about the area. "Water is on the back of the truck. Come and see me when you're ready," he said as he scribbled something on a clipboard.

I nodded my acknowledgment and moved to my instruction sheet. All it said was "GREEN: Your next RV is located at..." and gave the eight-digit coordinates of the new location.

I plotted the spot on the map and reported to the sitter.

"Show me where you are and show me where you're going," he directed.

I did so, received the inevitable "Have a good 'un," and moved out sharply on the new route.

The rest of the day was much the same. The legs between RVs were four to seven kilometers in length. The terrain stayed pretty much the same except for one good-size creek I had to wade. Occasionally I would cross paths with other candidates, but otherwise I was alone. It was a good workout, vigorous, but not overly demanding.

My only apprehension was a slight worry about whether I was moving fast enough. But I knew this was a good pace. I was covering ground quickly and my navigation was accurate. I *could* go faster if I had to, but that raised the risk of getting hurt or becoming overfatigued, and my navigation becoming sloppy.

I arrived at my sixth RV in the late afternoon and called out my color and number as soon as the sitter looked up at my approach.

"Roger, Green Six. Go across the road to those pines, take off your rucksack, and sit down." He pointed to a clump of pines about thirty meters away.

I stood there uncertainly for a second and asked, "Am I finished?"

He merely repeated, "Go across the road to those pines, take off your rucksack, and sit down." He said it in a level, calm voice as if I had never caused him to repeat his statement. No exasperation, no snideness, no emphasis, just the statement of instructions.

"Right," I said, as I moved away. *Just do as you're told and don't ask questions unless the instructions are unclear.*

I crossed the street and shucked off my rucksack. It felt good to get that bastard off my back. You can become accustomed to carrying a ruck, but it never becomes comfortable. I plucked my canteens from their covers, drained the last one down my throat, and filled them both from one of the water cans nearby. Then I sat down and leaned back against my ruck, propped my feet up a tree, and thought about the day as I sipped a canteen.

This must be the finish point for the day and I must be doing okay, I thought. *I'm the only one here so I must be first. No, maybe I'm late and a truckful has already gone in. No, that can't be right, to get here faster than I did you'd have to run all day. But maybe the others didn't come from my starting point; maybe they came from other points and had different legs, maybe.... Maybe, hell! I don't know and I'm not going to worry about it or waste energy trying to figure it out. I'll just do my best, and if that's not good enough they can send me home.*

But within a few minutes, another guy showed up at the RV and came over to the rest spot under the pines. I had not seen him before now. We introduced ourselves as he dropped his ruck and settled down.

His name was Ron Cardowski and he was a tall, lean master sergeant stationed with the 10th Special Forces in Bad Tolz, Germany. Bad Tolz is one of my favorite places and I have many friends stationed there, so we chatted about mutual acquaintances, favorite ski slopes, and Bavarian *Gasthauses* as more candidates began to arrive at our location.

After a half hour or so there were about fifteen men lounging in the shade of the pine grove. A little later, a deuce-and-a-half pulled up and the RV sitter told us to climb aboard. One guy had to ask if the truck was going back to camp, and he seemed a little put out when the sitter merely repeated, "Get on the truck." The guy climbed aboard, muttering to himself.

I retreated into myself as the truck bounced along the dusty sand trail and thought about that guy, about my question, "Am I finished?" and other things I had noticed. The factor of the unknown was subtly but persistently at work here.

The Army lives and operates on published schedules. In peacetime, the document that regulates life is the unit Training Schedule.

The Training Schedule is published weekly and announces each day's activity in detail: time of formations, hourly activities, uniform requirements, classes and the names of the instructors, activity locations, mealtimes and what type rations are provided, special notes, and what time the duty day ends. Other notices such as the Duty Roster round out these detailed instructions.

For field and combat operations, the Operations Order provides all the instructions for the conduct of foreseen activities. As most people suspect, military life is a highly regulated affair. And for experienced soldiers, that amount of regulation gives a certain sense of comfort. It provides the framework they need to plan, conduct, and pursue their duties and their lives. The inevitable changes wrought on the training schedule—just because all things cannot be minutely regulated—always produce some degree of turmoil in a unit.

So you can imagine the effect this minimal instruction was having on everyone in the Selection course. We were all affected to varying degrees. I have always prided myself on my adaptability and my ability to overcome obstacles, but I could feel a sense of anxiety about the unknowns of this course hovering in the back of my mind.

What was going to happen next? Was I moving fast enough? How long was it all going to last? Were there "spies" in the course watching, listening, and reporting back to the cadre? I thought about these things and others on the truck ride and came to the conclusion that I didn't give a damn about any of them. The factor of the unknown was exhilarating and I enjoyed it. I always have.

But one of us had reached a different conclusion by the time our truck arrived back at camp. He was a well-built, tough-looking sergeant first class serving on drill sergeant duty with a basic training brigade. When we piled off the truck, he went to the cadre member standing nearby and reported that he wished to voluntarily withdraw from the course. Those of us present were surprised to see it happen; this guy was no slouch. The cadre member merely directed him to the orderly room for out-processing and then told the rest of us that instructions were on the bulletin board.

Word filtered out later that he told Sergeant Major Shumate he was jacking it in because he couldn't stand not knowing what he would be doing, not just after the next event, but the next day and the day after that. He said he realized he required structure and organization and that this just wasn't for him. I never saw him again.

I went to the hooch to put my gear away, had a good shower, and enjoyed an excellent supper. The meals here were extraordinarily good.

Later that evening, they were showing a movie in the mess hall. *Marathon Man.*

The next six days were much like the first one. Point to point, I covered just about the entire western half of Fort Bragg. Every day we had a different color and number, and every day we started and finished with a different group.

Some days had fewer RVs to hit, but the legs were longer and more difficult. Some days saw more RVs, and one time, I was nearing the Overdue Time when I finally finished. The end of some days found as many as twenty of us at the final RV, but on another day, only four of us got on the same truck back to camp.

Cadre members would show up for a day and then disappear. But no matter who they were, the RV sitters always acted the same, with a calm, deliberate, dispassionate, "just the facts, ma'am" demeanor. You never saw any of them get ruffled or have the slightest flutter in their composure. They didn't smile, they didn't frown, and they didn't gesture. But they always watched.

Everything happened when it was supposed to. If the bulletin board announced truck departure at 0600 hours, they rolled at 0600. If someone missed the truck, he was never seen or spoken of again. The steady disappearance of men was downright eerie, made noticeable only by the diminished size of the crowd each night in the mess hall. No one saw them leave, no one heard them leave, they were just . . . gone.

The Midnight Hook, as we called the mechanism behind these vanishing acts, had already snatched three old comrades of mine. I was reading *The Gulag Archipelago*, so perhaps my antennae were somewhat sensitive to the mystery of disappearing men.

Day seven was a very short day. We returned to camp at 1300 hours and headed straight to the classroom for another round of psychological testing. It felt peculiar, sitting at a school desk, dog tired and soaked through with sweat, methodically taking a written examination knowing you'd never see the results. All you'd be able to do was wonder if you had passed, failed, or fallen somewhere in between.

There was a formation that evening after chow. Major Odessa, the Iron Major, as I thought of him, was in charge.

"Men, this last week has been a practice session. Some of you have been away from tactical units for a while and needed to hone your navigational skills. Some men, who have since departed, didn't really want to be here, and just needed a little time to realize that fact. Up until now, the only men who have returned to their units have been those too injured to carry on or those who have voluntarily withdrawn from the course. That all changes tomorrow."

Holding himself perfectly still, he paused, as if gathering his thoughts. I held my breath and felt myself freeze along with him. Then he continued, and I breathed again.

"Tomorrow you begin Stress Phase. You will be relocating to a remote, mountainous field location. You will be bivouacking in the open. Prepare for a ten-day stay in the field and pack your duffel bag accordingly. All meals will be C rations. Potable water will be provided; do not drink from any streams or other bodies of water.

"After this formation, you will report to the supply room to draw a weapon and the map sheets you will need. Keep those items with you at all times. You will carry your weapon in your hand; they do not have slings attached and you will not rig a sling or tie the weapon to your body.

"Replace or draw any additional equipment you need this evening. Pack anything you will not need for the field and store it in the supply room. Privately owned vehicles will stay here.

"As of tomorrow, your movement between RVs will be timed and you will be judged against a set time standard for movement. Do not worry yourself trying to determine what that time standard is. Just do the best you can.

"There are those of you here now who will fail to meet course standards and will be removed from the Selection course for that failure. Those men will be returned to their units with a copy of a letter that will go to their commanding officer declaring that man to be both an exemplary soldier and a credit to his unit, but not, unfortunately, selected for service with this unit at this time. Indeed, all of you are excellent soldiers or you would not still be here.

"Things have been rather easy until now. The difficulty will increase tomorrow. Pay attention, follow instructions, and do your best. That's all we require.

"Since there are no questions, you are released to prepare for tomorrow. Additional instructions are posted on the bulletin board. Have a good 'un." And with that, the major turned on his heel and walked out of the room.

You mean I've been walking for fun this whole last week? What the hell? But I knew I'd profited from the last seven days of practice. My navigation was razor-sharp, my conditioning was even better, and I was becoming accustomed to being on my own and not having a forty-four-man platoon to shepherd about.

But it wasn't all freedom. The cadre had been watching and keeping notes on us all along—and not just our RV times. They weren't surreptitious about it, but neither were they very open. If you paid attention, you could see they observed everything that went on and would sometimes write in a notebook before moving on with whatever they were doing.

Some guys were really agitated by it and worried about what was being recorded in those notes. I thought the observation reports were genuine, but that some of the note-taking was designed purely to create consternation. I later found this to be true.

I checked the bulletin board for instructions and headed for the supply room. Sergeant Major Shumate was standing nearby, smoking a cigarette and watching the sunset.

I greeted him as I walked by, "Evening, Sergeant Major."

He was holding his cigarette at arm's length and squinting at it with one eye as if trying to detect some defect.

"Hey there, Ranger," he said, looking up. "Still hanging around, eh? It must be that you like the chow... 'cause there sure ain't no booze or pussy hereabouts."

The cigarette must have passed inspection, because he reeled it back in and took an elaborate draw while eyeing me from beneath his brows, while that amused smile I had seen before lifted the ends of his mustache.

"I guess that's it, Sergeant Major, and besides, I've been needing a little vacation anyway."

He snorted in reply as he exhaled through his nose, and then tilting his head back, with elegant grace blew a slow, rolling ring into the still air.

"A lot of these guys wouldn't know what you meant by that," he said, glancing around the yard. "But I remember what it's like to be a platoon sergeant, and I think it was easier back then than it is now. So yeah, enjoy what you can, none of this lasts forever. Maybe I'll see you when you get back," he said in dismissal.

"I hope so, Sergeant Major."

"Yeah," he replied, and returned his attention to the sunset and his cigarette.

I glanced back as I opened the door to the supply room. From where I stood he looked like a man surveying the universe from some secret vantage point.

Maybe he was.

Somewhere in the Uwharrie Mountains National Forest.

The Uwharries are an eruption of rugged terrain about fifty miles northwest of Fort Bragg. A quick study of the map sheets told me the land was not gentle. In fact, it looked very similar to the Appalachian Ridge and Valley region where I had grown up in north Georgia.

We had mounted up early for the ride to our new location. I thought we would set up camp first, but a couple of hours into the trip, our convoy started to disintegrate, and pretty soon our truck was traveling alone. We turned onto a narrow paved road and then came to a halt. A cadre member called us off the truck four at a time. I was itching to get going and glad to be in the first group.

The RV sitter was a cadre member named Carlos. He sent me around to the front of the old bread delivery van that was his vehicle to read the instructions posted on the hood of the truck.

The weapon I had been issued was a "grease gun," the old .45-caliber submachine gun that had been Army standard since the Second World War. It was reliable as sin, but very heavy for its size and awkward as hell to carry, particularly without a sling. I tried to lay it on the hood of the truck as I plotted the coordinates on my map, but the damn thing kept sliding off. I didn't want to lay it on the ground because the grass was wet from a heavy dew. After looking around for a decent place to put it, I stuck it, barrel first, into the grille of the truck and let it dangle there.

I took my map over to Carlos, showed him were I was and where I was going, slung my rucksack on my back, and hauled ass out of the RV on my initial heading.

This was it—the first leg of the first real day—and I was fired up. I felt so strong my feet barely touched the ground as I left the RV. As soon as I crossed the road I had to negotiate a barbed-wire fence on the other side. But that was no problem. I threw my right hand on top of a fence post and bounded over in one great leap, and while in midair over the fence, I saw my empty left hand.

Oh, shit. I left my weapon at the RV. I hit the ground on the far side of the fence with the exhilaration hissing out of me like air from a punctured beach ball. Carlos watched me all the way back to the truck, where I sheepishly pulled my weapon from the grille and departed, this time at a more moderate pace.

His dispassionate "Have a good 'un" stung like a shotgun blast of rock salt, particularly when I realized that he hadn't said it on my first departure. He knew I was screwing up all along but had given no hint of it.

Well, it was a good lesson. My pride was bruised a little and I'd lost a few minutes. Probably had even gotten a notation of "dickhead attack" beside my name in Carlos's notebook. I'd make it a point not to let it happen again.

The terrain here was much more difficult to negotiate than on Fort Bragg, but I felt I needed to cover just as much ground per hour as before. I would have to be smarter in my route selection because I wouldn't be able to beat down the mountains. If I tried to assault them, eventually they would overpower me. All I wanted was their indifference. In return, I promised to make my passage as unobtrusive as I could.

My routes that first day seemed positively screwy. From RV to RV I found myself contouring clockwise, midway up the slopes of various ridges. I wanted to cross their spines, where I could get on their tops and run the long axis. But on every leg, doing that would have carried me so far out of the way as to be not worth the effort. A waste of precious energy. I spent the majority of my time on the slopes going in wide circles with my left foot downhill. It was so continuous that I got one of the few foot blisters I've ever had in my life—just under the ankle on the outside of the left foot, the perpetual downhill side.

I saw only one other person between RVs that day. Sometime in the afternoon I came across Captain Jim Bush limping along.

Jim had also come to Selection from 1st Ranger. He had commanded our company until earlier in the year, and since that time had been serving as the assistant operations officer for the Battalion, a job he didn't particularly care for. Jim was one of those hard-core combat officers who prefer to be in the field with the troops. And though staff positions are important, they naturally chafe a man like Captain Bush. He was also as tough as shoe leather—and if he was limping, he was hurt pretty badly. Still, Jim Bush could limp faster than most men could walk.

I broke the code of silence and asked him what happened as our paths crossed.

"Caught my foot between two rocks coming down the slope of a mountain and twisted my ankle. Didn't hear or feel anything crack, so I'm hoping it's just a sprain. I'll know tonight when I pull the boot off," he said between compressed lips and gritted teeth.

"Okay, Cap'n. See you later." And we continued on our separate ways.

Luck. Pure-ass luck was going to play its part in this endeavor. The luck not to fall and break a leg, the luck not to get a stick jammed in the eye, the luck not to be bitten by a snake or do something so stupid you couldn't recover from it. Luck is always in the mix, and I just hoped to avoid the bad side of it.

To help that along, I had brought my best talisman with me.

It wasn't anything special—just the jungle fatigues I was wearing. They had become good luck through use. I had worn the same set every day so far and would continue to wear them as long as their luck held up, no matter how rank they became.

I had brought three sets of fatigues with me to Selection. One set was in reserve, one set I wore in the evenings after cleaning up following the days' activities, and the other set I wore every day. They weren't as ripe as you might think. I had already washed them out once or twice and hung them up at night. In the mornings, they were no more wet than when I had taken them off, soaked in sweat, the evening before. They had accumulated luck, and luck attracts more luck. And I didn't want to do anything that might break the cycle.

Late in the afternoon I was finally told to drop ruck and sit down. Again I was by myself until within minutes, another candidate, Ron, joined me at the finish point. It had been a tough day and I was bushed. Our load had been increased by five pounds and my feet and knees were tired and sore from contouring in the same position all day.

I was hot and soaked with a sticky sweat. But just about the time Ron arrived, one of those serendipitous blessings of nature also showed up: a good shower of rain. We covered our rucksacks with ponchos and moved to a small clearing in the trees to let the rainwater sluice over our bodies. It was delicious and it was just the right amount. The rain fell steadily for about fifteen minutes and then the sun returned. The air was washed and clean and so was I. What a treat. If you've never experienced such a pleasant, simple thing, you have my pity.

Within a half hour we were joined by about a half dozen other men. I could also hear men being sent to another location about fifty meters away on the other side of the road. Two trucks pulled up at the RV, and a cadre member came over and told our group to get on the first one. We grabbed our rucks and climbed aboard.

As the truck rumbled off, I looked at the other group, but they were still sitting there. I quickly wondered which of us was going where, and just as quickly dismissed the thought. The men in the other group weren't my concern, and as for me, I'd know the destination when I got there.

We rode for about a half an hour and then pulled up into a logging road. Several men were called off and the rest of us continued along. At a second stop, I was called off the truck with four or five other men. Marvin was waiting there for us. He had been the sitter at my second RV that day. As soon as we dismounted he gave us our instructions.

"This is where you'll make camp tonight. Your bags are on the back of my truck. So are water and C rations. Stay in a group within twenty-five meters of the truck. Fires are authorized but must be doused by 2200 hours, keep them small and under control. The medic will be here later if anyone needs to see him. Scales are slung in front of the truck. Rucksack weight for tomorrow is fifty pounds. You will receive your color and number for the day at 0545. The vehicle departure time in the morning is 0600.... Don't be late and don't be light." And with that he focused his attention on his clipboard.

I nabbed my bag and looked for a good spot between two trees to set up a poncho hooch. I was almost finished when another truck pulled up and dropped off a half dozen more men who received the same briefing from Marvin. I paid little attention to the new arrivals until Virg Parks brayed in my ear.

"Hey, Bud, that looks like a good spot you got there, I'll just join you!" he shouted from a foot away. Parks always stood as close to you as possible, as if he were going to whisper some intimate secret, and then hollered like he was calling hogs. He threw his kit bag and rucksack in a heap on the ground and started digging through his pockets. I knew what was coming next.

"Hey, Bud, ya got a cigarette?" he asked, rooting through his pockets for what he knew wasn't there.

"No, Parks, I quit smoking. It got too expensive supporting my habit *and* people like you," I replied as I got a clean set of jungle fatigues out of my kit bag. It was no joke. Parks was the biggest mooch I'd seen in my life.

"Well..." Parks began, eyeing my poncho hooch and planting a just-found cigarette in his mouth. "I'll just tie my poncho to yours and we'll make one big hooch. Got some more of that suspension line?"

"Sure, Parks. Here." I handed him a few feet of cord. Then I moved away a bit to give myself a canteen cup bath, shave, change clothes, and hang up my lucky uniform to dry and air out.

The following morning at 0600 hours, the trucks rolled as promised. I was glad to get moving out of the first RV. My legs were a little stiff and my uniform was still damp and cold, but both discomforts would rapidly go away.

What a day. I was moving right at the ragged edge of my capability. Every route to every RV was a struggle. The drift of the land was contrary to every one of my routes. I was never able to use a valley or a ridge to advantage. Every slope was rocky, rugged, and covered with deadfall. The low ground was worse—a tangle of wait-a-minute vines and briars. Whoever had laid out today's course had done so with studied devilment in mind. It was impossible to maintain good time, and I was worried about being too slow.

I was bashing along a wide, relatively flat spot on the side of a slope when I came across an old abandoned farmstead. The place was overgrown with brush and blackberry briars, but right in the middle of what had been the front yard, I found a bush full of ripe Tommy Toe tomatoes. The Tommy Toe is a perennial plant, and that bush had been dropping fruit here for no telling how many years.

I stopped for the few seconds it took to fill the cargo pockets of my fatigue pants and took off again, popping those sweet and juicy little tomatoes in my mouth one right after the other. What an unexpected and uplifting treat. Even now, writing this more than two decades later, I can see that place clearly and taste those delicious little tomatoes.

The day became even rougher. The slopes were so steep that even tacking back and forth, I had to pull myself from tree to tree to reach the top. The descents were even more hazardous. One misplaced step, one slip, one leaf-covered stump hole or slick tree root, and that would be it.

As the day wore on I started to get worried. It was less than thirty minutes until Overdue Time and I was still more than a kilometer from my next RV. I poured on my reserves of energy and picked up my pace. I came stroking into the RV with about five minutes to spare, shouting my color and number as soon as I saw the sitter.

He consulted his watch, jotted down my info, told me to hang my ruck on the scales at the RV, and pointed to one of the sheets of acetate paper situated around the area. "Come see me when you're ready," he said.

I hung my rucksack on the scales and went to plot my next RV. *I'm screwed now. There's no way I can get to the next RV with what, two minutes left until Overdue Time? Why hadn't I moved faster? Why hadn't I picked better routes?* I'd moved as hard as I could. I'd picked the best routes I could figure. It just wasn't going to be good enough. I went to report to the sitter.

He glanced up as I started to spread my map and go through the drill. "Take your ruck off the scales and go sit by that big rock," he said, gesturing to the other side of the clearing.

I looked in his eyes briefly for a clue as to how I had done but saw no hint of information. "Okay," I replied as I hoisted my rucksack off the hook and went to the place he had indicated. *Man,* I thought as I sat down and propped my feet up. *If I've screwed this day up, Superman himself would have had a tough time.*

I sat there sipping water and studying the routes I had taken that day. No, I couldn't see how I could have picked better routes. And even though the routes were more difficult today, I had still managed to make what I considered to be good time. But if that wasn't good enough, I was in trouble.

Within the next half hour, other guys came rushing into the RV, uniforms ripped and torn, sweat-soaked, faces splotched red from exertion. They all received the same treatment I had and each of them eyed me quizzically when they saw me sitting down, apparently finished, while they plotted their next RV.

The fourth man to come into the position stared longingly at the three of us sitting together on the far side of the clearing when the sitter told him to hang his ruck on the scale and move to his instruction sheet. He just stood there, shoulders slumped, chest heaving, and hands at his side. After a short pause, he took a ragged breath and said, "I voluntarily withdraw."

The sitter replied, "Take your rucksack and move over there, down the slope, and sit down," and pointed to a position that would be out of sight of the RV.

The poor guy stumbled away and out of sight. He never looked back. Our little cluster kept our mouths shut and only lifted eyebrows at one another in communication.

What was the lesson here? Simple. Don't quit. Never quit no matter what. Keep going until someone tells you to sit down. Keep going as long as you're able to move, no matter how poorly you think you may be doing. Just don't quit.

Camp that night was in another location with a completely different group of men. We received the same instructions as the evening before and settled in for a night's rest. But that evening, the medic had a number of visitors when he stopped by on his rounds.

Next day: more of the same, or as they say in Panama, *"Lo mismo ... pero peor."* The same ... only worse.

Long, grueling legs over terrain never lending itself to route selection. I was never able to plot a route that approximated a line between RVs. To use the terrain to any sort of advantage, I had to make lung-busting climbs up-slope to top a long ridge that would carry me only vaguely in the direction of the next RV. There was simply no margin for error. But the more tired I got, the more difficult that became.

About midafternoon, things got hectic. I had just dropped off a ridge top and was zeroing in on my RV when I was overrun by civilians blasting through the woods on cross-country motorcycles.

There were dozens of them all over the place, motors squalling like angry hornets. I felt like a slow ship with kamikazes buzzing about me. They seemed to be going in the same general direction that I was taking—up a broad but rapidly narrowing hollow to a pass in the mountain called Gold Mine Branch.

Just as I came in sight of the RV, a motorbike came whipping past me with a passenger wearing a rucksack holding on to the rider. Yep, that's right . . . a Selection candidate.

The bike stopped next to the RV sitter's truck, and as the candidate got off the back of the bike, I heard him say to the sitter, "I reckon that was a little too far, eh?"

"Put your ruck in the back of my truck and make yourself comfortable. A vehicle will pick you up shortly," said the sitter.

The guy turned back to the biker he had hitched the ride with and told him with a wave, "Thanks for the lift, man. I'll catch you later." Then he threw his rucksack in the truck and sat on the bumper while the biker blasted out of the RV in a shower of dirt and leaves.

Wow! That was some kind of a championship screwup. I plotted my next RV and looked the guy in the face as I walked past him toward the sitter. He threw up his hands with a shrug of his shoulders and a grin that said, "Aah, what the fuck, I tried."

I grinned back at him and shook my head as I walked by. I watched the sitter as closely as possible as we went through the departure ritual. If Easy Rider had surprised him or upset his equilibrium, I wasn't able to detect it.

And so another guy went into Delta Force legend. Even now, when we old hands get together and talk about Selection and the things we've seen over the years, someone will inevitably say, "Remember that guy who came into the RV on the back of a motor-cycle?" Fellow, whoever you are, I want you to know that your place in history is secure. Somehow, I think you'll be pleased.

The rest of the day passed in a sweat-blurred flurry of up-slope, down-slope, and traverse-slope. Of heaving chest, burning lungs, quivering legs, and aching back. Of counting terrain features, pace-count, and compass sightings. My body was drenched in sweat; my face and hands were cut and scratched by sticks, briars, and thorns. Eventually it came to an end. When I finally sat down, I felt like a toothpaste tube that had been squeezed empty. It was an effort to throw my rucksack aboard the truck and climb up after it.

We departed that final RV differently that day. Instead of our group getting on the same truck, we were called individually by color and number and sent to several different trucks.

A question immediately arose in my mind—and doubtless in the minds of the other men. *Is this truck taking me to camp or is this truck going back to Fort Bragg?* The question was answered when we were dropped off at a new campsite. All right, I thought. I'll be here at least one more day.

Camp was unusually quiet that evening. The rule of no conver-sation during the day had seeped into bivouac as well.

Daylight and at it again on another tremendously difficult day. Agonizing climbs up-slope only presaged hazardous descents. To come down-slope without sliding out of control, you have to lean forward, putting the weight of your upper body downhill and over your feet, much like skiing.

But if you trip in that position, your rucksack will drive you face first into the ground or a tree—and with nothing to cushion the fall, you may not recover. I had taken a few falls already, but each time, I had been able to twist around and fall on my side so that my rucksack wasn't on top of me when I hit the ground. So far, my luck was holding.

Throughout the morning and into midday I saw no other candi-dates between RVs. It was like I had the mountains to myself. By late in the afternoon, I was tracking along the top of a long, narrow ridge that, for once, was taking me in the direction of my next RV.

Earlier I had gone almost a half kilometer out of the way to gain the top of this ridge by way of a long, sloping finger offering a somewhat gradual route up the otherwise precipitous sides. But it had paid off. I was making excellent time by virtue of the energy I had saved.

Then I heard a human voice. Not a conversational voice, but the voice of someone wailing in deathlike agony. It was coming from just ahead and off the side of the ridge. I trotted over to a place where I could see down the mountain slope, and spotted him a hundred meters below. He was midway up the steepest portion of the whole mountain, hauling himself tree to tree and rock to rock up what can only be described as a cliff—only to lose his grip and slide back again. He was yelling and bellowing like he was being disemboweled with a rusty file. I watched him for a few seconds, then shook my head in wonder and moved on. The sounds of his battle faded behind me as I continued on my trek. I never saw that man again.

With the sun slipping low in the western sky, my day finally and mercifully ended. A new camp location, a different group of guys, a couple of familiar faces. I didn't bother to count heads, but the camp population was decidedly shrinking.

I slept the sleep of the dead that night, and if I dreamed, I never knew it.

I didn't know it when I set out that morning, but I was going to become intimately familiar with the relief and topography of Gold Mine Mountain. The day would become known as the "Day of the Star," because when drawn on a map, the routes resembled a six-pointed star.

All day long, I crossed that damned mountain from one side to the other. On the map the mountain looked like a big, dead, contorted octopus. The main body was lumpy and irregular; the top writhed snakelike in a series of sharp-crested saddles. The fingers and ridges running off the sides of the crest were gnarled and twisted like the arthritic hands of an old man.

I would arrive exhausted and breathless at one RV only to be sent to the next RV back on the side I just came from. The mountain was too big to contour around and the lay of the ground was such that I could never make anything approximating a direct approach, or maintain the hard-earned high ground for any length of time. Never getting anywhere, back and forth across the same mountain. It was a masterful torture. But then I had a revelation:

What difference could it possibly make if I crossed back and forth over this same mountain until doomsday?

A mountain was a mountain, time was time, and route selection was route selection. The only thing that mattered was speed and ground made good. My destination was determined by time; the physical position of that ultimate destination was only incidental to my reason for being here. The frustration and mental torture I had been suffering were completely of my own making—and completely within my power to disregard.

I dropped all thoughts of anything other than making the best possible approach to the next RV, and it was amazing how much mentally and physically stronger I felt.

From then on it was just a hard day in the mountains. And as happens with all days, no matter how difficult, this one, too, came to a close. I finished the day at RV Easy Rider, the spot where Biker Boy had brought his Selection to such a notable conclusion.

Eventually about twenty of us had arrived and were sitting in one group instead of the normal two or three widely separated clusters. After the trucks came and went, I was left sitting with only six or seven other guys. What was the significance of this?

Before long, a truck arrived with our bags and we were told to make camp right here. A few minutes later, another truck arrived and dropped off three or four more men.

I didn't know it until later, but this was the day of the Big Cut. Those who had collected enough late points against them got the ax at the end of that day. This winnowing of the harvest had brought us down to about thirty men. Thirty out of the original 163 who had started out that first day back at Aberdeen Camp.

I've talked about the unknown or unannounced time standard of the Selection course. After going through Selection, and later working as a cadre member of Selection, I'm still not sure what the time standard is. The only people who know for certain are the Selection detachment commander and noncommissioned officer in charge (NCOIC).

No one else is privy to that information. Not even the Delta Force commander himself. It is one of the best-kept, most well-compartmentalized secrets in the Western world. It ensures that no candidate will ever have an advantage over anyone else, even those who have to come back for a subsequent try.

Every man who ultimately makes it through Delta Selection has had to gauge his performance by his own internal yardstick. He's had to give his utmost because he couldn't be sure just how good was good enough. It keeps everyone honest.

The evening in camp passed in a leisurely fashion. A small group of us sat around talking about our different units, the Army, politics, and national events. Keekee Saenz was in our cluster that night, and we put up a hooch together. I had taken a distinct liking to the guy and was glad to pass a restful evening in conversation with him. I had no suspicion at the time that it would be many years before we were to meet again—and then under very different circumstances.

That evening I also realized something that was really only obvious in its absence: We had started the course with a normal complement of pro-football-player-sized men, but now that I thought about it, most of those had disappeared after the Eighteen Miler. And the two or three who had started Stress Phase were now missing in action.

As I looked around at my campmates and thought about the men I had seen in the last couple of days, it hit me that every man here was more or less average. All shapes, sizes, and builds—but no massive men. We did have a few big guys make it into the unit, but they were greatly outnumbered by men of below-average size.

Selection taxed all your abilities, mental and physical. The mountains would win if you took them head-on, so you had to out-think them. But craftiness alone wouldn't get you from RV to RV on time, much less allow you to keep it up day after day. That required superior physical conditioning, but conditioning and tenacity are not dependent upon size alone. Only a tough body coupled with a tough mind bought a winning ticket to Selection. One without the other could not and would not succeed.

What a great day this was turning out to be. The easiest ground I had crossed so far. The slopes were still high and steep, but the terrain was even and regular. The trees were big, mature hardwoods with very little underbrush. The ground was smooth with few rocks. It was a place to make good time. And I was taking advantage of it because I was certain that conditions would change very soon. They did.

I was stroking along toward my next RV when I came across a twelve-foot-high chain-link fence stretching out of sight in each direction. The question was, go under it, over it, or around it?

I had a sneaking suspicion that I would encounter something worse if I attempted to go around it. The skirt of the fence was anchored in the ground (probably as a barrier to wild hogs), which prevented me from going under. That left over the top. I'm a good climber, but I had an additional seventy pounds on my body and it wouldn't be easy.

Here's what I planned: I'd put my grease gun down the front of my shirt, then climb to the top of the fence and throw my rucksack to the other side. Then I could climb over and down with ease.

Here's how it played out: The climb up wasn't very difficult, but once up top, I discovered I would have to sit straddling the top of the fence to take off the rucksack and let it drop to the ground. But the top of the fence was slack and wobbly, so when I tried to slip the straps off my shoulders, I got to swaying back and forth until the weight of the damn rucksack pulled me off balance and over the other side.

I was hanging upside down, dangling by my left leg from the top of the fence. The grease gun had slid out the top of my shirt and popped me in the mouth, splitting my upper lip and loosening two teeth. That damn rucksack was dangling below my head and it had my shoulders locked. I couldn't shake it loose or my leg would give way and I'd fall headfirst.

Ever so slowly, I worked my right hand over until I could find the quick-release tab on the left shoulder strap. *Let's see . . . it's upside down so I have to pull it the other way.* As soon as that one shoulder was free, the rucksack hurtled earthward and hit with a crash. Then I had to do a long sit-up to get to the top of the fence, right myself, free my leg, and climb down.

Both feet on the ground once more, I looked around, hoping no one had seen that little episode, and then I gave that treacherous rucksack a vicious kick. Bastard! You've just been waiting for the chance to do me in, haven't you? Well, I'll keep an eye on you from now on; you can count on that. With the metallic taste of blood in my mouth, I shouldered the brute and took off again.

I hit the top of the mountain and came into my RV with a rush. Carlos was the sitter and he sent me on to the next stop. From there I was sent right back to Carlos and his RV. *What's going on now?* I thought. A variation on the Day of the Star?

Carlos pointed me to a different set of instructions and then changed his mind. "No, go over there and sit down," he directed.

Wow, I was finished for the day and it wasn't quite 1030. I went to the spot Carlos had indicated, still in broad view of the RV. I shucked that bastard ruck off my back, dug out a C ration, propped my feet up a tree, and leaned back to enjoy my brunch. I was reclining there enjoying the good life when Virgil Parks came crashing into the RV like a roller-coaster car that had jumped the tracks. He saw me sitting there and stopped like he had run into an invisible wall.

"What the hell are you doing just sitting there?" he asked with an incredulous look on his face.

He obviously thought I had quit, but just didn't want to believe his eyes. I decided to have a little fun. I hung my head and in a whining, self-pitying voice slurred, "This is it, Parks . . . I'm finished. I . . . I . . . I can't go any further today. I've reached the end."

A furious look of disgust enflamed his face as he raised his grease gun menacingly and stalked toward me. "Why you, you . . ."

Carlos called him off, and it was the first time I saw a break in the stone-faced detachment of a cadre member. "Hey, you!" and he barked Parks's color and number. "Get over here and worry about yourself. That man's finished for today and you're not."

Parks lowered his grease gun and looked at me with surprise as he turned away to check into the RV and get his new instructions.

"God damn!" he said as he walked past me when he departed the RV. "You're finished already? You must be hauling ass!"

"Have a good 'un, Parks." I grinned as I lifted a can of C ration peaches in salute. "Have a good 'un." *Ah, that was fun. And these peaches sure are good,* I thought as I slid another one over my tongue.

It was thirty minutes before anyone else came in to stay, but then four or five men arrived at the RV almost simultaneously. Shortly thereafter a truck with half a dozen other men aboard came to pick us up and took us to a spot on Blewitt Falls Lake. Major Odessa was waiting for us along with our bags. Another truck came in right behind us and disgorged its passengers. We numbered about twenty in all.

The major called us over to him.

"Short day today, men," he said, surveying the crowd. "I suggest you take this opportunity to apply soap and water to your bodies. Some of you are getting rather ripe. When you finish, I'll have further instructions."

I dug my shaving kit out of my bag, grabbed a bar of soap, shucked off my uniform and boots, and plunged into the lake. Man, did it ever feel good. I waded back to the bank, lathered up, and plunged back in again. I did that several more times and then just floated in the water, enjoying the sensation of weightlessness.

What a treat. We laughed, joked, and made the most of this unexpected break before climbing out and putting on a clean uniform. I felt like a million bucks. Once everyone was squared away, Major Odessa spoke to us again.

"Men, tomorrow is the big day: the Forty Miler. Those who successfully complete the event will stay for a bit more testing and an interview by the Commander's Evaluation Board. Those who fail to satisfactorily complete the event will be returned to their units. This is no time to slack off and no time to rest. Some of you are not doing so well and are hanging on by the skin of your teeth. I'd recommend that every one of you give tomorrow your utmost effort.

"Now, as it appears that the matters of hygiene have been completed, you will be taken into the town of Troy, where you can obtain something other than C rations for the noon meal. Take your instructions for the rest of the day from Marvin." With that, the major turned to walk away.

An old acquaintance, Frank Trout, and I were walking up the trail together toward the trucks and we passed close to Major Odessa, who was standing just inside the tree line watching the group file past. As we came near, he leaned forward, pointed his finger at us, and whispered in a forcefully contained voice, "And you're two of them I was talking about!"

Startled, we looked at him as he spoke, but we kept walking. *Holy shit! Was that right? No . . . that had to be bullshit. He was just keeping up the guessing game. Yeah, that was it, he was just playing games. I'm doing okay. But what about Frank?* Frank looked pretty rattled.

Well, tomorrow would tell. Tomorrow the fat lady would sing, after a forty-mile opera.

I pitched my kit bag and rucksack into the back of the baggage van and climbed aboard the truck to town. From there we went into Troy and scattered about the few places where you could get a meal. I had a decent lunch at a small diner, but to tell you the truth, I would have just as soon gone straight to camp and had a C ration. Once I'm in the field I don't like to break my field attitude until it's all over. But no harm done.

That evening we were issued eight different map sheets and instructions for an 0200 hours departure. I turned in as soon as I had folded my maps and readied my gear for the next day. I heard no conversation in the camp that night.

Eighteen of us left the final camp that morning. We arrived at the start point, the head of the Uwharrie Trail, at 0300 hours, and after a few simple instructions, we were released at three-minute intervals.

Major Odessa had given the short briefing: Use of roads and trails was authorized until instructed otherwise. We were allowed to follow the Uwharrie Trail until it terminated and then were to take further instructions from the RV sitter at trail's end. The trail would split at a point designated on the map, and we were to take the branch marked as the "New Trail." Cadre members would be posted where the trail crossed any roads. Have a good 'un.

And off went the first man.

I had been leaning against my rucksack for at least thirty minutes, drumming my heels on the ground and watching the other candidates depart. There were just a handful of us still sitting there in the dark, and I was anxious to get going. *Hurry up and call my color and number.* I should have relaxed and napped. I was the last man released from the start point.

Daylight was still a couple of hours away and the night was moonless, but I could feel the clear, hard-packed trail beneath my feet. It wasn't hard to follow and I didn't need to use a flashlight. It would just ruin my night vision, anyway. The chill air felt good rushing past my face, and since I was on the trail, I dropped my compass in a breast pocket of my jungle shirt instead of letting it dangle and bounce against my chest where it normally hung from its lanyard.

Move hard while it's cool, before the sun comes up and starts sucking water from your body. Until then, moisture loss is mainly from breathing and that's minimal. But later today, water's going to become critical. Push hard now, push hard and make the most of this time. You were the last one to start and that means you have to make up for the head start the rest of them have on you. Push hard.

I did. I moved as swiftly as I could on that black trail through the woods, and it wasn't long before I could see the light of a flashlight bobbing along the trail in front of me. I caught and overtook the owner of the flashlight and then started overtaking and passing other flashlights. *Yeah, this is it. This is the way to make up for lost time.*

Within an hour and a half I had caught and pulled ahead of at least half of the group, but after that I saw no one else. An hour later the darkness started to subside. Sunrise was a while off yet, but it would soon be light enough to see well. A gray smear showed through the trees in front of me. *Hmmm. That should be off to my right, because the trail is going north.* I reached for my compass. *Nah, probably just a temporary turn to the east before the trail swings north again.*

But the trail kept heading east and soon started to bend back to the south. *This isn't right,* I thought, as the trail finally broke out into a clearing and I had enough daylight to check my location. I dropped ruck and got out my map and compass.

Let's see, I should be about here on the map, about twenty kilometers up the trail. But the terrain looked nothing like it should.

At this distance from the start point, I figured I should be on a long, narrow ridge running almost exactly due north. Instead, the trail was turning southeast and passing through a wide shallow valley that opened out to the east. The terrain wasn't distinct enough to do a resection, so instead I did a terrain analysis.

Wide shallow valley to the east, large rounded hill mass to the southwest, prominent ridge to the north, running from southwest to northeast. Nope . . . doesn't fit. But just for the sake of argument . . . if I had taken the Old Uwharrie Trail branch instead of the New Uwharrie

*branch I would be . . . exactly where I'm standing now! Holy rat's ass!
Good God a'mighty! How could I have been so stupid?*

Of all the pecker-headed rookie mistakes! I had saved all my potential screwups to let them loose in this one big, Fourth of July,
Atomic Dumb-Ass Attack! Man, oh man.

*Now, let's see if I can unravel this Mongasso Knot. I'm twelve kilo-
meters from the branch in the trail, which means that I should have
been twelve kilometers up the new trail. That would put me about here,
if I hadn't screwed up. That's a total of twenty-four kilometers if I back-
track, but just twenty kilometers if I cut cross-country to intercept the
trail where I'd be right now if I hadn't fouled up. But I might as well go
ahead and intercept the trail where it crosses this hardtop road instead.
That makes for a cross-country total of about twenty-seven kilometers
or sixteen miles before I see the trail again. Well, I ain't gettin' there by
standing around this clearing with my face hanging out. I've just
turned the Forty Miler into a Fifty-five Miler.*

I saddled up and started moving.

So far throughout the course, I had taken a short break every
hour. Sometimes the break was for ten minutes, sometimes for five,
and occasionally as short as three minutes. The length of the break
was always predicated on how well I thought I was doing. Even a
short break of a couple of minutes gives you a mental and physical
lift that always leaves you stronger than when you sat down. But my
breaks had to be severely limited now.

I pushed hard for two hours and then made a two-minute stop.
Fortunately, I didn't have to stop for water but could get at my canteens and drink on the move. It was critical that I drink plenty of
water—at least a quart an hour—because if I became dehydrated,
I'd eventually go down.

I stopped at a small spring bubbling from the base of a hill and
filled my canteens. Then I dropped two iodine tablets in each canteen to purify the contents. My movement would thoroughly mix
the tablets with the water and it would be completely purified
within thirty minutes.

On and on I pushed with a sense of urgency like never before. I
adjusted my heading to hit the trail a few hundred meters before it
intersected the road. I had trouble enough as it was without risking
being caught by a cadre member on or too near a hardtop road.
Shortly after noon I struck the trail and, a few minutes later, came

out on the road. Major Odessa was waiting there and seemed not the least bit surprised by my sudden appearance.

"Seeing some of the countryside, are you?" he quipped. "I do wish you hadn't taken the wrong turn in the trail. It does so add to an already lengthy day."

"Yes, sir, and I'm sure it hurts you more than it does me," I retorted as I crossed the road and reentered the trail.

"No, not at all," he replied. "I'm remarkably comfortable and pain-free. But you, on the other hand . . . you know you can quit at any time. Wouldn't you like to quit now? There's no one here but you and I. It's an excellent time to quit. You know it's almost impossible to catch up. Why not quit now and save yourself an exercise in futility?"

He said the last sentence to my back as I walked past him and into the woods on the far side of the road.

"No thanks, Major," I said with a glance over my shoulder. He was beaming at me like I had just won Best Dog of Show. *Why did it have to be him? I'll bet he's been there for hours waiting for me, just for the pleasure of watching my humiliation.*

Well, it wasn't much as far as humiliations go. I had never been lost, just befuddled for a while. But now that was behind me and I was back on track again. I pressed on with the strength born of desperation.

A couple of hours later I finally caught up with someone. It was Gorilla Man, and he was limping up the trail like he had a flat tire.

"What happened to you?" I asked as I got close to him.

He looked up. "Once it got daylight, I took off my boots and put on my running shoes to wear between RVs. But I think I've got march fractures now," he said between gritted teeth.

"Why not put your boots back on?" I threw it over my shoulder as I passed him.

"That's not a bad idea," he said wonderingly, as he stopped and looked down at his feet. He sounded genuinely amazed at the advice.

Thank goodness for guys like that. Whenever you're feeling really stupid, they can show you that you're just an amateur in the field.

Within the next hour or so, I caught and overtook several other men. I had covered just slightly over thirty miles by now, but still had more than twenty to go. It was getting more and more difficult to do speed computations in my head. My hands were tingling from the rucksack straps cutting into my shoulders, pinching the nerves and arteries, and restricting the blood flow to my arms.

I was bent forward against the weight of the rucksack. It felt like I was dragging a train behind me, and my feet hurt all the way up to my knees. I don't mean they were just sore, I mean they felt like I had been strapped to the rack and someone had beaten the balls of my feet with a bat. I tried to calculate the foot-pounds of energy my feet had absorbed so far today, but had to give up the effort. I only knew that the accumulated tonnage of all those thousands of steps was immense. And it was only going to get worse.

There was an RV at trail's end. My rucksack was weighed there, and I was sent up a gravel road through open farm country. After a while on the road, I started meeting guys coming back from the direction I was going. None of us had the spare energy to even nod to one another. We only exchanged pained glances of recognition.

The sun was only about one fist above the horizon now, there was roughly an hour and a half of daylight left, and I still had a long way to go. I came to an RV at the end of a long, sweeping bend in the road. I had been able to see it for ten minutes across the fields, and it was absolute torture to make my way there.

Carlos was the sitter. I plotted my next RV and reported back to him. "Change the batteries in your flashlight and then show me that it works," he instructed.

I did what he directed and then clipped the GI flashlight to the shoulder strap of my rucksack.

"You may continue to use roads and trails, but you are not restricted to them," he said after I had shown him the location of my next RV. I nodded my understanding of what he had said, adjusted the straps of my rucksack, and was off again.

I continued to study my map as I made my way back down the road again. The gravel of the road was especially painful to my feet. I walked in the ruts of the road where the gravel had been smashed to the sides, but the stray stones there were even more painful.

It looked like my best route was to follow this road for another kilometer, then move due west, cross-country and over a sharp ridge to pick up a road paralleling this one in the next valley over. That road eventually intersected the one where the RV was located.

Darkness caught me before I reached the top of the ridge. The slope was covered in a tangle of mountain pine saplings and brush, but it was some relief to my legs to get off the road and climb. Once on top, I looked for the best way down. Far below, at the bottom of the slope, I could make out a light winking through the trees. *That must be the security light on the church down there.* My map showed a country church located along the road at the base of the ridge. As I made my way down the brush-tangled slope, that light was like a shore beacon to a sailor on a stormy sea. I zeroed in on it and ignored everything else.

When I was almost to the churchyard, I heard a voice call out, "Oh, Jesus! Somebody's finally there. Help me out of here! Help me! Come and get me."

It could only be one person.

I had been so focused on the light in the churchyard that I hadn't seen him. Parks was fifty meters to my left, tangled up in a two-acre patch of kudzu. He was thrashing and flailing like a man caught in quicksand, going down for the last time.

"Over here, Parks. Take your time and walk straight to me. Stop fighting it and just walk slowly toward me. The more you fight it, the more tangled you're going to get."

It was agony just standing there and waiting for him to wade out of that field of kudzu.

"Okay, man, okay," he mewled. "Just don't leave me. Wait until I get out."

Don't get me wrong. I wasn't in agony over Parks's predicament. It just hurt worse to stand still than it did to keep walking. As soon as he was almost to the edge, I continued lurching downhill to the church.

I was so exhausted now, and my body was such a throbbing mass of pain, that every little decision was a major undertaking. Parks caught up with me in the churchyard. I knew I had to go to the left on the road in front of the church, but it took a deliberate effort to tell my right from my left.

"Which way do we go?" Parks whined. "I don't think that's the right way," he said to my back as I turned and walked away. But I could hear the gravel crunch under his feet as he fell in behind and followed me down the road.

I slogged down the road into the growing darkness. I was done for. I no longer had any idea what time it was. I just knew it was some time after dark. My legs were a solid aching mass, as heavy as concrete. My arms were completely numb. I could only maintain a hold on my grease gun by tucking the gun's magazine well into the front waistband of my fatigue pants and pressing it there with my unfeeling and clublike hands. My neck ached terribly from fighting the weight of the rucksack. My head had been thrust forward all day like a tortoise's head shoved out in front of his shell. My eyes pulsed with the pain of utter exhaustion. I was ready to quit.

That's it. The next RV is the last one . . . no matter what, I'm not going any farther. I can't go any farther. But damn, the next RV just has to be the last one, doesn't it? Sure, it has to be. How far have I come? I don't know, I can't remember. I can't think anymore. All I can do is put one foot in front of the other. Left, right, left. One step and then another step. Just one more step. If I can just keep taking one more step, then I can keep going. Yep, I can keep going. I've come too goddamn far to quit now.

"Parks, shut up! Just shut the fuck up!"

Parks had been trailing along in my slipstream, keeping up a continuous babble. "This is the wrong way. You're going the wrong way. We'll never get there this way. Is the next RV the finish? How much farther do you think it is? I can't make it anymore. I'm gonna quit. Don't leave me here! Don't leave me!"

I had to get away from him. His incoherent prattle was robbing me of what little energy I had left. From somewhere within the depths of my bowels, I summoned up a reserve of strength, and increased my pace just as I hit the road junction. I turned to the right, in the direction of the RV, and left Parks standing at the intersection, mumbling to himself, whimpering that I was going the wrong way.

I stumbled down the road into the darkness and walked right into the RV. I almost bounced off the sitter's truck and stood there swaying like a tree in the wind while Marvin gave me instructions. I could hear him clearly, but it seemed that it took a few seconds to understand what he said. It was like listening underwater.

I plotted the next coordinates and reported back with my current location and the position of the next RV.

"From this point forward, the use of roads and trails is no longer authorized," said Marvin from the glow of his flashlight.

Oh no, that means I'll have to cross that river and I don't have the strength to swim it. I left the RV on wooden legs, laboriously working out a plan in my head. *I'll have to find a steep bend in the river, build a poncho raft for my rucksack, and let the current push me to the other side. All I have to do is hang on. Then I'll change clothes . . . and leave my wet uniform behind because I can't carry the additional weight of a waterlogged uniform. This is gonna be tough, but I can do it, I know I can.*

Just as I had taken a few steps away from the RV, someone stepped out of the darkness and stopped me with a hand on my chest. It was Major Odessa.

"Haney, you look like you're in pretty bad shape. Why don't you give it up before you hurt yourself."

"Major, I'm not gonna quit, but I can't argue with you about it. Just let me go." I staggered as I tried to walk around him.

He kept his hand on my chest. "Hold it a second. Does your flashlight work? Does it have fresh batteries? Show me."

Goddamn it, goddamn it! What's he screwing with me for? I don't have the energy for this. I fumbled with thick useless fingers, trying to find the sliding "on" button of the flashlight, and after much effort, spilled a thin beam of light out across the road.

"Okay. That's good," he said as I leaned my weight forward to step away. "But you don't have to go any farther, Haney. You've finished. You have successfully completed Stress Phase and the Forty Miler."

For a second I thought it was another trick, and I just stood there rocking back and forth as I tried to make out the meaning of what I had just heard. But as the words "successfully completed" finally came to rest in my consciousness, I saw the smile that had broken out on the major's hitherto stonelike face.

It was finally over.

Someone stepped up and pulled the rucksack from my back and other hands guided me off the road, down a pathway into the woods. I was led to the side of a fire and lowered to the ground with my back propped against the bank of the path. Smiley, the medic, gently took my boots off, inspected my feet, and propped them up on my rucksack.

Someone else brought me a canteen cup of something from a kettle sitting on the fire: hot spiced wine. God, how delicious. I never tasted anything so perfect. Cadre members came over and shook my hand and said congratulations. Major Odessa came down and knelt beside me.

"You had me worried for a while this morning, Haney. I thought you had walked off the edge of the earth," he said with a smile.

"No, sir, but it was damn near off the map sheet," I said, and took another sip of wine. It was a little peculiar. Everyone was all smiles, everyone was concerned, everyone was helpful—where previously, it had been so impersonal. It felt good. It felt good to be finished. It felt good to be sitting here drinking. It all just felt damn good.

The cadre members drifted away and I was left resting against the bank, comfortably slurping hot wine. My legs were as stiff as rails. Same for the arms. But they would be all right tomorrow, and for now, it felt great just to be still and not have to move.

I looked at my watch: 2150 hours. I finished about fifteen minutes ago, so let's round that off to 2130. I started this morning at 0330, so that means I had walked for . . . eighteen hours. I had covered more than fifty miles in eighteen hours, and my feet sure knew it. But they had held up good and served me well. I couldn't have asked any more of them. I wriggled my toes and flapped my feet back and forth. *Thanks, feet.*

I heard voices up on the road. I could hear Parks arguing with Marvin, but I couldn't make out what was being said. A few minutes later I heard Parks shouting and carrying on in an elated voice—the major must have told him he was finished.

So Parks had made that last turn in the right direction after all. A few minutes later, he was carried down and propped against the bank of the trail across the fire from me. He looked like hell, but he was almost delirious with joy at having completed the march.

He received the same postmarch ministrations I had enjoyed, and soon we were left alone to savor our victory in shared solitude. And for once, his turbulent soul seemed at peace as we lounged there in silence, staring into the muttering fire and floating on our thoughts of this day.

Within an hour, three more fugitives had increased the size of our happy campfire brotherhood. After they had been tended to and allowed to decompress a bit, we were guided and carried back up to the road, helped into the back of a truck, and stuffed down in sleeping bags for the trip back to Aberdeen Camp.

I never heard the sound of the engine cranking and knew nothing else until we were being helped out of the trucks back at camp. Two of the men could not be awakened and were carried into the barracks like sacks of grain and dropped on their bunks.

I hobbled in on terribly stiff sore legs and painful feet, fell on a cot, and went immediately back to sleep. The sun was up many hours before I was.

Before breakfast, we were herded outside in front of the trucks, where Sergeant Major Shumate took the "after" picture, as he had promised.

There were eighteen men in the photograph. Eighteen out of the original 163 who had started. But the Selection course still wasn't over. The Commander's Board was still to come.

Our little band of walking wounded spent the rest of the morning limping around camp, cleaning and turning in our equipment. In the afternoon, we sat down in the classroom and filled out a peer report questionnaire. Since we didn't all know one another's names, we were identified by the numbered chair we sat in. The questions were all subjective in nature:

Who do you think showed the most character? Who seemed the most competent? Who was the weakest? Who would you most want by your side in combat? Who would you least want by your side in combat? Who do you most trust? Who do you least trust? If you had to reject one man from this group, who would it be and why? After completing the peer report we were free for the remainder of the afternoon.

I was physically spent and achingly sore in every part of my body. But as I reflected on what I had undergone, I felt a calm sense of satisfaction and contentment. I had not just survived an ordeal, because survival in a sense is just passive. No, I had conquered. But conquered what? I had to think about that awhile, and then I realized: myself.

I had undertaken a tremendously difficult challenge. Many men had tried and failed; only a few of us had stayed the course. And I don't think a single man among us felt he did not merit the success he had earned. I was certainly sure I deserved to be here. It had been difficult, but I had done it solely on my own abilities. I was just glad this part was over. But the Commander's Board was still ahead. That, and an interview with the unit psychologist.

After supper that night, we found a schedule posted on the bulletin board listing the times of our meeting with the shrink. We had already been reminded that this was still an individual effort and we were still forbidden to speak with any other candidate about the interview process.

I was the first one to report to the psychologist the following morning. I found him ensconced in an easy chair tucked deep in a shadowed corner of the room. He didn't look up from the folder of papers he was studying, but with a languid wave of a white hand indicated that I take a seat on the steel chair in the center of the otherwise empty room.

I had expected a less austere setting and found my hackles starting to rise unexpectedly. *The only thing missing is a blinding white light shining in my eyes.* I sat down and waited. The psychologist casually flipped back and forth through the papers in his lap and continued to ignore my presence. If his intent was to piss me off, it was working.

As I searched out the man in his darkened corner, I saw that he was a pudgy, effeminate-looking person with the longish hair of an academic. Behind his glasses his eyes appeared weak, as though they seldom saw the sun. A smug, superior air seemed to surround the man, and when he finally spoke to me it was off to one side, as though I was not worthy of his full attention. With no preliminaries and no mutual introductions, he launched straight into his program.

"Haney," he began in a sibilant voice. "I'm going to outline a hypothetical situation and I want you to tell me how you would accomplish the tasking you are given." His tone made it clear he considered it a distasteful duty to speak to me.

"Your commander has selected you to take out a terrorist who has been located in San Francisco. Due to the need for secrecy and the delicacy of the task, neither the local authorities nor the FBI can be made aware of the mission. You must eliminate the terrorist and then make your way undetected out of the city and back to Fort Bragg. You can leave no trace of evidence that would lead back to this unit. Tell me how you would accomplish this task." The unmoving shadow in the corner fell silent.

A simple tactical exercise. Not exactly what I had expected in this interview, but oh well, let me see how I would do this. I thought about the situation for a few minutes, and then following the format of an Operations Order, I outlined how I would go about accomplishing the mission.

The shrink remained motionless while I talked, looking only at the papers he held on his lap. When I finished speaking he maintained his silence for at least a full minute, still studying the papers that fascinated him so. Then, at last, he lifted his eyes to me for the first time and hissed at me from the shadows.

"You ignorant redneck. Have you never heard of the Posse Comitatus Act? Don't you know it's against federal law for the military to be used for operations within the United States?"

Venom fairly dripped from his tongue.

"And the mission wasn't to kill a terrorist at all, but to assassinate your commander's wife's lover. The reason he selected *you* for this mission was he knew you were such an unthinking simpleton and a mental nonentity that you would do what he wanted without question." He paused a second before continuing.

"You stupid cracker. It's a good thing we have an army, so white trash like you can have a place to go rather than to the local chain gang, where you would doubtless be otherwise."

He watched me from behind hooded eyes before concluding with "What do you have to say for yourself now?"

Had I been my normal self, I could have laughed it all off and asked the man to try again. But in my still near-exhausted state, and without the full power of my faculties, his words hit me like a physical blow. No, that's not true. If it had been a physical assault, I would have known how to fight back. As it was, I was stunned and reeling. *How dare that fat bastard speak to me that way.* I felt belittled and at a complete loss as to what to do or say.

As I stared at my nemesis in anger, I soon realized it had been a setup. But I was enraged and embarrassed just the same. It was one thing to be made to look stupid, but he had denigrated my background, and that was an assault on my honor. It was completely infuriating, and I was consumed with rage. The only thing saving the man from a severe beating was the fact that he was an officer.

It was obvious to me now that the interview had one purpose: to mount a full-scale psychological assault and hit me where it would hurt. It had been masterfully executed. The man's objective had been to shake my self-confidence and see what kind of noises I would make under duress.

This is just like a prisoner-of-war interrogation, I thought—and I knew that whatever I said would be wrong. I uttered one expletive and refused to talk anymore.

Every few minutes the guy would sneer a comment in my direction, but I had said all I was going to say and I wasn't going to be deceived again. For the next ten minutes I sat in my chair and stared at my interrogator while the angry sound of my racing pulse pounded relentlessly in my ears.

Eventually he too must have realized this wasn't going any further and that he had all he was going to get from me. He waved the pudgy white fingers of one hand in my general direction, and shifting his gaze back to his papers once again, twittered, "We're finished here. Why don't you go away."

With pleasure.

I felt beat-up, violated, and helpless to do anything about it. By the time all of us had undergone our interview with this man, I found out I wasn't alone in my reaction. In fact, he had managed to so completely destroy the sense of trust necessary for his position that none of us would ever speak to him again. He was rendered ineffective as a unit psychologist and soon left the Army to pursue "other opportunities." Subsequent unit psychologists were aghast that we had been subjected to such stupid treatment.

All the interviews were finished by late that evening, and since a new class of candidates would be arriving the next day to start Selection, we were sent back to main post at Fort Bragg to await our appearance before the Commander's Board. In the meantime we would be staying at Moon Hall, where we had originally signed in.

Moon Hall is a military hotel complex, and by any standards, it's quite a facility. There's also a great NCO Club annex in one of the buildings and a mess hall that would knock your socks off.

Every Friday the mess was open all afternoon—from lunch

through supper—continuously offering up a succession of steam-ship rounds for sacrifice. Breakfast every day was a thing of beauty, and brunch on Saturdays and Sundays was out of this world. The only thing missing was a fountain of Bloody Marys.

The mess sergeant (or "dining facility manager," as they were called in official Army newspeak) was a national award-winning chef who was hired for an astronomical salary by a New York hotel when he retired. And considering the acclaim of everyone who ever ate in his mess, he deserved every cent of that salary.

We loafed around Fort Bragg for several days. The Commander's Board would not convene for a while, and until then, we were to relax and recuperate. We had an informal formation in the lobby every morning at 1000 hours and then were released to our own control.

I was glad for the downtime. It turned out that I had gotten a march fracture in my left foot during the Forty Miler. I thought I knew when it happened, but by that point in the march, my feet were so numb the pain couldn't register. After a few days' rest, I felt fine.

Doc Smiley met us in the lobby one morning and told us the board would convene the next day. We were to report in fatigue uniform to Aberdeen Camp the next morning at 0800 hours.

So the last hurdle was at hand. Tomorrow I would learn my fate—acceptance or rejection. I would not even contemplate being turned away. But if that happened, I'd face it in its own time. And tomorrow I would finally meet the commander of the unit, Colonel Charlie (not Charles) Beckwith. I knew almost nothing about the man—I'd never heard of him prior to my arrival at Selection. But most of the SF soldiers knew of him, and a few had served near if not with him, in Vietnam and other locations around the world.

The reports on Colonel Beckwith were a mixed lot. Some said he was a hell of a commander; others said he was a megalomaniac with a reputation for getting his troops killed. But the reports made little difference to me.

Commanders come and commanders go. If the unit has decent troops, it will survive. With a good commander, a good unit could prosper; with a bad one, a good unit could hold its own. And after what I'd seen during Selection, the mere handful of men in the unit so far told me this was going to be one hell of an outfit.

If Beckwith was crazy, I suspected it was a good kind of crazy. He was, and it was—but all that in good time.

My board appearance was scheduled for 1500 hours. We were severely cautioned against speaking to one another about anything that was said or done within the board.

The morning and afternoon dragged by like geological epochs. I'm a patient man, but on this day, I could barely contain myself. I'd sit inside the waiting room for a while and then go outside to talk nervously with the other "waiters." Men were called and would disappear inside. The first three men to be interviewed came out of the room ashen-faced, and refused to look at us as they reported to the orderly room for orders to return to their home units.

Rejected. Not accepted for assignment. Cold, hard, devastating words. My guts chilled and settled into a hard freeze as I watched those men, one by lonely one, walk away. Just like the dead and wounded seen stretched out after a firefight, they had my sympathy, but I was glad it wasn't me.

I was also glad they left camp immediately and didn't say any awkward farewells. They were social lepers and I didn't want to risk catching the infection they carried. I'm not proud of feeling that way, but I have to admit to the truth of those thoughts.

Finally two men in a row came out of that room so elated they looked like they would explode. You could tell they wanted to jump up and down or dance from the sheer pleasure of winning. Smiley led each of them away before they could say anything to those of us still waiting in limbo.

Then it was my turn.

Okay, Eric, this is it. Compose yourself, keep your wits about you, and be ready for anything. Smiley told me to walk to the front of the room, halt in front of the chair, and report to the commander—just like any other board appearance. I gave my uniform a quick check, brought myself to the position of attention, picked up a thousand-yard stare, took a deep breath, and marched through the door and into the lion's den. *Leave us go amongst them.*

I halted in front of the chair, with just enough space in front of me so that when I turned about, I could sit straight down without having to look for the chair or back up to take my seat. I executed a parade-ground about-face, whipped up a quivering salute, waited two counts, and growled out in my best platoon sergeant voice, "Sir! Sergeant Haney reports to the commander!"

It was my first view of Colonel Beckwith. I was looking at a point in space just above his head, but I could still see him clearly— a big man sprawled across the folding chair directly in front of me.

His face was fierce; almost belligerent. It was the face he used for most occasions. He had a shock of slate gray hair, a wide forehead, and piercing eyes set deep in his face, with dark circles underneath. His cheeks were high, but not prominent. His nose was hawklike, but not large. His jawline looked like it had been shaped by an ax. His lower lip was pushed out slightly, creating an insolent air. His chest and shoulders were deep and wide, and his belly was expansive. All in all, he looked just like what he was—a warrior chieftain surrounded by his lieutenants.

He let me hold my position while he looked me up and down several times before he finally returned my salute and told me to sit down. Then the attack commenced.

"Haney, I understand you don't like officers" were the first words he hurled at me, dredged up from somewhere deep within his chest.

I had told myself before this started that I would be brutally honest and not tap-dance around any question. They were going to get Eric Haney, Staff Sergeant by the Grace of God, in the raw and in person. I was going to give them the whole log, with the bark still on it, and to hell with the consequences.

"That's correct, sir." I fastened my eyes on his as I spoke. "I despise most of the officers I've ever met."

He came unglued. His face swelled and turned red, and the veins bulged out in his neck. But I was determined to take no shit.

"Goddamn it, Haney, that's mutinous!" he shouted at me. "What the hell's wrong with you? How could you make a statement like that?"

"Sir, most of the officers I've met spend the majority of their time scheming for career progression and looking for ways to stab each other in the back. The only good thing about that is they usually leave the NCOs and the soldiers alone to get on with unit business—at least until they want to put on some kind of dog-and-pony show to impress someone with how great they are."

From the corner of my eye I could see Sergeant Major Country Grimes trying to suppress a grin. *Ah, just maybe I have one ally in the room.*

Beckwith ranted and raved until eventually his anger lost steam. He looked at me like I was a biological specimen. Then he leaned back in his chair, swelled out his chest, and asked in an arrogant voice, "Well, Sergeant Smart-Ass, what did you think of Stress Phase?"

"Sir, I kept waiting for the stress to start."

"You what!" He leapt from his chair, spraying spittle through the air. "You kept waiting for stress to start? What in God's name do you mean by that? Are you out of your mind?" His face was so swollen with rage, I thought he might have a stroke. He stood there gasping for air and gaping at me.

"Sir, I ate four meals a day and slept at least eight hours every night. No one was shooting at me. I never stepped on a land mine. The weather was good. I never got frostbite or had heat exhaustion. I was responsible for myself and no one else. Yep, it was hard. In some ways, the hardest thing I've ever done. But, sir, there are more difficult things in life than Selection."

He huffed and puffed about that until he thought up something else to slap me with. And that was the way it went.

We took turns yelling at one another. He would tell me the Rangers were a bunch of pansies and I'd tell him he was full of mud. He told me I was just a parade-ground soldier and I countered that he obviously hadn't read my record because I'd never served a day in anything but combat units.

Beckwith would rant until he literally ran out of breath, and then someone else in the room would come at me with something else. I was getting it from all sides, like a bear with its back to a cliff and a pack of hounds lunging in and snapping at its flanks. It got so intense I thought I was going to have to fight.

At one point, Beckwith said he'd had enough of my shit and was just going to have Sergeant Russell here kick my ass, indicating a big, hard-looking man seated in the front row.

I stared at Russell, turned back to look the colonel straight in the face, and told him that was one order he better not give unless he wanted to see me thrash his man. Russell held my gaze and smiled slightly, and I got my feet under me, ready to jump if I had to. If

Beckwith ordered Russell at me, I planned to kick him in the face and take him out of the fight before he could get out of his chair. I'd only get the one chance.

We took a breather then. It was like the bell had rung and the colonel and I fell back in our chairs, panting like two boxers between rounds. I'd been taking some big punches but felt like I had thrown a few good ones of my own. Then Sergeant Major Grimes broke the heavy quiet.

"Haney," he said in his Pennsylvania mountain twang, "the peer reports of the other men indicated they don't think very highly of you. Said they thought you were a pretty poor example of a soldier." His voice was calm and measured and he watched me intently, one eye squinted like he was inspecting a rifle barrel.

I thought for a few seconds about what he said. Then I answered. "Sergeant Major, that's bullshit and you know it. You're just trying to rattle my cage. I'm the best goddamn soldier those men have ever met in their military lives."

Grimes stifled another grin.

Someone on the other side of the room—someone who just had to be an officer—wagged his finger at me and accused me of being evasive and mealymouthed. Said I'd refused to answer all the questions in my psychological battery.

I asked him what he was talking about, and he held up a sheet of paper and read aloud, "I love my mother, but . . ."

"Why didn't you complete the sentence?" he yelled at me, shaking the rolled sheet of paper in the air.

"There's nothing to complete," I said. "I love my mother, no buts about it. Don't try to put your feelings about your own mother off on me."

"Colonel, I've had enough," he said, turning to look at Colonel Beckwith. "This man can't give a straight answer to the simplest question. He's been nothing but insolent and disrespectful since he walked in the door. I, for one, have seen and heard enough."

The colonel nodded his agreement. Looking back at me, he said, "Get out and wait till I call for you." He dismissed me with a jerk of his thumb toward the door.

I stood, saluted, and started for the door. He waved what could only vaguely be called a salute in my general direction as I marched for the door and exercised the utmost of my self-control to keep from slamming it behind me. I stalked to the far end of the hall and paced back and forth in a four-foot square. I was wound up tighter than a two-dollar watch.

One of my Selection mates, Jimmy Johnson, could stand it no longer and came down to talk to me. I cut him off with a raised hand before he opened his mouth and drew breath.

"Jimmy, don't ask me a damned thing. You know I can't say anything, and you'll put us both in a trick if you don't just go away. Now, leave me alone." With that I turned my back on him and paced in the other direction.

The men at the other end of the hall stared at me like I had anthrax.

A few minutes later, Smiley came out of the conference room and beckoned me to come with him into another room. It was the medical station.

"Read the chart on the wall," he said. "All lines, top to bottom."

"With my glasses or without?"

"With."

I read them and then asked, "What the hell is this all about?"

"The colonel wants to know how well you can see. Very few men who wear glasses have made it through Stress Phase. Now come with me. He wants you back inside. Just take your seat, you don't have to report again."

I went back to my chair and stared at Colonel Beckwith. He looked at Smiley and asked, "Well?"

Smiley nodded. "Colonel, his vision is fine with his glasses."

The colonel turned his eyes to me. His gaze was still fierce, but the belligerence was gone. "Well, Haney," he said with just the slightest lilt of humor in his voice, "you've got a little bit of a temper on you, once you get roused, don't you?"

"Yes, sir, I'm afraid I do."

"And you've got a smart mouth to go along with it, don't you?"

"Yes, sir, I have one of those too."

"And you're kind of prone to shooting from the hip, sort of rapid-fire-like, when somebody pokes at you, aren't you?"

"Yes, sir, I'd say that's also true."

He pushed out his lower lip and paused in reflection for a few seconds before continuing, "Well, hell, son, so am I, and it ain't necessarily bad all the time. The trick is knowing when it'll work and when it won't. But I like your style and I want you with us."

He stood as he said the last sentence and extended a bear paw of a hand in my direction. I looked at his hand, looked at his face, and smiled. I grabbed his still-outstretched hand, gave it a good shake, and felt the power of his grip. The other men in the room crowded round and offered their congratulations.

"Welcome aboard," they said. "Good to have you with us."

Grimes grinned at me. "Just rattling your cage, eh?"

"Yes, Sergeant Major. That's what you were doing, wasn't it?"

"Yeah, it was, and I thought I'd gotten to you for a second there."

"You came mighty close, Sergeant Major, you damn sure did."

And that was it. I had made it. I was a member of the newest, most elite unit in the national inventory.

When the board completed its business, there were twelve new members of 1st Special Forces Operational Detachment—Delta. Of the original 163 men who started Selection, eighteen had passed Stress Phase and twelve had survived the Commander's Board. Four men had been rejected outright and two others were told they could try again at a future date. Both did and both were eventually selected.

The success rate for this Selection course was slightly above 7 percent. It would turn out to be the highest in Delta Force history.

I returned to Hunter Field to out-process and move my family to Fort Bragg. Jim Bush and I were the first men from the Ranger Battalion to make it into that mysterious new unit. And the fact that we couldn't say anything about it just added to our celebrity.

I packed up, said my farewells, and headed out for a new phase of life. I had no idea what I was in for. When I look back at the young man I was then, I can only shake my head in wonder at the good fortune he carried with him to that new assignment.

Life would be difficult most of the time, and dangerous almost all the time—and every once in a while, it would be deadly.

PREPARING
THE FORCE

THE SELECTION COURSE IMMEDIATELY FOLLOWING MINE PRO-
duced eleven more successful candidates. So I and the twenty-
two other most recently added members of the country's newest
and most mysterious unit signed in to Delta Force in November
and December of 1978.

With our arrival, the size of the unit was doubled. Now there
would be enough people to run Selection, to train the men already
in the unit, and conduct a formal training course for those of us
who had just arrived. Critical mass had been reached, though just
barely. We were still short of the numbers needed to bring the unit
to operational strength; that would take at least one more year.

When I reported for assignment it was to the Fort Bragg Stockade, our home and headquarters for the next eight years. The unit
needed a large secure facility, and this was just about a perfect fit for
our needs at the time.

The Army was changing its method of handling prisoners. Soldiers convicted by courts-martial and sentenced to incarceration
were no longer being held in local installation facilities but instead
would all be remanded to Fort Leavenworth. At Fort Bragg that left
a big, beautiful, brand-new, high-security facility almost empty.
Colonel Beckwith snapped it up.

All we had to do to convert it to our use was cut the bunks loose
from the floors in the dormitory bays and put up a few walls for
class and conference rooms. We screened the chain-link fencing surrounding the compound to restrict the view from outside, and last

but not least, we planted rose gardens around the building's entrance. A nice touch.

The civilian guards who controlled access at the front gate and patrolled the grounds of the compound were all retired Special Forces sergeant majors, a hard, dedicated, serious group of men.

Chief Guard Hugh Gordon was one of my favorites. Gordon had been one of the very first members of Special Forces back in the early 1950s. During World War Two he had parachuted into Normandy with the 82nd Airborne Division on his nineteenth birthday. He was indicative of the men who provided our exterior security, and you can believe me when I tell you that security was never breached. Not even by us.

One night after a training exercise, Doc Smiley decided to take a shortcut to the building and climbed the back fence rather than walk all the way around to the front gate. The next day, he told us that he was straddling the top of the fence when he heard a pump shotgun rack a shell into the chamber and a calm voice announce, "Just drop your ass to the ground on this side of the fence."

All the way to the ground, Smiley kept saying, "Don't shoot, Huck. It's me, Smiley." Mr. Huckaby then walked him to the front gate and logged him in. When he turned to walk away, Huckaby said he'd known who it was all along—otherwise he would have shot him off the top of the fence. None of us tried hopping the fence after that little incident. Huck died at his post about ten years later. He was found dead, sitting on the ground, his back against the fence and his shotgun across his lap. He had suffered a heart attack while patrolling the perimeter. God bless all those old veterans.

Our band of new members received the designation "OTC-3," which stood for Operators Training Course Number Three. We were the third group of men into the unit. The first spurt had been Colonel Beckwith and his handpicked staff, the second group were selectees from the first two Selection courses, and our group was the result of the following two Selection courses.

We settled on the name "operator" to designate an operational member of the unit (as opposed to a member of the support staff) due to some legal and political situations. We couldn't use "operative" because that name had certain espionage connotations from the CIA. The term "agent" had some legal issues.

An agent carries a legal commission to perform certain duties and a governmental authority empowered by a state or federal constitution issues that commission. In our case, we would perform our duties under the authority of the federal government as administered by the Department of Defense and the Department of the Army.

But in the military, only officers carry legal commissions from the President and are confirmed by Congress. Sergeants, who are noncommissioned officers, are authorized to perform their duties by virtue of appointment by the Secretary of the Army. Sergeants therefore cannot be agents of the government. And since almost every operational member of Delta Force is a sergeant, we needed to choose a different name for ourselves.

Hence, operator. If that sounds sort of convoluted, it's because it is. But if you work for any governmental entity, it will make perfect sense to you.

Delta Force was loosely patterned on the organizational structure of the British 22 Special Air Service Regiment.

The smallest unit was the four-man team. Four or five teams, along with a small headquarters element, constituted a troop. Two troops—an assault troop and a sniper troop—formed a squadron. Each squadron had a small command element. When OTC-3 finished its training, we formed two squadrons: A Squadron and B Squadron. These were known as the Sabre Squadrons.

The Selection and Training Detachment, like the Sabre Squadrons, was composed of operators. We also had a signal squadron, which provided direct communication support for the unit, and the normal contingent of administrative, intelligence, operational planning, and support elements.

At the top of the pyramid were the commander, the deputy commander, and the executive officer, the command sergeant major, and members of the commander's staff such as the unit surgeon and psychologist.

The very best people in the Army within their respective disciplines filled Delta Force's nonoperational functions. Operators always knew that we were backed up and supported by the absolute masters of their professions, no matter what their specialty—parachute riggers, administrative or finance clerks, cooks, supply personnel, communications specialists, or gunsmiths. You name the job, Delta folks were the best at it.

Delta's original plan called for three operational squadrons, but it would take more than ten years to realize that goal. Even the first year, we had a difficult time keeping up with attrition, and further growth proved slow and painful. The third Delta squadron was finally formed in 1990, prior to Operation Desert Storm.

Our training program was scheduled to start the first week of January 1979, immediately after the holiday season. Until then we busied ourselves with labor and construction projects such as readying the compound, finishing the newly constructed shooting house, and building our new range complex. While we were preparing the facilities, our instructors were preparing to lead us through the training program that would mold us into counterterrorist operators.

Colonel Beckwith had personally selected the team of four men who would be our lead instructors. Earlier in the summer, they had been trained in counterterrorist tactics and techniques by a visiting team of training experts from the British Special Air Service. In addition, we would receive assistance from visiting instructors and lecturers from other government agencies such as the FBI Academy, the CIA, the State Department, the Federal Aviation Administration, the Bureau of Alcohol, Tobacco, and Firearms, the Defense Nuclear Agency, the Department of Energy, and the U.S. Marshal's Service.

We would also have the benefit of guest speakers and experts on terrorism from the academic world. From the very beginning, Beckwith was determined that the Operators Training Course would be the most extensive and in-depth program of instruction of its kind, and that it would produce the most skilled and capable counterterrorist fighters on the face of the earth. And it only got better with time and experience. It was a very different approach to the task, one never taken by any organization before. And in truth, everything in our lives would be different from then on.

Upon assignment to Delta Force, we ceased to exist in the regular Army. Delta Force was (and is) a *secret* organization. It had no official existence on the rolls of Army units and neither did its members. We simply disappeared from the system. Our records were pulled, and from then on were managed within a secret system known as the Department of the Army Security Roster (DASR).

We had a cover organization on Fort Bragg that we used as our "official" unit. That organization has an official address, a commander and first sergeant, and someone to answer phones and provide a backstop. It provides a first level of "cover for status" and is useful for those mundane matters of life such as listing your employer or unit of assignment on credit applications, or telling your neighbors where you work. The name of the unit and its phone numbers change every few years so as not to get worn out from overuse.

We disappeared from the military in other ways also. We lived on civilian clothing status and almost never wore a uniform. A relaxed grooming policy allowed us to grow longer hair and beards, making it easier to blend in when operating undercover. And after all, if we needed to look military, it was much easier to get a haircut quickly than to reverse the process.

As Mao says, "The guerrilla swims in the sea of the people." And in Delta Force, we operated like guerrillas. Or terrorists. Because the reality was, in order to become experts at counterterrorism, we had to first become expert terrorists.

We became completely insular in our relationships with outsiders. We didn't talk with anyone outside the unit about what we did—no, not even with our families. Even within the unit, we operated strictly on a need-to-know basis. If a teammate or friend happened to disappear for a while, you never asked where he had been or what he'd been doing when he returned. If he had been on a new type of mission we needed to know about, we would be told of it in a briefing session to all the operators.

So in very short order, operational security (OPSEC) became our underlying religion, and we naturally tended to restrict our dealings with outsiders. It became such habit that, even today, when someone asks me what I do for a living or where I'm from, my first reaction is to give an evasive answer.

During that formative period, Delta's Operator Training Course (OTC) was six months long. Later years saw the addition of an Accelerated Military Free-Fall Parachuting Course, but the principal areas of instruction, and the length of the course, have remained constant over time.

Our particular course would last from January to the end of June 1979. During that time, we would master the skills we needed to accomplish our mission. We would also develop new tactics and techniques for use within the organization.

Shooting is both a science and an art. The science of shooting is principally concerned with exterior ballistics: what a projectile does in flight, how fast it initially takes off, how well it retains energy, its flight path in relation to the sight path, how it is affected by atmospheric conditions, what it does upon impact, and how it delivers its energy to a target.

A few other scientific matters are concerned with the mechanics of the equipment—the consistency of powder loads and bullet weights and shapes, the accuracy of the barrel, and the gun's inherent tightness or sloppiness.

The art of shooting is purely human. That comes into the picture when we hold a gun with this pulsing, trembling, quivering, and shaking body of ours. When we calculate all sorts of variables and try to make the round go off at just the precise instant that will cause the bullet to impact a tiny spot exactly where it was intended to go. Even when you're very good at it, you're never quite satisfied. And when you first start out, it can be a humbling exercise.

But the mastery of this skill is ground zero for the Delta Force operator. Without it, he would be some other type of being. Because when it gets right down to it, a Delta operator is an extremely skilled killer. He is like the wolf that becomes a shepherd. He will guard the flock, but make no mistake about it—he remains a deadly predator.

Shooting is divided into two categories, short guns and long guns, and so are operators. Assault team members are known as short gunners, and sniper/observers are called long gunners.

Everyone in OTC is trained on the long gun. Men chosen for sniper troops will be given specific—and exhaustive—training following their assignment.

Instead of training with a fancy sniper rifle, we used the Army's standard M-14, the predecessor of the M-16. The M-14 is the lineal descendant of the M-1 Garand of World War Two fame.

The M-14 is heavier than the M-16, fires a much larger round, and has greater range and power. Gussied-up and accurized, it is an excellent gun for target match shooting. Modified and mounted with a ranging telescope, it was used by the Army as a sniper rifle for years. Delta snipers still use it for certain tasks, but for the purposes of training, we used it in its plain-Jane form. There's no point learning to drive a Porsche until you've mastered a Ford.

We spent our first three weeks of the course on the rifle range. It was a good, stress-free way to get to know one another. It gave us a chance to change some initial impressions we had of the other men in the course—especially some I had made.

There were two guys in Selection I disliked on sight, and it turned out the feeling was mutual. Even though we probably never spoke to one another during Selection, my dislike for them continued to build in the weeks before we started OTC.

One guy was a stocky Californian from the 5th Special Forces Group at Fort Bragg. The other was a dark, muscular guy from the Infantry Brigade in Alaska. I don't know why I disliked them so much in Selection, but by the time we got to OTC, I was prepared to despise them. And they were equally prepared to return the favor.

The Californian, Jerry Knox, was a fireball of a man. He had a sly sense of humor and more intensity of character than almost any man I've ever known. The muscle man, J. T. Robards, was utterly courageous. One of the most courageous men I've ever met.

J.T. hated parachuting—said he was terrified of it. I was jump-mastering a jump one day, and as we were chuting up, J.T. kept up a running commentary about how much he hated jumping and how much it scared him. Checking his equipment prior to boarding, I asked him in exasperation, "If you hate it so damn much, J.T., why've you stayed in airborne units for the last fifteen years? It's voluntary, you know."

He looked at me in surprise and said, "Hell, Eric, I just like being with the kind of guys who *like* to do it."

During OTC, we developed profound respect for each other and formed lifelong friendships. And this extended to every member as we jelled into a cohesive unit. This was the best group of men I've ever been associated with in my life.

We had our differences now and again. That's only natural in any tightly knit clan—all the more so when it's a clan populated by tough-minded men. But we always worked out our differences, even if the working-out got a little heated.

But there was one ironclad rule in Delta: You never laid an angry hand on a brother operator. That was unforgivable, and would result in immediate dismissal. It happened only once during my eight years in the organization, and I don't believe it has ever happened since.

So those first few weeks on the rifle range were valuable for a number of reasons. We got to know the character of our comrades and we laid a common foundation on which to build core skills. Potential snipers were identified, chosen both for their natural talent and inclination to serve in that capacity. In those early days, we didn't have the luxury of taking years to develop sniper troops.

The clock was already ticking, faster than we realized.

The principal tools of the Delta Force assault team member are pistols and submachine guns. Initially, both of our short guns fired the same round: .45-caliber automatic pistol.

Our submachine gun was the old World War Two–era M-3 "grease gun." We used that model over a more modern design because Colonel Beckwith snagged a warehouse full of them free from the CIA, and Charlie never could pass up a good deal. One of our guys complained about having to take so many of them, but Beckwith retorted, "Hell, you ain't got to feed 'em, and you don't have to shovel shit out from under 'em, so what are you bitching about?"

With practice, the grease gun is an easy weapon to use. Even given its poor sights and limited range, that .45-caliber round gives it some pretty impressive power. Within a year, we adopted the German-made Heckler and Koch model MP-5 to replace it, but we kept a few grease guns around to use as silenced weapons. It was unsurpassed in that mode. The round is subsonic, so it doesn't give off a crack as it passes through the air, but it's heavy enough to retain a lot of energy and killing power.

Our pistol was an accurized version of Colt's M-1911A1, the old Army standby. This .45-caliber pistol is a big, hard-hitting weapon, inherently accurate but difficult to master. Each operator has two, and they are the weapons he uses more than anything else for close-in work.

Pistols are trade-offs. You trade power, range, and accuracy for portability and concealability. With the .45, we kept the power we wanted, and constant intensive training gave us the range and accuracy.

Our primary pistol shooting method was called "instinctive fire," and it is considered a fundamental skill for deadly combat at close range. Here's why. Most shooting is based on the methods used in target shooting; that is, staring at the front sight while shooting. The same thing holds true with a pistol—if what you're concerned with is target shooting. But a close-range gunfight is a world away from target shooting. And then some.

Combat shooting is more akin to wing shooting—shooting birds on the wing—and you can do it only by watching the target and giving it your whole concentration. Rather than smoothly squeezing the trigger until it goes off, you have to slap the trigger at just the right instant to hit the target. And before you can shoot a target, you must identify it. You have to determine *who the terrorist is.* You have to separate the deadly threat from the innocent by-stander. And to do that effectively you have to look at people instead of your sights. If your training has taught you to look at your sights, and suddenly, out of sheer survival instinct, you find yourself looking at your opponent, you'll shoot high at best. More likely, you'll have no idea where your gun is in relation to your opponent and you'll miss him altogether. That's why so many cops fire shots that miss during an armed confrontation. They're looking at their opponents, but they trained looking at their sights.

There's an old saying in the Army that you should "train the way you fight." For the most part, the Army ignores it. That's why regular Army units almost always get their asses kicked in their initial battles, unless they have a long train-up period before their first taste of combat. Under those conditions, units will develop training programs that actually prepare men for combat. But for some strange reason, the generals and other senior officers see to it that peacetime training has little resemblance to reality.

But in Delta, the only unit in the entire Army on continual war footing, we didn't have the luxury of wasted training time. When the bell rings, we have to come out of the corner not just swinging but landing killing blows. You have to look at your enemy and hit him—right where you want to hit him. Kill him and take him out of the fight before he can cause any harm. If you're in a deadly fight in a room or the cabin of an airplane, you can't afford to do anything else.

Initially we fired one round at a time. When we could consistently hit the spot we were looking at (told to look at, told to hit), we increased the distance. When we had that distance down, we moved close to the target again and practiced slapping double-taps—two very fast shots—in the same spot. The intention with the double-tap is to create a terrible wound that's sure to be fatal.

We did it over and over and over. Soon the fun went out of it, and it became work. And about that time, it became painful. The .45 is a powerful pistol with sharp recoil, and the tight grip we used meant we absorbed the full force of the recoil in our hands and arms.

Soon, like everyone else, I had a large, painful blister in the web of my thumb from the pounding of the gun in my hand. It would heal just enough at night to really hurt the next day. After a while, the blister turned into a big callus that stayed on my hand for the next eight years. The surest way to identify a Delta Force Assault Team member is by that telltale callus on his firing hand. They all have one.

Shoot we did. Eight hours a day, thousands of rounds downrange. We shot till our targets were destroyed and then we put up new ones. When we had the technique down standing in one position, the instructors taught us turning movements left and right. When we mastered that, we learned to turn our backs to the targets, face about, and shoot on command.

Then we learned to walk and shoot. At first we walked directly toward the target and then parallel to it. Then away from it, spinning and firing on command. We worked in four-man groups led by one of the four instructors—Bill, Mike, Bob, or Allen. We changed instructors every day. Our skills increased along with our confidence in one another and we stood closer and closer to the other members of our team while firing.

Soon we were shooting multiple targets, first in twos and threes, then whole groups. Next we added "good guy" targets mixed in with the "bad guys." The targets got closer together and the bad guys were sometimes partially covered by the good guys.

Then we mastered shooting on the run, always closing with the targets, always being aggressive. We would transition from the submachine gun to the pistol or from the pistol to the submachine gun. Our instructor would load a pistol for us and intentionally induce a malfunction or load only a partial magazine so we would have to execute a transition to another weapon, or a reload drill, or clear a malfunction. Our response to the unexpected had to be routine.

Then we did these things in teams of twos and then threes, and then fours. We would engage a group of targets as a team, closing with them and distributing fire while remaining acutely aware of the man adjacent to you, often shooting near him and he near you. The point was to calculate angle of fire on the move, hitting the bad guys without the rounds going through them and hitting a good guy.

To hit a good guy meant an immediate "Chinese Self-Criticism Drill." Everything stopped and you had to explain to the instructor and your teammates why you shot a good guy. It wasn't taken lightly and it wasn't funny. Short of shooting a comrade, it was about the worst mistake you could make.

We were training to rescue hostages, and if we couldn't keep from hitting them in a fight, we weren't doing our job. If we were no better than that, then a squad of infantry could do the job. They could just go in and kill everybody.

We worked at this for over a month. One solid month on the range. At the end of the day we would put our weapons and equipment on the truck, change into running kit, and run back to the compound a little more than five miles away. It was a good way to bleed off the intensity of the day. When we got in, we would clean weapons, talk about the day, clean ourselves, go home, and come back to do it again the next day.

Everyone sees rapid improvement in his shooting ability at first. Then you reach a sort of plateau where improvement seems slow and incremental. After that, every gain is made by working on the finer points of technique. By this time, we were splitting hairs with our shooting.

And then we were introduced to the Shooting House, where we'd spend eight hours a day for the next month.

The Shooting House was back at the compound. In fact, it was just out the back door from our OTC bay. I had helped build it, putting up drywall just before we started OTC, and the guys ahead of us in the unit were already shooting there several hours a day.

That original Shooting House was a simple affair with four rooms, two on each side, and a central corridor down the middle. Each room's lighting could be controlled from the hallway and raised or lowered as needed. Three of the rooms could be set up to resemble almost any type of dwelling, office, or warehouse space. The fourth room was the Aircraft Room, a section of aircraft fuselage complete with airplane doors, passenger seats, and overhead luggage bins.

The place was ruggedly constructed to withstand the impact of all the bullets and explosives used inside. The door frames in each room were made of heavy timbers and slightly recessed so we could breach them with explosives and then put up new doors.

There was a central ventilation system to pull out the smoke, but unfortunately, it pulled air in at the bottom of the walls and exhausted through the ceilings so a lot of lead dust and vapors went right up our noses. We changed the ventilation when we realized the problem, but within a year, several guys had dangerously high concentrations of lead and had to limit their time in the Shooting House.

The Shooting House could be a very eerie place. The day our instructors took us in for an introduction was a real eye-opener. Each room was furnished differently; one was like an office, one was like a living room, one was an industrial setting, and of course, there was the aircraft room. It looked so real it was weird. The furniture was new, the carpets were clean, and the place was peopled with manikins in natural poses and dress. Some were terrorists and others were hostages—there were even children. If I hadn't realized before how serious this business was, I sure knew it now.

This was where all of our range work came together. In the Shooting House, we added tactics to shooting. The formula became infinitely more complicated and hazardous. Our instructors demonstrated. With live fire.

Our OTC class, all twenty-three of us, was taken into the big room of the Shooting House. Some were seated on the sofa, some sat around a card table, more were scattered around the corners, and the rest stood in the center of the room.

Intermingled among us were bad guys—FBI silhouette targets in the shape of a man holding a pistol. Bill, our chief shooting instructor, placed a handheld radio on the table in the center of the room and told us to listen carefully when the radio came on. Then he stepped outside and closed the door.

Seconds later the radio crackled to life with these words: *"I have control—stand by. Five . . . four . . . three . . . two . . . one—Execute! Execute! Execute!"*

What happened next was so fast it was impossible to follow. The room erupted in noise and violent action.

On that first *"Execute!"* the door to the room blasted open and I could see Allen coming through at a run. At the very instant he came in, something flew from his hand toward the ceiling at the center of the room and exploded. I tried to watch the team as they came in, but my eye—and everyone else's—had been irresistibly drawn to that flying flash-bang. When it exploded above our heads I hardly heard the pistols and submachine guns going off all around us. I was stunned motionless.

It was over in less than three seconds. Our instructors were posted all about the room. Allen was in one corner and Mike was in the opposite diagonal corner. Bob was just to the left of the door and Bill was just to the right. Smoke hung in the air, and I could taste the acrid fumes of the flash-bang in the back of my throat.

Bill looked to Allen and said, "Search."

Weapon at the ready, Allen moved over the sector of the room he had assaulted, checking the dead "terrorists" for signs of life. Bill covered while he checked each target and then returned to his position in the corner.

When Allen was back in position, he gave Bill an affirmative nod and Bill shifted his attention to Mike, giving him the same command. Bob covered Mike as he checked the "dead," and twice Bob moved a step forward or to the side so that he could easily cover a target while Mike checked it. Mike never stepped in front of an unchecked target in a way that would have prevented Bob from shooting if he had to.

I looked around the room and saw that each "terrorist" had two bullet holes in a vital spot: either the head, the center of the chest, or the throat. *How the hell had they done that with us all around the room and intermingled with the targets?* It seemed impossible that all those bullets missed us. Someone should have been hit—but we were all whole and unperforated. It was unreal.

Bill asked, "Did everybody see what happened during the assault?"

"Hell no, Bill," somebody croaked. "All we saw was that damn flash-bang and then you guys were in here."

"That's the way it's supposed to work," replied Bill. "Now we'll do it again at a walking pace and I'll explain it as we go along.

"Under normal conditions, we would've blown the door with explosives, but in this case, it would've been too much of a distraction."

As Bill spoke, Allen walked through the room in demonstration.

"The first man in the room, the number-one man, threw the flash-bang," said Bill, "and made an instant decision to turn left. He did that because the left side was the 'heavy side' of the room, meaning there were more people on that side than on the other. It could also mean that it was a longer side of the room—you'll learn more about that later. The number-one man always goes to the 'heavy side,' which usually means the more dangerous side."

Allen was walking the left side of the room, simulating shooting the targets he had engaged on the live-fire run-through.

"Staying close to the wall, he goes down that side of the room engaging any targets in that area. He turns at the corner and goes down that wall, still engaging targets. He halts at the far corner and faces back into the room."

We all looked at Allen.

"On the first time through, did anyone follow Allen until he stopped in his corner?" Bill asked innocently, though he knew the answer.

We all shook our heads.

"Why not?" he asked.

Several people said they'd been distracted by the flash-bang. Guy Harmon gave another reason. "I tried to watch him," he said, "but instead I noticed Mike, coming in right on top of Allen, but Mike turned right and that drew my attention away."

"Did you see him shoot?" Bill asked.

"No, I didn't," said Guy. "I knew he was shooting, but I was making myself small and covering up. My mind was on surviving."

Bill nodded. "Okay," and then he continued. "Mike came in right on top of Allen, but he turned right when Allen went left. Mike immediately engaged the targets on the far wall opposite the door, then went down the wall to the first corner, turned, and came to a halt watching into the corner farther down the wall, and out into the center of the room."

Mike walked through each step as Bill narrated.

"Do you see what happened here? It's impossible to keep an eye on movement in opposite directions. If you're the terrorist, you can't keep up with what's going on because your attention is divided—and fatally so. But the assaulter is only concerned with what's in front of him in his sector of the room.

"Who saw me and Bob as we entered the room?" he asked.

No one really had. When the shooting stopped, I noticed they were in the room on either side of the doorway. I had felt their presence but didn't really see them until the action stopped.

Bill went on with his explanation. "Rather than pile in right on top of the first two men, we hesitated a split second before entering the room. That way, the attention of the terrorists was no longer on the door but on the two men in the room, who are still on the move. With attention drawn away from the door—numbers one and two men kept moving—we came in unnoticed.

"I went to the heavy side and started engaging targets in that area to assist the number-one man. I worked from the center of the room to the left. Bob stepped to the other side and worked from the center to the right." As he said this, they positioned themselves as described. It was perfect.

"Look at us now. Look at our positions and the areas we're covering. There's not a square inch of this room that's not covered by fire and observation. If a piece of furniture presents an obstacle to one man, at least two others can see—and shoot—around it. We have completely dominated the room. We own it and everyone in it.

"Had you men actually been hostages," Bill went on, "as team leader, I would've started talking to you as soon as the shooting stopped. We want the hostages to stay calm and comply with our commands. We'll ask if they know of anyone or anything else in the room that is still a threat to their safety. We want to know if any terrorists are hiding in the room or among the hostages, and whether or not there are any explosives. But the last thing you ask is, 'Are there any bombs in the place?' We don't want to start a stampede."

As if the flash-bangs and submachine guns weren't enough.

"When we've determined everything is under control in here, I'll render a situation report to the troop commander. I'll tell him the room is clear, ask for medical assistance if we need it, and tell him we're prepared to evacuate the hostages. We'll continue to talk to and engage the attention of the hostages until they are moved out to the hostage holding area, where they will be initially questioned and identified.

"When the hostages are out, we brief ourselves on what happened in the room. In turn, each team member demonstrates and explains his actions in the room. He'll recount where he went, who he shot, how many rounds he fired and where; and he'll account for each shot fired. Not until we all know exactly what the team did inside the room will I report to the troop commander that I'm ready to turn the room over to troop control. The only exception to this would be an emergency evacuation, caused by, say, an uncontrolled fire or the discovery of explosives."

Jimmy Masters raised his hand for a question. Jimmy, a Creek Indian from Oklahoma, was one of the sharpest men in the class. When he had a question or a comment, it was always valuable.

Bill acknowledged him with a nod and said, "Jim, I'm going to ask you, and everyone else, to hold the questions for now. We're going to take a break and reconvene back in the classroom. Colonel Beckwith wants to speak to you. Then we'll answer all your questions and take it from there. The Shooting House is going to be your full-time home for the next month or so. Okay, that's it—classroom in fifteen minutes."

And we were dismissed.

Even though I had seen it up close, the room assault was hard to believe. The suddenness of it was astounding. One moment all was calm, then hell erupted, and just as suddenly—calm returned. There was a mental factor at work here that intrigued me.

The assault team had exploded into action when they assaulted the room, but when it was concluded, they immediately went back to a very calm, controlled mental state. It appeared seamless. They didn't have to stop after their explosion of intensity and regain their composure—they went smoothly from one mode to the other. They knew when to rush, and when to go slow, but their self-control never deserted them. They never became overly or visibly excited, as most men would have.

I could now see where all those shooting drills were leading us. If we stopped right now, we would be damned good combat shooters—infinitely better than any other military unit I knew of. But this next phase of training would take us to an altogether different level.

And deep in the core of my being was a kernel of dread: *Could I do that? Could I shoot that close to another person and run the risk of killing an innocent hostage or one of my mates?*

The honest answer was—not yet. My skills were close, but my confidence wasn't.

"Gentlemen, the unit commander."

We jumped to our feet and the position of attention as Colonel Beckwith swept down the center aisle of the classroom like a hungry bear headed for a bee tree. This was the first time Beckwith had addressed us as a class.

"Sit down, men, sit down," he growled, and waved us back into our seats. He stood there at the front of the classroom with his fists in his hip pockets and for a full minute looked us over with a penetrating glare.

He looked and sounded a lot like the old cowboy actor Chill Wills—but in a malevolent sort of way. His gravelly voice rumbled up from deep within his chest. He had on dirty suede desert boots and wore his khaki trousers slung low under his belly. Up top he wore an open-necked, blue oxford shirt underneath a navy blazer. He looked like the clothes had been thrown at him and more or less landed in the right places. He also looked like he could not have cared less. And this from a man who later hired a fashion consultant to teach us how to dress. Finally he spoke again.

"Well," he drawled. "You boys just got a little taste of what we're all about, eh? We ain't sellin' shoes or makin' cornflakes 'round here. It's serious bidness we talkin' about. You gotta kill and ya got to be damn good at it...cause we ain't takin' no prisoners. We ain't sendin' no terrorist bastards to prison just so they buddies kin take more hostages to git 'em loose. No sir, we gonna drop 'em dead on the ground and make martyrs out of 'em. That's the best way to go about it.

"And you cain't be shootin' no hostages while ye doin' it!" he thundered. "I ain't gonna be 'splainin' to the President why we went in and shot up a bunch of innocent folks we was 'sposed to be rescuin'."

Beckwith had slipped into the Georgia cracker dialect he favored for speaking to us on serious matters—or when he was angry. As I came to know him, I realized it was an affectation he used for dramatic effect. Beckwith was in deadly earnest about the subject of terrorism, but he was always a showman.

"So ye got to be good and ye got to be smart," he continued as he paced back and forth across the front of the room. "I'll take care of the luck."

He stopped dead center in the room and leaned toward us, a smile creeping across his face.

"And I'll tell ye what you're working towards," he went on. "Soon's you boys finish OTC we'll have enough bodies here to officially form this unit. Then we gonna take about six months to do our unit training, and after that I'm gonna tell the President we ready to go. And then you better grab yer asses, 'cause I'm gonna keep ye busy. I tell ye, things gonna be so good—we gonna do such great things, it'll be like pickin' up diamonds from right off the ground. Yes sirree, diamonds big as mule turds.

"So ya'll pay attention to what Bill and his team are teachin' ye. This phase of training is about to git dangerous and I cain't afford to lose none of ye yet. Awright, Bill, they yerz. Carry on."

And with that he launched himself down the aisle and out the door so fast we barely made it to our feet before he was gone.

Well, that was entertaining. Diamonds big as mule turds, eh? We'll have to see about that. One man's diamond is another man's turd. And he can't afford to lose any of us yet? Hmmm. I wonder when he can afford to lose some of us?

But he was certainly right about one thing—the next phase of training had the potential to be very, very dangerous. However, I had every confidence in our crew of instructors. They had gotten us to this point in a masterful fashion, and I was certain they would bring us through the next hurdles.

We spent the rest of the morning in the classroom while Allen diagrammed the steps of room combat on the blackboard. He drew the sequence of each team member's movement and actions just the way Bill had talked through their steps for us in the Shooting House.

On the board it was easy to see how the room was divided into overlapping sectors of coverage. In the room, it hadn't been so readily visible.

Speed, surprise, and violence of action. Those were the keys to success and survival, those and the ability to shoot what we intended to shoot and nothing else. We were not just going to go in harm's way. We were going to charge down harm's throat, grab a handful of his guts, and turn him inside out.

The individual attributes of an aggressive and adventurous spirit were such fundamental requirements for this work that it was just taken for granted that each man had what was necessary. Selection had seen to that. Now we were just adding the skills.

We started in the Shooting House as we had on the range: first walking through without weapons, then with, but dry-firing. Next walking through live-firing with one target, then adding targets. We increased our speed until we could move at a full run.

It was exciting. Standing outside the door to a room in the ready position, muscles tensing, wound up like a coiled spring, guns going off in the other rooms. Bill, Mike, Allen, or Bob holding the handle to the door, counting down with voice and fingers—*"Three . . . two . . . one—Execute! Execute! Execute!"*

You blast inside and immediately make a turn left or right. Sometimes a target is right in your face—right inside the doorway. You have to shoot on the move; shoot and keep moving at full speed and keep shooting until all targets are taken out. Then you assess the room for other dangers, other threats. Your heart is still pounding from that burst of speed and energy, but your mind has to remain calm and detached. It's like you have to observe yourself and the scene from outside your body—from a spot on the ceiling where you can take it all in with a fish-eye lens.

Soon it feels good; it feels fluid. You start to clear the room with a style that feels automatic. If a target is in your sector, you shoot it without even looking to see the hits—because you know where the shots went before they were fired. Your pistol or submachine gun follows your eyes while your mind ranges ahead. You can feel the gun moving in your hands, sense and count the shots as they're fired, but you never really hear the sounds of the shots going off.

Somewhere about that time, we added hostage targets to the equation. Then our instructors switched to cartoon targets that sometimes held weapons and sometimes didn't. That caused a little hesitation and embarrassment at first, but soon it made no difference at all. We either shot for the weapons held by the targets or at targets identified as "bad" (whether they had weapons or not) just as the instructor flung open the door and we hurled ourselves inside to do battle.

Then we started working in pairs. Two men in at a time, the first man in taking the heavy side, the second man going to the other side of the room. That added a whole new dimension and feel to the exercise. Hearing and feeling the fire from a partner, knowing the angles of fire were shifting and changing and that a "friendly" was in the room. The angles and elevations of your shots took on added importance. You didn't want to hit your mate—or he, you—but sometimes the rounds you fired would miss him by inches and his would pass just as closely by you.

Next we added teammate-down drills: how to pick up a partner's side of the room if he was shot and incapacitated or his weapons malfunctioned. We shifted from room to room and partner to partner, and each scenario was different from the one before. When we were fluent clearing a room as a two-man team, we started rotating through the aircraft room.

To clear a section of an aircraft cabin, two men would rush down the aisle looking for all the world like a set of deadly Siamese twins. The lead man low and his partner right over his shoulder, one clearing left and the other right. Head shots were the norm, because that's all that could usually be seen of a target over the tops of the seats and the heads of the "passengers." To make those shots running at full speed—and not touch a hostage—was the most difficult task imaginable. All our shots passed within a hair's distance of a "friendly," but there was no excuse for so much as grazing a hostage. To do so meant the dreaded public self-criticism drill.

When we could function and function well as two-man teams we formed into four-man teams. We shifted around the Shooting

House between rooms and team members. An instructor was in charge of each room, and we rotated from station to station. Every room presented a new problem and a different situation to overcome.

When clearing the aircraft room as a four-man team, we would enter the cabin by the over-wing emergency exit and immediately break into a pair of two-man teams—one team clearing forward and the other team aft. We worked on emergency evacuations and how to move stunned and frightened passengers with a minimum of effort and fuss.

I felt confident—not only in my own abilities, but also in the abilities of all my comrades. There wasn't a single man in the group I had the slightest hesitation about going into a room with and letting loose a storm of gunfire.

About that time, Bill made an announcement.

"You've all done well, guys, and you've come a long way in a very short time. You're actually much farther along than we were in the same period of training."

It was hard to imagine those four men ever being novices at close-quarter battle.

"But now we're going to take a break from the Shooting House. I'm going to turn you over to Dave Donaldson. He and his crew will be in charge of your breaching training. Some of it is mechanical, but most of it is concerned with explosives. You'll be working with Dave for a couple of weeks, and then you'll come back to the Shooting House to apply what you've learned. Give Dave and his team the attention you've given us, and we'll see you again later. . . ." He paused.

"Just make sure you come back with all your fingers."

And with those words, I saw Bill smile for the first time.

Mentally and physically, Dave Donaldson was a perfectly proportioned human being. He wasn't quite average height, maybe five feet seven inches, but he had the presence of a large man. He was an old Special Forces engineer, a demolitions specialist, and he knew more about the practical use of explosives than any man alive.

That message didn't come across because he talked about what he knew, but because he could show you what to do and how to do it. With all ten fingers.

Just as there are no old, bold pilots, there are no old, fearless demo men. You have to handle explosives the way you would handle a large, bad-tempered rattlesnake. You never take the snake for granted and you never, ever, let your attention wander.

With demolitions, you check everything over not just once but three times. And you never take shortcuts. If you do, you may become atomized pink goo on the nearest undemolished hard surface.

We were already experienced in the use of standard military explosives. For the combat infantryman, the Ranger, and the Special Forces soldier, explosives are just another tool for making a hole in something or knocking it over efficiently. And if you can harm your enemy in the process—so much the better. But Dave was going to teach us breaching—which means getting into a place causing the least damage and using the least material.

Dave and his crew were already pretty knowledgeable on the mechanical end of the spectrum, but to prepare for the course, they talked to the real experts: convicted cat burglars and escape artists serving long-term sentences in maximum-security prisons.

The prisoners really warmed up once they understood that they were helping a secret military organization by divulging their techniques and unique abilities. We all came away duly impressed and better informed. It's sort of funny—those guys ply their skills and the government sends them to prison. We ply the same skills on behalf of that very same government and get paid to do it.

We started by learning to quietly break into buildings. We learned to scale the outsides of buildings to get to upper floors; to descend to lower ones or drop unharmed from roofs. Using a push drill and a straightened coat hanger, we opened window latches from the outside. Then we went to work on door locks. We learned about the various styles of locks and their internal workings. We made duplicate keys, jimmied locks, and picked locks. Once we got through the locks, we defeated inside security chains with a rubber band, a paper clip, and a thumbtack. For sliding bolts we went back to the drill and coat hanger.

We opened padlocks with fingernail-shaped pieces cut from a beer can. (If you've noticed, I'm not explaining how to do all this. You'll have to learn that somewhere else.) We finished every day with a practical exam: defeating an array of different locks within a set time period. This included escaping from handcuffs.

We used any tool that could help us break into any place. We became proficient with cutting torches, metal cutting saws, jacks, cranes, hoists, and the famous "Jaws of Life."

Next came vehicles. We opened locked doors and defeated locked steering columns. We started vehicles with hot-wire kits made under Dave's expert tutelage. These became part of the car-theft equipment we kept with us ever after. It's probably not much of a surprise these days, but a decent car thief with a three-tool theft kit can get into and start your car about as fast as you can with your keys. So can a Delta operator.

We spent days on the demo range reviewing the basics and doing simple work with standard explosives. We made craters with dynamite and cut trees with TNT to form obstacles. We built and detonated things like "earmuff" charges to destroy bridge supports, and fashioned C-4 into special shapes to cut railroad rails, I beams, and thick steel rods. Using specialized shaped charges made from wine bottles and C-4, we cut into safes. We blew up, first a large delivery van, and then a house, using a bag of flour, a pad of steel wool, and four ounces of TNT.

We made easy-to-use, safe-to-handle explosives with a trip to the local hardware store. An ammonium nitrate charge, for example, came from two hundred pounds of fertilizer, ten quarts of motor oil, and five pounds of dynamite. Bury a charge like that in the ground and you can make a crater thirty feet wide and fifteen feet deep.

Then we worked with specialized breaching charges. These were explosive materials that allowed us to make very precise and surgical cuts into the doors and walls of any building or other man-made structure. Using these charges, we could slash our way to the inside of any target in a manner that was safe not only to ourselves but to the hostages inside.

Now we were in business. No barrier could keep us out. And after our training period with Dave, we headed back to the Shooting House to put our newly acquired skills to practical application. With all the fingers we started with.

For the next three days, Bill and his team put us through a series of tactical situations in the Shooting House. Each drill required us to explosively penetrate the door of the room we were assaulting.

When we hit three rooms simultaneously, it made some kind of a blast. One charge going off in the confines of the Shooting House hallway was really something, but three going off simultaneously was like standing under an Atlas rocket at liftoff. The noise, shock wave, and fireballs from three charges detonating together were horrendous—and we were standing right in the middle of it. The lead man of each team was only inches from the door charge when it exploded, and the only protective gear we wore in those early days was foam earplugs. Only later did we go to protective eyewear, and later still we added protective vests. Live and learn. Thankfully, we lived while we learned.

On day three of that week, we got a real treat: we went out to the range for some joint work with the unit snipers.

The facade of a two-story building had been built down-range to allow the snipers to shoot targets that rapidly appeared and disappeared in the windows and doorways. For this training session, the long gunners guided our movements to the target by radio, telling us when it was clear to move and halting us when targets were present. On our final approach to the target, and as we placed our charges on the doors, they covered our every movement by fire.

Together we worked on coordinated assaults. This is when the assault teams have approached the target undetected, have placed charges on the breach points, and are in position for the assault. When all teams signal ready, the commander takes over and sets the assault in motion with the radio command: *"I have control—stand by. Five ... four ... three ... two ... one ... Execute! Execute! Execute!"* On the count of two, the snipers fire on any exposed terrorists, right over the heads of the assaulters crouched under the windows. On the count of one, the charges are blown. At *"Execute!"* the assaulters launch themselves inside the room and unleash hell.

Then we worked on a very important variation of the coordinated assault. We made our approach as before, put everything in place, and all teams would signal ready. Then—nothing.

The commander would hold us in position. Or start and stop the countdown. Or call us completely off the target and back to the assault position. It was an exercise to teach us that we were a disciplined force; once we were *switched on*, we could also be *switched off*. But I have to tell you, it's difficult to back off that target once you're primed and ready to go—even in training. It's like calling a dog away from a cat he's just cornered; he might back off, but he ain't got to like it.

We did each of these assaults again after dark, using the night as our principal ally. It made everything easier for us. Wearing night-vision goggles, we could see in the dark and shoot just as accurately as in the daylight. Another benefit of the instinctive shooting technique is that even without goggles, you shoot as well in the dark as in the light.

We finished late that night and were back at the Ranch—the unit compound—cleaning weapons when Bill made an announcement.

"Guys, you all did well. The snipers told me before we left how much they enjoyed working with you today, and you can bet that Colonel Beckwith will know about it by tomorrow.

"We have just one main Shooting House training objective left to accomplish during this phase, and it happens tomorrow and the next day. Remember how you were introduced to the Shooting House that first day? Well, now it's your turn."

The room went silent.

"Each of you will take turns playing the hostage and sitting in the hot seat while your mates conduct a live-fire assault. You will be a hostage four times. You will also rotate through every position on the assault team. Each assault will initiate with an explosive breach. Meet in the classroom for the mission briefing at ten hundred hours. Get a good night's sleep, see you in the morning."

And with a nonchalant wave of his hand, he dismissed us.

This is going to be some final exam, I thought as I finished cleaning my pistol. *Pass, and it's just another training day. Screw up, shoot and kill a friend, and you fail.* That's a high penalty for flunking a test.

I looked around the arms room at my friends and comrades. *Do I trust my ability and skills enough to hurl deadly missiles within millimeters of their heads? One misstep, one flinch, and it could be catastrophic. My little girl plays with the children of the guys in this room. Yeah, Bill. Get a good night's sleep. That's a good one. I'll never close my eyes tonight,* I thought, as I put my gear away and walked to the parking lot.

I started to open the door of my truck but just stood there for a minute, looking at the cold night sky and watching the vapor cloud of my breath. It was a clear, moonless night and the stars stood out in bright relief, winking against the eternity of space.

The cold door handle felt good in my hand. I slid behind the wheel and coaxed the little engine to life. *Man, I've got to rebuild the engine of this thing when I get the chance.* I wheeled out the gate and waved goodnight to the old veteran on the night shift.

Now it was my turn. I was sitting in a leather armchair in one of the rooms of the Shooting House. The place was furnished like a living room with sofas and chairs, coffee and end tables, mirrors, pictures, and bookcases. There were even books on the shelves.

The lighting was dim. Manikins and paper targets were positioned about the room. Some held guns and some were empty-handed. They were the terrorists and I was their hostage. There was an armed manikin crouched behind me with one hand on my neck and the other on my shoulder, pointing a pistol at the door. Another terrorist stood on my other side, pointing a submachine gun at my head.

Within the next ten minutes, the door would be blown in and four of my classmates would assault the room using the close-quarter battle techniques we had learned. Within three seconds of the explosion, they had to kill the terrorists, gain positive control of the room—and rescue me. Bullets would rain throughout the room and someone would be firing live rounds within inches of my head. If they missed a single terrorist or hit me by mistake, the team would fail this phase of training.

I sincerely wanted them to pass the exam.

My team and I had successfully passed the first test this morning. Marty Johnson had been the hostage and he had only blinked his eyes when a pair of double taps from my .45-caliber pistol knocked the heads off the terrorist manikins so close beside him. Then we changed positions within the team and made three more assaults in different rooms with other comrades occupying the hot seat.

Now that I was here, I realized it was harder to be the shooter than the hostage. To be on the assault team required great confidence in your abilities. To be the hostage required faith in your comrades. It was easier to think of being shot than of shooting a mate.

As the minutes ticked by so slowly, I thought about the long, hard path we'd taken to this point. We had spent untold hours on the range, and in the Shooting House, and had fired hundreds of thousands of rounds to get here, to this room, to this chair.

I heard an explosion down the hall, then the immediate stutter of pistols and submachine guns in another room. The firing was over in just a few seconds.

I hope that went well. I glanced down at my watch. The assault should be any time now. *I sure hope these guys pass their test, I most sincerely do.* The door exploded with a flash and a clap, and a shock wave hit me like a punch in the face.

I could see the team hurling themselves into the room, see the splashes of fire from the muzzles of their guns, and feel the slap of overpressure as bullets flew by my face. But I can't honestly say I heard any one distinct sound or that my brain registered any one distinct image. It happened so fast, so suddenly, that even though I was expecting it, it was so completely overpowering that my system was unable to respond until it was all over. The ferocity of the attack stunned me. It was like being struck by lightning—a pure and elemental force.

J.T. was the team leader. As he gave commands to his team to conduct the search, I unfroze enough to turn in my chair and check the terrorist over my shoulder. The manikin's head was lying on the floor a few feet away, with one hole just under his right cheek and another slightly in front of his ear.

The terrorist on my other side had a pair of holes at the base of his throat. The rest of the manikins and cartoon targets around the room had at least two hits in the kill zone; some had four where the three and four men had added their shots to an already hit target.

When the team finished their room search, J.T. gave me a toothy grin from under his lush mustache. "You okay, Bubba?" he asked as he looked me over from head to toe.

Allen had just stepped into the room and he looked me over along with the rest of the targets.

"Yeah, J.T., I'm fine," I replied, using the same nonchalant phrase I would later use to answer the same question in a much more dangerous setting.

Allen finished his scrutiny of the room. "All right, boys, that's a go. Now do it three more times and you're Shooting House graduates. But don't let that pressure you or anything." He smiled as he marked his clipboard. "Paste up the targets, put a new head on that dummy, and get ready for the next run-through. J.T., have a seat and make yourself comfortable. It's your turn in the barrel."

"Give me your equipment, J.T.," I said, cheerful again as I got up from the chair. "I'll put it down by the reload table in the hallway. And don't worry about a thing, old buddy. We'll be gentle—I know it's your first time."

"Yeah, thanks" was all he said as we cleared out of the room. He was uncharacteristically quiet while we hung a new door on the hinges and locked it into place.

It all came off without a hitch. Everyone had multiple turns as a hostage, and as an assaulter with a live hostage in the room. Nobody was hurt and no targets were missed. And the confidence that life-or-death final examination gave us—in ourselves as much as in our mates—stuck with us for life. I trusted myself and I trusted my comrades in a way that was unshakable. From that point on, no matter the situation, no matter how dangerous, we would prevail.

I believed that to the core of my being. I still do.

"We do more observing and reporting than we do shooting— so perhaps we would be better called 'observer-reporters' than 'snipers,'" explained the long gun chief, Larry Freedman.

"In fact," he went on, "when dealing with outsiders, we use the term 'sniper/observer' and not 'sniper,' because so much of what we do is scene observation and collection of immediate intelligence. And that's what you guys are going to get a taste of this week."

Master Sergeant Larry Freedman (also known by his self-proclaimed radio call sign, "Super Jew") loved life like few other human beings I've met. He was intensely interested in people and always amused with life's surprises. He would soon become one of my best friends. Years later, after retiring from the Army and while working for the CIA, he would become the first American killed during America's "intervention" in Somalia.

"Some of you will be selected for assignment to a sniper troop when you've finished OTC," said Freedman. "But all of you have to understand how we do our business. At one time or another on a site, every one of you will pull duty in the TOC—Tactical Operations Center—so it's vitally important you learn our reporting methods and procedures. Also, as you saw on the range last week, snipers will often overwatch your movement and guide assault teams to the target. Or an assault will be sniper-initiated.

"But more than any of that jazz," he said, jabbing his finger at us, "we don't want you getting in our way and screwing up a shot— and you sure don't want us shooting you." By this time, he was wearing a huge grin that threw deep laugh wrinkles across his face.

Larry Freedman had a head full of wiry, prematurely gray hair he was inordinately proud of and a great, thick mustache in luxuriant bloom across the middle of his face. Permanent laugh lines radiated from the corners of his eyes. He would often laugh so hard at some antic he had witnessed or a joke he was telling that the tears would run down his cheeks.

Larry worked hard to maintain the chiseled Mr. America body that helped earn him his code name, but he was also a superman in many other ways. He looked after his snipers like they were his own flesh and blood, and whenever anybody in the unit needed a helping hand or some wise counsel, it was usually Larry who knew what to do or say.

He was also known for the battles royal he had with Colonel Beckwith whenever Charlie tried to interfere with what Larry thought was best and right for his snipers. The yelling matches they had were legend in the unit. Years later, while he and I were huddled together in some godforsaken spot of the globe, Larry told me that Beckwith had fired him on six separate occasions.

"But I'm still here," he crowed, "three commanders later." The fights they had were merely lovers' spats; Beckwith thought the world of Larry, and Larry thought the same of our commander.

This day, however, was our introduction to the world Larry loved so much, the world of the long gunner.

"First we'll spend a couple of days getting down the basics of reporting," he said, "and then we'll go out to the range and run some practical exercises. You guys are going to enjoy this—I guarantee. Now let me introduce your intructor, Branislav Urbanski. He'll be your guide the rest of the week."

Branislav Urbanski was an extraordinary character, and he, too, became one of my best friends. Branislav escaped from Poland in the late 1960s and made his way to America when he was just a teenager. Once here, he discovered that the fastest way to an American citizenship was via the military, so he joined up. His use of the English language and view of American culture had been learned in the U.S. Army, specifically in the old separate Ranger companies, and because of that, both were a little off-center of the prevailing societal norms.

In Branislav's face you could see the Tartar blood deposited in the Slavic gene pool by the armies of the Khans. He had high cheekbones, a broad brow, and wide-set eyes that disappeared into slits when he was either deadly serious—or highly amused. He looked like the middleweight boxer he was, with a strong jaw and chin, broad shoulders, long arms, and an almost neckless head that sat squarely on his shoulders. He was fluent in Polish, Russian, German, and English. Like most expatriate Poles, Branislav was a rabid nationalist, and I've never seen a man rejoice as he did when Poland slipped the Soviet yoke some years later.

But beyond all that, Branislav was one of our premier snipers, and now he took us under the wing of his knowledge and ability and explained things we would have to know, starting with how to look at a building and report what we saw.

On the face of it, that sounds like a pretty simple procedure. But with sniper teams posted all around a crisis point, it takes some hard-and-fast reference points to keep the situation from turning into a Tower of Babel. Branislav taught us how to impose order on potential chaos. The idea is simplicity itself.

Buildings are given a color code to designate a specific side. The front is designated white. The back of the target, black. The target's own left is red, and its right is green.

Floors or levels are given a phonetic alphabet designation, in ascending order. Thus the first floor is labeled Alpha, the second Bravo, the third Charlie, and so on. (Yes—some buildings have more floors than the alphabet has letters, and we had a means of handling that.) All openings in the building, whether doorways or windows, were numbered on their respective floors from left to right.

For example, if I were observing the front of the building and saw something happen in the sixth window on the seventh floor, I would record and report the location as follows:

"White, Golf, Six."

Back at the sniper TOC, the information would be logged and plotted on the target schematic. All other sniper teams would immediately know what happened and where, and as soon as I said "white," the teams on the other sides of the building knew that it was something outside their own zones of observation.

We used the same means of identification on planes, trains, buses, and boats. In fact, it was adapted from the method of marking the sides of ships and planes with navigation lights: red for the left or port side, and green for the right or starboard side of the vessel.

Brani pointed out that by patient, careful observation and reporting, the snipers could build up an extremely valuable body of information on a terrorist crisis scene. Details such as which areas were used, and just as important, which areas were not. The location of hostages. The actions the terrorists would take during periods of heightened tension. Their leadership, rest schedule, and a million other things that helped build accurate profiles of them as individuals.

Delta Force snipers are chosen only after extensive additional psychological testing and evaluation. There are a number of attributes you look for in a sniper, and there are two of paramount importance to avoid.

The first characteristic is what we called the "Texas Tower Syndrome," referencing Charles Whitman's massacre of fourteen people from the bell tower of the University of Texas in 1966. That characteristic manifests itself when a sniper starts shooting and he can't stop. It just feels so good—such an overwhelming sense of power— that he can't turn it off when there are no more legitimate targets left. He'll continue to shoot anyone in sight. It is a very real compulsion, and I've heard its Siren call in my own ear.

The second characteristic takes a much different, more understandable form. This one we termed the "Munich Massacre Syndrome."

Think of it like this. A sniper spends most of his time watching. Observing. Getting to know his targets. Through his high-power spotting scope, a sniper can see the features on the faces of the terrorists as clearly as if he were in the room with them. He sees them when they smile, and sneeze, and eat a sandwich, and get drowsy, and as they manifest all the other little things that identify each of us as uniquely human.

But they don't know he can see them. They have no idea where he is—they don't even know he exists. The terrorists represent no personal threat to the sniper whatsoever. They are far away. They can't harm him. They can't kill him. As the sniper spends hour after hour observing his targets through his spotting scope, he gets to know the people he is watching as human beings and he becomes intimate with them. And then, when the order to shoot is given, he can't do it. He can't kill these people he has come to know; these people who are no threat to his life.

That's what happened at the Munich Olympics massacre in 1972. When the order was given to shoot the Black September terrorists who had taken eleven Israeli athletes hostage, the German police sharpshooters couldn't pull the trigger. They had observed the hostage-takers for such a long time, and developed such a sense of empathy for them, they couldn't bring themselves to kill people they felt they now knew. The terrorists were then able to kill the Israeli Olympic athletes under their control.

The psychological niche where you'll find the man who can shoulder aside these two behavioral opposites is very narrow. The ideal is a man who, from the safety of long range, can kill when it is required but is immune to the impulse to continue killing when the situation is resolved. A man whose psyche is strong and so fundamentally rooted in a personal philosophy or religion that he doesn't suffer unduly from taking human life under appropriate conditions. The snipers of Delta Force are decent, thoughtful, intelligent, and unshakable men. By their demeanor, they could easily be taken for academics—very fit, powerful, and deadly academics, perhaps—but professorial just the same.

After our talk, the class divided in half, and Branislav took my group into the other classroom to begin our practical exercise. On a large table in the middle of the classroom was an eight-story building in miniature, so perfectly detailed it could have been part of a movie set. It had windows and doorways, wide canopied primary entrances, fire escapes, a rooftop garden, and an outdoor restaurant.

Inside the "hotel," as we called it, lights could be turned on and off in various rooms. There were even miniature cardboard cutouts of people, some of whom were armed, who could be made to appear and disappear by a series of strings running up through the bottom. Outside there were a few sidewalks and trees, and cars and trucks parked in the adjacent streets.

Branislav gave us the instructions for the training session. Half of us were positioned around the room in observer positions that gave all-around coverage of the building. At each position were a notebook and pen, a pair of binoculars, a camera with telephoto lens, a compass, and a radio.

Larry Freedman had taken the other half of the class to another room where they would establish and man a sniper TOC. Some would operate the radios in the TOC, others would transcribe the received data, and still others would plot the reported activity on a sketch of the building drawn from data radioed in by the observers. When film started to come in from the observers, other students would develop it in the sniper "fly-away" darkroom set up in another room. The photos would be posted along with the building sketches to help build useful information as the situation developed.

Then each group settled in and set to work. From our observer positions, we had to label the sides of the building and work on individual sketches of the side of the building we were assigned. We immediately began taking photos of the site, but as Branislav explained, neither sketches nor exposed film would be sent back to the TOC for several hours. Instead, the TOC would have to build its initial picture of the site from our verbal reports over the radio.

Brani came over to my position, and I asked him why we didn't immediately send sketches and exposed film back to the TOC. It seemed to me that it was especially needed just after arrival on the scene. He was ready for me.

Two reasons, he explained. One, because he wanted the guys

manning the sniper TOC to produce a picture of the site based upon our radioed reports—it was a good way to get on the same sheet of music and it was a good way to practice radio discipline.

Second, in the first flush of setting up at a site, people are so busy, there usually isn't a man to spare running back and forth between the various observer positions. And sometimes, depending on the target, we couldn't move between positions without the risk of being spotted. In that case, movement would take place only after dark.

We stayed in our positions until six o'clock that evening before we broke for the day and both groups reunited to compare notes. It was uncanny what the guys in the TOC had accomplished. The first prints from the film we had finally sent back were just now coming out of the darkroom, but the target sketch they'd produced—solely from verbal reports—was amazingly accurate.

Larry summed up the day for us: "Guys, the whole point in what takes place, both here in the TOC and out on site, is to build a body of information you can use to make the best possible decision about when, where, and how to conduct an assault. There is no such thing as a matter too small to be reported and logged. There is no such thing as too much intelligence. We will do everything in our power to make the assaulter's job easier. If we can resolve a situation solely by sniper fire—so much the better. But no matter what, we want to tip the odds in favor of the short gunners when they have to hit the place.

"Since the cat's out of the bag now with our miniature building, we'll go out to the range for the rest of the week and do the same thing we did today using the facade. The group that was in the TOC this afternoon will be on the line, and you other guys will be the TOC bunnies tomorrow. And since there are no questions," he smiled, "I'll see you all here in the morning."

That was a really good day's training, I thought as I drove home that evening. *In fact, I think I learned more today than on any other one day of the course.*

I thoroughly enjoyed that week with Larry and his crew. I gained a whole new appreciation for what the long gunners did and how they went about it. I realized that shooting *was* only a part of what they did; a vital part, to be sure, but not the only part. And I made some new, lifelong friends.

Things were rocking along now. More and more I was beginning to feel that we were part of the unit. We were still some months from being full-fledged operators, but I felt confident we could function well if called upon.

"The toughest thing we're ever going to have to do is recover a terrorist-held airplane," explained Colonel Beckwith. "We've been working on how to go about it, and so have the British, the Germans, the French, and the Israelis. So far, nobody has a real good grip on the problem. But it's a problem we've got to solve and we've got to solve it soon."

Charlie was dressed in a rather presentable fashion today—and so were the rest of us. We had been told to be in casual dress attire, and had also been given an order against chewing tobacco in the classroom while this particular visitor was with us. The colonel obviously wanted our guest to form a favorable impression of the unit, and that meant we all had to do our part. We didn't want to come across as a bunch of knuckle-draggers.

"You're going to spend a few days here in the classroom with some visitors, and then go down to Atlanta this weekend for a visit the FAA's helped us arrange with Delta Airlines. Delta has agreed to let us conduct research and training on planes they have in for scheduled maintenance. This will be our first real chance at working with a civil air carrier, so the whole outfit will be coming down, too. We want to make the most of this opportunity.

"I want to remind you again that all of our guests are here under our nonattribution policy. Whatever they share with us is for our use only—we don't divulge their identities, and whatever they say stays right here in the unit. So be smart, pay attention, and give a big hand to our guest, Mr. XXXX of the Federal Aviation Administration."

Beckwith led the applause as our visitor made his way to the front of the classroom. Charlie Beckwith was a master at this sort of thing. He knew our future depended on the goodwill and help of some of the other government agencies, and he was shrewd enough about human nature to know how to go about gaining that support. He invited people from the highest and most influential levels of government to come to the unit for a visit or to be a guest speaker.

We took them to the range and the Shooting House for live-fire demonstrations—some of them even sat in the hot seat. We let them shoot a few guns and fire off an explosive charge, showed them all sorts of "secret" stuff, and told them they were one of the few outsiders *ever* to see any of this. We'd let them share a meal with the guys in the mess hall, swear them—as a new "associate member" of the unit—to undying secrecy, and send them on their happy way home with excited memories of everything they'd seen and done.

Everybody likes to be in on a secret, so by the end of the visit, we would have a new ally. Then our guest would whisper to a few people about what he had seen and done down with that secret outfit at Fort Bragg and before long, other people who deemed themselves important would angle for an invitation.

This sort of thing paid big dividends for the unit in the years to come, and the reality was, we always learned something valuable from our guests. Our current visitor was a case in point. He was a very high-ranking official of the FAA, and the information he gave us about aircraft hijacking incidents and the things aircrews were trained to do if hijacked was invaluable.

Coupled with what we learned from the FBI's training academy group the following day, we found that there was a very distinct line of demarcation between the authority of the FAA and the FBI when it came to responsibility for a hijacked plane.

Very simply put, as long as the doors of the plane were closed, it belonged to the FAA. But once the doors opened, the enforcement of federal airplane piracy law became the responsibility of the FBI. What that really means: once the plane lands, the FBI takes charge.

But in those days, no agency in American law enforcement was prepared to wrest control of an airplane away from an armed and determined terrorist band. The FBI didn't have the training, the manpower, or the organization for the task. Neither did any of the large metropolitan police SWAT teams.

Everybody knew there was a glaring problem, but no one was doing anything to address it. Aircraft hijackings had been a growth industry during the 1970s, and any organization that gave it even the slightest study soon realized it was a problem of monumental proportions. Everybody was hoping somebody else would take the lead, and it looked like we would have to be that somebody.

During that week in the classroom, we studied every successful example of a Western power taking a plane back from hijackers. It didn't take long. There were only two.

The French counterterrorist service, GIGN (Groupe d'Intervention de la Gendarmerie Nationale), had resolved a hijacking principally by the fires of their snipers. But a wounded hijacker had killed the commander of the force when he led a detachment onto the plane.

In the second instance, the German federal police CT force GSG-9 (Grenzschutzgruppe 9), assisted by two British SAS members, had executed an assault to retake a hijacked Lufthansa 737 that had been flown to Mogadishu, Somalia, in October 1977. Although ultimately a success, the assault could easily have become catastrophic. Once in the plane, the German force got bogged down in a protracted gunfight. During the battle, the terrorist leader, who was in the cockpit, managed to throw two hand grenades into the passenger cabin before he was killed. Fortunately, the seats absorbed the worst of the blast and shrapnel.

In the official after-action review the Germans shared with us, they freely admitted they had been unprepared for the assault they undertook and the plan they had put together to retake the plane was ad hoc. Though pleased they had recovered the hostages, they knew they might not be so lucky the next time. There had to be a better method of executing an aircraft assault.

Our guys were already at work on the problem. By studying all the terrorist hijackings in the last decade, we determined that there were very few occasions when snipers alone could resolve a situation. But one obstacle for the snipers turned out to be not as large as anticipated.

The leader of a hijacking force usually would position himself in the cockpit of the plane. After all, that's the control center. Often enough, other members of the terrorist force would gravitate to the cockpit as well. If the snipers could kill any terrorists located in the cockpit when the assault was initiated, it would greatly enhance the mission's chances of success. But there was a problem.

Most sniper units believed that a bullet fired through the extremely thick glass of an airplane cockpit would be deflected enough to cause a miss—or worse—veer off path and hit one of the airplane's crew members. The FBI and Secret Service snipers thought so, too, but no one had made any empirical studies of the problem until we came along.

We got a truckload of cockpit glass from many different types of aircraft, mounted it in metal frames, and started shooting. Our snipers determined there wasn't much of a problem after all. The deflection was so slight that, within the confines of an airplane's cockpit, it made little difference to the accuracy of the shot. They could hit and kill the terrorists and still leave any crew members in the cockpit unscathed. It even turned out that any glass shattered by the bullet, and flying around inside the cockpit, had the consistency of sand and presented little danger to the crew.

The assaulters were confident we could hit a plane in the same fashion as a building: to enter simultaneously, in a violently executed rush, through every access point. If we could do that, we could be on top of the terrorists so fast we could overwhelm and kill them before they were able to make an effective response.

But how do you get up to a plane without being seen? And how do you get in all at once? How could we divide the plane into areas of responsibility and sectors of fire? And speaking of fire, just how vulnerable was a plane to catching fire during an assault? We planned to answer those and many other questions while we were in Atlanta.

So after we had pumped our visitors for all they knew, we spent the rest of the week divided into teams trying to come up with some preliminary tactics. We went out to the Shooting House and worked various assault drills. It didn't take long to figure out that by simultaneously entering all the entrances of a plane, we would have some teams moving and shooting directly toward one another. Or teams with their backs turned to their mates.

We soon realized that while our small, twelve-row section of fuselage was great for training a single four-man team, it was far too short for multiple team training. We needed a full-length fuselage to work on these problems. Until we could get access to the real thing, we would have to be content with chalkboard drills.

But all in all, a lot of progress was made in those few days with every member of the Tribe focusing attention on killing this mastodon. This is a good example of how operational plans were developed in Delta Force.

Beckwith laid down the law early on. Operators would develop their own tactics and operational methods. He had chosen us because we were all experienced fighters and no one needed to tell us how to go about our business. The men on the teams would determine the *how* of a mission and Beckwith and his subordinate commanders would provide assets and coordination. But no one would ever *dictate* tactics to us or tell us *how* to risk our own lives.

With that as a given, I can tell you that some of our tactics discussions became pretty heated. If you threw an idea on the table during a skull session, you had to be ready to defend it from all sides. But this was the only way we could have gone about developing these ideas. In those early days everything we did was plowing new ground. There was no tested methodology. And mistaken ideas would be paid for in lives—not just the lives of the hostages we were supposed to rescue, but our own.

By the close of business Thursday, we had a few preliminary plans we wanted to work on. Friday morning we loaded our bags and set out for Atlanta. Later that evening we loaded into our vans and made the short drive from the hotel to Delta Airlines' maintenance hangar on the back side of what is now called Atlanta's Hartsfield International Airport.

Our caretaker then and for many subsequent visits was Delta Airlines' chief of security, Mr. Joe Stone. But the tone for the relationship was established by a senior vice president of the company when he greeted us upon our arrival at the hangar and told us we would have any and all support we needed. The reason was simple, he told us. First, it was the right thing to do; and second, it could easily be one of their planes and their passengers and crew we would need to rescue someday.

That was an easy statement to make—but Delta Airlines put its money where its mouth was. I have no idea how many tens of thousands of dollars the company sacrificed to lost productivity during our visits. We were always given their two most senior and experienced maintenance men as technical advisers, and any plane in the hangar was at our disposal. They would always have a variety of planes in the hangar, but if we wanted a particular model to rehearse on, they would make it available to us, even if they had to pull one in from another city. We worked with all the other major airlines over the years, but none of them ever showed the concern and enthusiasm for what we were trying to accomplish that Delta Airlines did.

Maybe it had something to do with sharing a family name.

We started by learning ground operations. We got to drive baggage trucks and tug motors; load and unload baggage from all types of planes; drive fuel trucks and refuel airplanes; and crank up and operate ground power units (GPUs), the trailer-mounted jet engines that blow air into and crank a plane's engines. Our favorite ground job of them all was operating the "SST"—the shit-sucking truck—the all-important vehicle that pumps out the toilets. (Trust me, if you are ever on a plane that's taken hostage and held for more than a day, you'll cheer the arrival of the SST more than the rescue team.) By learning to fill the ground positions that care for the airplanes, we became comfortable on the busy flight lines and adept at blending into the environment of an airport.

We spent several hours in the wheel, tire, and brake shop and discovered something that blew one of our theories. Shooting out a plane's tires wouldn't be much, if any, help in an assault. Not only could jet planes still taxi around with blown tires, the damn things could even take off—they have that much power. But there was another vulnerability we found that would allow us to immobilize a plane, and that immediately went into our growing playbook.

Then we got inside the planes—all kinds of them. First the narrow bodies: 707s and DC-8s; 727s, 737s, and DC-9s. We even snagged a few Convair turboprops that were still in service. Then we tackled the wide-body planes Delta flew: the giant Boeing 747 and the Lockheed L-1011. We became familiar with their internal layouts, the locations of their emergency equipment, and areas of particular danger such as the routing of fuel and oxygen lines.

Aircraft doors became an obsession. We learned how to operate the doors of each plane, not just from the inside, but what was more important, from the outside. It was imperative that we be able to rapidly open any door or emergency exit. We had to know how to get into any plane—in the blink of an eye—and we quickly learned how to go about it.

The next problem was what to do when we got in. In practice, we found this to be less of a problem than we had anticipated. From our point of view, the passenger compartments, cockpit, and galley areas of an airplane weren't very different from the rooms in a building, excepting that an airplane was absolutely crammed with people.

But tactically, we could clear a plane in almost the same manner as we approached a building. Even though the plane would be filled with hostages, of necessity most of them would be down in their seats. And as we found out through experimentation, the seats of an airplane are extremely tough and offer great protection from gunfire and shrapnel. Locked cockpit and lavatory doors also proved to be no problem. We found a way to get through those like there was no lock on them.

Next we were going to need data on all the different commercial passenger planes in the world. We would need to know how high the planes sat off the ground, how high it was to the threshold of each door, which direction the doors turned, and how to disarm the emergency slides. We had to know where the emergency lighting system switches were mounted and where the fire extinguishers were. Fortunately, that information was easy to obtain from the aircraft manufacturers and individual airlines.

This was only the beginning—but it was a good beginning. Within the next six months, we compiled the greatest database of this sort in the world, covering every commercial passenger plane in existence. We reproduced the data, illustrated with dimensional sketches, and created a small handbook we christened the "Encyclopedia Aeronautica." Every Delta team had a copy.

As new airplanes came out or older planes were modified, it was a simple matter to incorporate the updates.

Airlines and airplane manufacturers were most helpful with this, and made the new models available to us for research and training. We were caught short only once, and that was easily rectified.

We finished our session in Atlanta in good spirits. The unit's only real deficiency now was numbers—we didn't yet have a sufficient number of operators to completely cover all the positions needed to take down a 747 or an L-1011. If our growth rate held, it would be another year before we were large enough for that task. We just hoped that until then, we wouldn't have to respond to the hijacking of a wide-body airplane.

When we got back to the Ranch, Walt Shumate was in the hallway talking to one of the clerks. He looked up as I walked by and smiled that sly grin that always made him look like he had a really good, really dirty secret he'd been keeping to himself.

"Hey, Haney," he said, twirling the end of his mustache. "Didn't break no airplanes down in Atlanta, did you? Colonel ain't got to pay for nothing you fucked up, does he? I know how you Rangers are around machinery." (Army lore holds that Rangers are so destructive they can unravel ball bearings and break anvils.)

"No, Sergeant Major," I said. "We just learned how to corral them—not throw them or brand them."

"Well, that's a good thing, I reckon." But he looked as though his spirits dropped for just a second before he continued. "But you know, I've always wanted to shoot down an airplane. That's got to really feel good if you're a ground soldier. Just think of all those planes and helicopters the Vietcong and the NVA shot down. Why, I'll bet some of those ol' boys got medals big as commode lids hanging around their necks for knocking down an American jet. Probably still drinking free beer at the NCO Club in Hanoi when one of 'em tells about that day on the old Ho Chi Minh Trail when he brought down an imperialist air pirate with his trusty AK-47.

"Shit," he said, kicking at a scuff mark on the floor. "Ya know, it just ain't fair that a Communist should be allowed to have that much fun. Hell, the little bastards don't even like fun."

Then he gave me a fierce look and said, "Let that be a lesson to you, Haney. Being right ain't necessarily fun." He shook his head wistfully.

"Uh, yeah, Sergeant Major," I answered. "I'll remember that. But right now I gotta help put this gear away."

"Yeah, Haney. Go do that, I'll catch you later." But just as I turned to walk away, he held my arm for a moment, and peered into my eyes as though he was searching for something before releasing his grip and walking away.

Strange man, I thought as I walked down the hallway to the OTC bay. But he was right. I'd always wanted to shoot down an airplane myself. I guess Walt and I were just on the wrong side—at least when it came to shooting down airplanes.

You can't have it all, I thought as I stowed my equipment away. *If we can't shoot 'em out of the sky, we'll just have to settle for saving them.*

" 'Tradecraft' is a catchall term that covers all the skills an espionage agent practices while plying his trade in the field. Dead drops, brief encounters, pickups, load and unload signals, danger and safe signals, surveillance and countersurveillance—all of these things and how you plan for them and put them into effect are part of what constitutes tradecraft."

Our instructor today looked like a high school chemistry teacher. He wasn't. He was a veteran agent with the CIA.

"Just as fieldcraft encompasses the skills a reconnaissance patrol employs to succeed and survive on a mission behind enemy lines, so tradecraft encompasses those skills we use to perform our job.

"But tradecraft is only a means to an end. And the end we work toward is the passage of information. Specifically, information delivery or retrieval by nontechnical means. Usually this is information in the form of a message, but sometimes it comes in the form of a person. Think of it as passing notes in class without the teacher catching on." He removed his glasses and gave the class a conspiratorial grin.

I'll bet he's had that experience, I thought, *but I'll also bet his students got away with it only if he chose to ignore it.*

Horn-rim glasses, Hush Puppies shoes, leather elbow patches on a tweed jacket, square-tailed knit tie, and a longish flattop haircut. The man didn't look like the ace CIA field agent he actually was. He was also, according to Colonel Beckwith, the best agent instructor on The Farm, as the CIA training center at Camp Perry, Virginia, is called by the cognoscenti.

It didn't surprise me when the man fished a pipe out of a coat pocket and puffed on it as we chatted in the hallway during break. But damn, did this guy ever know his business. And more than just knowing it, he could teach it—a rare thing.

The colonel had worked hard to strike some sort of deal with the CIA, and we had a close, cordial relationship with them until a later commander decided to cause an estrangement. But at present, we were still in the honeymoon phase. Two of our guys were in the CIA's new agent's course and our OTC class was receiving instruction from the agency's star trainer.

The CIA operatives I've met have been dedicated, intelligent, decent, mission-focused, and self-sacrificing citizens. I only wish I could say the same for the higher-ranking members of that organization.

We were bearing down on the end of OTC now, and the two major remaining portions of training would flow smoothly into one another. Many of the principles and techniques of tradecraft overlap with those employed in protective work. In fact, some Delta operators were already working a protective detail for former President Gerald Ford.

Our snipers had been shooting and cross-pollinating with the Secret Service snipers since early winter. So when former President Gerald Ford planned a ski trip, the Secret Service asked us to send them a couple of ski-qualified operators to help out. They just didn't have enough agents who could ski. Skiing is a common Ranger and Special Forces skill, so most of our guys were experts on the slopes. Charlie sent along two operators, the Secret Service gave them a crash course in executive protection, and they were assigned to President Ford's detail.

The guys briefed us on their return. Their mission was to sweep the slopes in front of Mr. Ford, then let him ski past while they observed and overwatched the party from above, their submachine guns slung under their ski jackets. Before a turn or a blind spot on the slope, they'd ski down past the party to clear the slope below. They would do this from the top of the slope to the bottom and then race ahead to the top of the next slope and do it all over again.

What a great job! All they had to do was clear and overwatch— none of the hard work of arranging motorcades, positioning vehicles, clearing rest rooms, and worrying about the crowds in the lift lines. Soon enough, we would all find out just how demanding, monotonous, and mundane most protection work really is. But right now, we were trying to master the basics of tradecraft.

Most of this sounds glamorous and intriguing, but I have to tell you that in the field, the practice of espionage is plain hard work— and most of it is pretty dull work at that. But it beats the hell out of being chained to a desk in an office or passing your life staring up a mule's ass on a farm, which is where I could have easily been.

Espionage has its moments of excitement, but we weren't learning tradecraft so we could be spies. Intelligence gathering was not a field we expected to have to plow—though as things turned out, we were wrong about that. We were learning these skills to become adept at slipping into and out of foreign territory and mounting operations in unfriendly or downright hostile nations. The first thing we learned was how to case a site and write a casing report.

Let's say we're going to conduct operations in a new city. We will need to plan methods for communication via message or meeting, including dead letter drops, personal meetings, brief encounters, and vehicular pickups. We have to find multiple sites for all these activities, and each site has to have an alternate in case it becomes compromised. As part of this, we need to set up routes that allow us to check for anyone who may be following us and places we can use to help shake off any suspected tail.

We have to have sites for day use and night use, and we have to be prepared for a site being rendered useless by construction work or some other unforeseen activity. We also have to make sure no one else is using a site we have selected.

That last part is very important. All surreptitious field agents (including criminals), regardless of their nation or government, use the same kinds of sites for their activities, and the same methods of tradecraft. It's like playing baseball. No matter who you play for— America, Russia, France, Israel, or whoever—the techniques are always the same.

It's wild to start casing a site for possible use and see signs that someone else is already using the location—as if some other dog has already watered a fire hydrant you were eyeing.

This is especially true with dead drops, because there are only two kinds of "load" and "unload" signals: chalk marks or thumb-tacks. (With the declining use of wooden telephone poles in large cities, the thumbtack signal has probably died out.)

If you live in Washington, D.C., or New York, look around sometimes when you're out on the street. If you see a chalk streak on a wall at about the height of a person's jacket pocket, or maybe a small piece of chalk crushed on the sidewalk near a street corner, you are probably seeing a signal left by an agent. Given the demise of the Soviet Union and the passing of the Cold War, it is amazing how much of this still goes on. If you are attuned to it, you'll see it. Our instructor told us that some sites in various world capitals were so covered with chalk marks, each nation's agents used a different color of chalk. It was a terrible breach of social and professional etiquette to use someone else's color. Talk about honor among thieves.

In most cases, a good site is "ordinary." It needs to be a place that no one pays any special attention to. Obviously, it also needs to lend itself to the activity taking place and the people involved. Mostly it just needs to be a busy place with lots of people and movement—another case of the successful guerrilla swimming in the sea of the people.

In those days, one favorite place for a dead drop was a public pay phone. They could be found just about anywhere, usually in a place that made it easy to conduct countersurveillance for the agent unloading the drop. The material to be passed would be placed in a magnetic key box, the kind you can buy at any auto parts store. To load the drop, you just stuck the magnetic box to the underside of the pay phone's shelf while making a call or looking up a number. The box is always stuck in a predetermined spot on the shelf (left front, right rear, etc.) so that when the drop is unloaded, the agent knows exactly where to reach and doesn't have to fumble around. The "loader" makes his "load" signal as he departs.

Why all this dancing around? Simple. To provide a cutout between people and groups. No one needs to know the identity of anyone else, especially between cells, and in the event of capture and interrogation, it helps minimize the knowledge any one operative can give up. It isn't foolproof. But it makes the work of the other side that much more difficult and time-consuming, and time is a precious and perishable commodity in intelligence work.

Even the best-laid plans can become exasperatingly fouled up. Some years later, I was in charge of the tradecraft portion of OTC. My team and I spent several weeks in Atlanta setting up sites and writing casing reports for the exercise, only to have most of our sites sealed off at the last minute because of a movie being shot downtown. It was a valuable lesson, because that snafu was exactly the sort of thing that could happen during an operation.

On another training session, one of our guys was supposed to follow an "agent" to a meeting site. Our guy spots the man he thinks is his quarry, believes he sees the "safe" and "follow me" signals, and proceeds to follow the man all over El Paso, Texas. After two hours of bus rides and mall-crawling, our guy becomes frustrated, steps close to the man he's been following, and hisses in his ear, "Buddy, don't you think it's about time we put an end to this shit?" The unintentional "agent" looks at the hulking, pissed-off stranger at his shoulder muttering what can only be a crazed and perverted threat, throws his hands in the air, and runs screaming down the street.

Fortunately for our guy, his teammates have been following along for sheer enjoyment. So they pluck their dumbstruck teammate off the street and whisk him to our safe house, where the rest of us—who have been getting constant radio updates on our "Wrong Way Ferrigan"—have gathered to complete our comrade's humiliation and sense of inadequacy.

That was funny when it happened and it's still a funny tale today. But that sort of mistake can have tragic consequences.

Years ago in Sweden, Israeli Mossad agents made a similar misidentification and assassinated a man they thought had been one of the Palestinian terrorists involved in the Munich Olympics massacre. This sort of business is like packing parachutes—you *always* have to be sure.

Surveillance and countersurveillance were the meat of the course and had the most pertinence for us. This included finding and following a subject on foot or by vehicle, knowing when to close in tightly on him and when to give him free range, and above all, knowing how to stay invisible. And to hone this skill, our instructor sent us on practice missions through the cities of North Carolina and Virginia.

Even in training it's a nerve-racking business. At the least, your activities can arouse the suspicion of the local police. And in our case, the police in every city we used had been alerted and were watching for us. It seemed unfair at the time, but our instructor had good reason to make the program as realistic as possible.

In preparation for the executive protection phase of training, we took a driving course. But not a normal driving course by any stretch of the imagination. It certainly wasn't "defensive." In fact, this was a course in "offensive" driving—in how to use a car or a convoy of cars as a weapon.

Two of our OTC instructors had been working with the State Department's Office of Diplomatic Protection and had undergone their program of instruction. From there they journeyed to Sear's Point, California, and attended Bob Bondurant's racing school. Now they brought home what they had learned.

The Dynamic Driving Course is one of those rare things that are just so much fun it never feels like work. Much like parachuting, the more difficult and dangerous the task, the more we enjoyed it. But I guess it's every man's dream come true—learning to handle a car like a stunt driver and getting paid to do it.

Some years later during our vicious little *guerrita* in Panama, my colonel's young Humvee driver asked me a question as we shared a canteen cup of coffee at the end of a hellish day.

"Sergeant Major, ya know what I like most about war?"

"No, Bowman," I said. "What do you like most about war?"

"Ya get to drive any way you want to and ain't nobody can do a damn thing about it." He smiled contentedly, wearing that old man/young man look on his face that is peculiar to combat soldiers. I understood exactly what he meant. And that was how I felt that first day of Dynamic Driving.

The first thing we did was go out and rent a dozen cars. Our instructors had learned the hard way that you don't use your own vehicle for this sort of thing. One of our guys had rolled his own car preparing for the class, and when he was asked if the unit would cover the repair cost, Beckwith said he was damned if he would pay for the damage because—in the colonel's own words—"That was just stuuuuupid!"

The rental car route worked well for a year or so, until just about every rental agency within fifty miles figured out what was going on. But by the time we were finally banned by the agencies, we had put together our own training fleet.

Early that morning we took our cars and equipment and moved out to the airfield at Camp Mackall. Mackall is a subpost of Fort Bragg, situated out near the golf meccas of Pinehurst and Southern Pines. During the Second World War it was where the glider units trained, but since the 1950s Mackall had been home to the first phase of Special Forces training.

It was the perfect spot for what we were doing. We could use the huge, triangular-shaped airfield with its six-thousand-foot runways and adjacent taxiways as our "skid pan" and racetrack. And because it was tucked away in such a remote location, we could train to our hearts' content in peace and security.

Donald Michael Feeney was our chief instructor. Donny is an Irish-Italian street kid from Brooklyn who, at the urging of a New York Juvenile Court judge, had found a home in the Army. We had just missed each other in the Ranger Battalion—he was signing out the day I arrived—but we knew each other by reputation and through mutual friends. When I arrived for Selection, Donny was one of the cadre members, and when we started OTC, he was one of the instructors.

Donny's demeanor has been described as "a terrier looking for a leg to piss on." He's as tough as a railroad spike, with alert flashing brown eyes and a keen intelligence. I believe he's one of the most courageous men I've ever known. You can have no better friend than Don Feeney. And no more relentless an enemy.

Even though he and I came from such utterly different backgrounds, and in some ways are about as opposite as two human beings can possibly be, Donny and I share a friendship tantamount to brotherhood. I think the highest compliment I've ever received was when Donny told someone a few years ago, "I trust Eric Haney with the lives of my children." I feel the same way about Don.

Out here on the skid pan, Donny was in his element: fast cars and few rules. Don's assistant instructor was Bill Oswalt, the cadre member who had issued my equipment when I reported in at Camp Aberdeen.

Bill's part Cherokee and hails from Tulsa, Oklahoma. He was a partisan of the "Okinawa Mafia," having served there with 1st Special Forces Group in the same company as Walt Shumate and several other current members of Delta. Neither of us knew it then, but when we formed B Squadron, Bill and I would be teammates for years and comrades forever. Bill is a compactly built, handsome man with eyes so dark you can't see the pupils. He has a wild sense of humor and is most definitely alive and kicking today. He, Donny, and I are still thick as thieves, and some people claim we constitute a three-man chain of cahoots—but that's never been proven in a court of law.

The next five days were a blur of motion and speed. Don and Bill took us through the basics of setting up a vehicle for high-

performance action and then walked us through handling dynam-
ics. We learned to feel where the weight was loaded on a car—front,
rear, and sides—and how that affects braking and control. We
learned how to hit the apex of a curve, use a roadway or single lane
to best advantage, and how to bring a car to a controlled stop in less
than a third of the normal distance. Next came controlled slides and
reversing movements: sliding 90-degree turns left and right, the forward 180-degree turn, and the reverse 180.

Then we put it all together and chased one another around a
track that had been marked around the airfield with traffic cones.
We had a good turn of luck when it rained that afternoon and we
were able to practice our newfound skills on a wet surface. The next
day we brought out several junkers from the property disposal yard
and practiced using a car as a weapon. Interesting little tricks such
as how to spin out another vehicle, how to hit a car and bring it to
an immediate halt without harming yourself, and how to punch
through a roadblock.

Most of it was a lot of fun, but as always, it was a highly com-
petitive atmosphere. Nobody wanted to be the one who inevitably
slid out of control and out of action. The only thing that gave me a
rough time was when Bill had me ride with him and operate a
video camera while he chased Donny around the track. By the
time we were into the second circuit, I was howling at Bill to stop
the car.

"What's the matter?" he yelled over the noise of screaming tires.

"I'm seasick!" I yelled back. "Let me out before I puke!"

Bill pulled over to the side of the track and stopped. I climbed
out, dry heaving, and wobbled around on shaky legs until I found
my equilibrium again. Bill thought it was a riot until I drove the
car and he tried his hand at watching a sliding, turning, braking, bouncing, accelerating world through a viewfinder. When I
pulled over to let him get his color back, it was no longer such a
great joke.

The last day and a half we spent on formation driving—how to
operate within a multicar convoy and use the vehicles as a weapon
to protect the "limo." This was the heart of what we were learning—lead vehicle, limo, follow car—and how to maneuver those
three vehicles as one.

We broke at lunch on Friday and got ready to depart. Before we left, Donny gave those of us who had been detailed to turn in the cars enough money to buy new tires for our rental vehicle.

"Scatter out to different tire stores in Fayetteville," he said, "and make sure you bring me back a receipt. I gotta account for that money!" He doled out twenty-dollar bills from a wad as big as his fist.

I had a little trouble with the man who put the tires on my vehicle. As soon as he realized it was a rental car, he became indignant that I was buying tires for it.

"I wouldn't pay for them tars if I wuz you, mister. Hell, the rental agency never shoulda let that car go out with 'em. Tars in that kinda condition . . . it's dangerous, you coulda been hurt." He shook his head in disgust as he looked at the bald tires with their steel belts shining through here and there.

"Shit, I'll call 'em myself," he huffed, moving heavily to the phone. "They'll have to listen to me. Ah'm a tar per-feshunal."

"No, man, that's okay, don't worry about it." I stayed his hand on the telephone. "I'll just have them call you if they have any problems with it. Just don't worry about it."

"Well . . . awright, mister, if that's what you want." He squinted at the wad of bills I had stuffed into his hand like it was hush money. "But it ain't right, and I wouldn't put up with it muhsef." He reluctantly gave me the receipt.

A concerned citizen, I thought as I drove back to the airport to turn in the car. Turns out I wasn't the only one to have that sort of reaction from a "tar per-feshunal."

From then on, at the end of every driving session, we replaced the tires ourselves at our own motor pool.

There are two principal methods of providing executive protection: the Secret Service way—and everyone else's.

The difference is asset driven. The Secret Service pulls out all the stops; in fact, they act as much like the Gestapo as any agency in the United States government.

When protecting a traveling president, vice president, their families, or presidential candidates, the Secret Service calls upon—and gets—the assistance of every police force and governmental agency within the jurisdictions through which the official party travels.

The men and women of the Secret Service do a hell of a job (one I do not envy) of protecting the biggest lightning rod for hostile intentions on the face of the earth. But without the tremendous assistance of those other host forces, the Secret Service could never provide the level of protection it gives to those in its charge.

The Secret Service is the best-dressed and most well-groomed group of people you have ever seen. This is an old joke, but it has some validity. If you don't know which person in a crowd is the American president, just pick out the seedy-looking man in the middle of a cluster of great-looking folks. The members of the presidential and vice presidential details are beautiful. There's just no other way to describe them.

From these beautiful people, we had our first lessons in what would become for Delta a very important tasking. Two senior Secret Service agents, Tommy and Francis, came from Washington to spend a few days with us and guide us through the classroom sessions of Protection. The single most important thing we learned from these men was the relationship you must maintain with your protectee, who is called "the Principal."

The first thing the director of the Secret Service tells a newly elected president, Tommy said, is this: that a whole lot of people voted against him, a whole lot of people hate him, a fair number of people wish him no good at all, and a substantial number of people would kill him if they could. Tommy said it's important to let the president know that regardless of the feeling of joy and light he gets from adoring crowds of well-wishers, and despite the genuine concern the vast majority of the nation has for its president, the feeling is not universal.

Then we were given a history lesson on the attempts that had been made upon the lives of presidents and presidential candidates during the 1970s.

Nixon had been the target of several credible threats, but Gerald Ford attracted dangerous kooks like a magnet attracts iron filings. George Wallace had been shot and paralyzed—and one of his Secret Service agents was shot through the throat during the same attack.

Next we learned the Secret Service theory (or more accurately, their practice) of providing security. Simply put, it consists of multiple concentric circles of protection placed around the Principal. The outer circles perform the missions of detection and deflection of potential problems, while the innermost circle "covers and evacuates" the Principal in the event of an attack.

If you remember the footage of the shooting of President Ronald Reagan, you've seen the textbook example of what happens in that situation. At the sound of the gun going off, the agents around the President dove on him, shielded him with their bodies, shoved him into the limo, and evacuated him from the area. They were operating on trained instinct: cover him up and get him away from danger.

On the street, the agent nearest the assailant at the sound of the shot yelled, "Gun!" and grabbed both the pistol and the hand that was holding it. His focus was on taking control of the weapon away from the attacker. The other agents, police officers, and citizens present piled on and crushed the shooter to the ground.

Most security work consists of making your Principal just a little more difficult to take on than someone else in hopes of encouraging the malintentioned to take their business elsewhere. The problem the Secret Service faces is, there is only one president of the United States. And someone intent on bagging a president—for reasons political or mental—usually won't settle for anyone else.

I worked with the Secret Service on only one occasion, as the counterattack team leader for Vice President Bush's detail when he visited Fort Bragg. That wasn't a particularly onerous task, since he was on probably some of the most secure ground in the United States.

But in 1994, in my postmilitary life, I took President Bertrand Aristide back into Haiti as a security detail leader for his protective staff. And I can tell you that it's a heavy responsibility knowing that the man you're looking after is specifically marked for death. Fortunately for President Aristide and myself, being marked for death was a fairly common occurrence in Haiti at the time.

We bid Tommy and Francis a warm good-bye, full of the sincere thanks and affection we felt for those tremendous men and the service they represented. The next day, we welcomed a pair of trainers from an agency we were to have a long and close relationship with—the U.S. Department of State. This is when we learned how the rest of the world has to go about protecting a Principal—with limited assets, poor-to-useless local support, and spotty intelligence.

In those days, the State Department's security service was called

State Department Security. It now goes by the somewhat more lofty title of Department of State Diplomatic Security. Then as now, it was charged with the protection of ambassadors posted overseas, the security of American embassies around the world, and providing security services for certain visiting diplomats in the U.S.

Back in 1979, State was having a difficult time. It had a very limited number of agents, and most of those wanted to be more diplomat than protection agent.

Up until then, life in an embassy posting overseas had been pretty benign, but that was changing rapidly. The American ambassador to Greece had been assassinated, American embassies in several countries had been attacked, and there were credible death threats on our ambassadors in such garden spots as Beirut, El Salvador, and a few other places where locals took exception to the American worldview.

For a lot of reasons, the State Department was having trouble coping with the threat it was facing. That's when Charlie Beckwith stepped in and offered them a deal they couldn't refuse. Ambassadorial protection agents did not have the massive resources the Secret Service could call upon. In the really bad places, they had only themselves and a handful of locally recruited (and often minimally trained) bodyguards. In the event of an attack, the protective force would not only have to "cover and evacuate" but also have to fight their way out.

Charlie told the State Department he would provide them with some men for posting to their most threatened embassies; men who could not only fight but train and lead local bodyguards—something we were good at and State didn't like doing. All State had to do was provide initial training in their methods. After that, we would train our own people. And to prevent any embarrassment brought about by the idea that State had to bring in hired guns, our men would operate under Department of State cover while on assignment.

It was a great deal for the State Department, and they jumped at it before Colonel Beckwith could change his mind. It gave us a permanent position in some really bad places in the world, places where we would probably have to operate in the near future. It gave us contacts and opened channels in an agency that had a very real and strong impact on our potential operations—and allowed us to start building trust with them. We would also be positioned to build personal contacts within the host nation, in the local government as well as with other factions and peoples. It would pay off for us time after time in the years to come.

Our two new guests, Alton and Raymond, painted a pretty bleak picture as they briefed us on what we were faced with around the world. And we couldn't have been more pleased. Then we dove into the subject at hand: how to protect an ambassador of the United States of America in a place where so many people were determined to kill him.

Avoiding situations and places that can become problems is the name of the game. If you are doing your job well, the boss will argue with you now and again about being overly cautious. But that's okay. It's a hell of a lot better than sitting in front of a congressional panel explaining how you managed to let *the* representative of the American people in a foreign country be killed while he or she was entrusted to your care. To this day, no member of Delta Force has ever had to answer that question.

Now it was time to practice what we thought we knew.

For a few days, Alton and Raymond took turns, with one of them being the Principal and the other one the detail leader, as we rehearsed our skills around Fayetteville and Raleigh. Then we started rotating in as detail leader, while one of the instructors provided a running critique and threw problems at us. Something as simple as a flat tire on the limo en route to an appointment in another city could throw a whole day out of kilter.

As we became proficient at handling the smaller, more mundane problems, our teachers would hit us with the big ones:

The Principal is at a dinner party in a private residence when the house is hit by rockets and catches fire and there is small-arms fire in the street outside.

An irate local national tries to assault the Principal at a press conference in a hotel lobby.

A local police checkpoint tries to stop the Principal's motorcade at gunpoint.

The Principal's wife wants you to send the detail's local bodyguards to pick up her friends for an official tea party she's hosting at the Embassy. She thinks it would be a nice touch.

The Principal suffers a heart attack at a diplomatic dinner.

Each one of these situations happened in situ and without notice, and it taught us a tremendous lesson. *Always expect something bad to happen and be ready to act.*

I was the detail leader when the Principal had his "heart attack" at the dinner party. I can promise you, it's pretty disconcerting to look calmly around the room and then back at your protectee just in time to see him drop face first into his soup as the room erupts into turmoil.

One of the most trying aspects of the job is that it's difficult to take care of the physical needs of yourself and your staff. Just getting a chance to go to the bathroom can be a challenge. And something as simple as getting everyone fed at mealtimes takes ingenuity and choreography. If the Old Man takes thirty minutes for a meal, that means you can only feed a few of your people during that time and you have to make arrangements for the others before and after normal mealtimes. It is the rare protectee who even realizes, much less cares about, something as simple as making sure the people protecting his life have time to eat.

The work is mentally demanding, not because of an intellectual challenge, but because it requires unrelenting vigilance and attention to detail. You are *never* able to relax, and that translates into physical fatigue, making it imperative that you maintain some sort of physical conditioning program. And that, too, has to be worked in around the Principal's daily schedule. Because like the Basic Training drill sergeant, "You get 'em up in the morning, you put 'em to bed at night, you're with 'em their every waking hour—and some nights while they sleep."

Once our instructors were happy with our local performance, we took our show on the road to Washington, D.C. It felt much more comfortable doing that sort of thing in Washington than it ever did in Fayetteville. A three-car motorcade in D.C. is part of the natural scenery, but back in North Carolina, it was like the circus band coming down Main Street.

In Washington the presence of a full-blown protective detail was so common that few people paid us any attention and we were able to concentrate on our work. Besides, Washington wasn't just a world capital; it was *the* world capital. So if we could do a professional job here, under the scrutiny of the best protective agencies on the planet, we should have no problems operating anywhere in the world.

Things went so smoothly all in all that it was a pretty dull exercise. In order for us to rotate everyone through the various positions on the detail, we broke into two groups and alternated working day and night shifts. That was what helped set up the incident I remember most vividly about protection training in Washington.

The detail I was working had the night shift that particular day, and for the evening, we would be taking the "President" to a performance at the Kennedy Center. That meant we had time to get in a little exercise before we took over from the other detail at 1600. So five or six of us took advantage of the downtime to go for a little run on the canal towpath that runs parallel to the Potomac River. After three or four miles, we turned around to head back to our hotel to get cleaned up and ready for work. A couple of guys raced on ahead while the rest of us loped back along the pathway, soaking up the pleasure of being outside and alive on a beautiful late-spring day.

Since we were so wet and nasty from the run, we entered the hotel from a side entrance that opened onto an elevator bank used mostly by housekeeping and room service. There was a set of swinging doors leading to the hotel's kitchen on the left of the elevators. On the other side was a back doorway to the main dining room.

At any given time, there is something going on at just about any hotel in the D.C. area. The one we were staying in was hosting a series of weeklong conferences for NOW, the National Organization for Women. A half-dozen or so NOW delegates were waiting for the elevator just as we stepped into the side entrance. Since we're basically decent men and didn't want to offend any of the ladies with our appearance or odor, we stood quietly behind them, intending to wait unobtrusively for the next elevator. Then, slipping silently and unexpectedly through the kitchen doors, came our comrade, Marshall Jones.

Marshall glanced at us and put a finger to his lips to command silence as he crept up behind Andres Benevides, our mate closest to the NOW delegates. Andres was just a few paces behind the women, with his back to Marshall, and was standing there with his hands on his hips, dripping sweat on the floor. Marshall crept forward, leaned down, and took the hem of Andres's running shorts between his thumbs and forefingers. In one fluid movement, he snatched the unsuspecting Andres's shorts down around his ankles and instantly dove back through the kitchen doors. It happened so fast we were all stunned—but no one more so than the poor victim of Marshall's Pearl Harbor–like sneak attack.

Andres glanced down at the shorts, crumpled forlornly around his feet like the skin of a dead animal. His eyes bulged out of his red and throttled face, and he gasped for air, looked wildly around him on all sides, threw back his head, and yelled, "Oh, Jesus Christ!"

Andres started hopping madly for the swinging doors to the kitchen, hands still on his hips, shorts tangled around his feet. He probably would have gotten away with it, if it hadn't been for his involuntary bellow of shock and horror.

Startled by the wail of despair behind them, the women waiting for the elevator turned, in unison, just in time to see a beautifully built sweaty man, wearing only a jockstrap around his *verquenzas* and terror on his face, frantically hopping sideways for the safety of the swinging doors. His quickness and the way he moved reminded me of a crab skittering across the beach for the refuge of his burrow.

We all stood there in stricken silence. Eight people thrown together by chance, frozen motionless and afraid to look at one another or acknowledge what we had seen. Sixteen downcast eyes followed the synchronized arcs of the swinging doors as they slowly came to rest. We were all too shocked to say or do anything.

Then the doyenne of the group, an expensively dressed, dignified, and very formidable-looking woman, arched an eyebrow, slanted her eyes at her friends, then at us, and dryly announced, "Hmm, I think I'll come here more often."

We fell on one another, choking and sobbing with laughter.

As you might suspect, Andres didn't think it was that damn funny. J.T. was his roommate and reported back to us that when he got upstairs, Andres was walking in tight circles, spitting angry curses, first in Spanish and then in English. Andres's dignity had been bruised and he was pissed. Even though he didn't have conclusive proof as to the identity of the culprit, he had his suspicions.

Later that day, when we poked fun at him about his Washington "debut," Andres smiled with deceptive sweetness, but nodded pointedly to Marshall and quietly intoned that old Army mantra of revenge, "Payback...is a Medevac."

We spent a few more busy days and nights in Washington under the careful eye of the State Department Security hierarchy and then quietly concluded our training with those very capable people.

After the out-briefing with our trainers, Donny and Bill told us to wait for them in the hotel until they got back. They would have some instructions for us when they returned from exchanging the official thank-yous and farewells at the State Department.

Something's cooking, I thought as we maneuvered through traffic. This bit about "stand by for instructions to follow" had a whiff of Selection to it. Well, we'd already been saying, "Selection is a never-ending process."

And no matter what, OTC was just about over and we would be forming into teams soon. Which didn't mean there weren't still a few surprises yet to come.

Gerhard Altmann was born in Germany. When just a boy of fifteen, he had been issued an ill-fitting uniform and a Panzerfaust antitank rocket launcher and sent into the rubble-filled streets of the dying city of Berlin to battle the omnivorous Red Army as it tore the throat out of Hitler's Third Reich.

Captured by the victorious Russians after twelve days of unspeakably brutal fighting, the young Gerhard was interned in a prisoner of war camp for several weeks until he and a number of other boy soldiers were able to make an escape. He returned to a destroyed Berlin, only to find his entire family dead and his neighborhood obliterated.

Gerhard survived that terrible postwar winter by his wits and the sheer toughness of youth. The following spring, he found work on a farm east of the city. Later that year he was turned in by an informer for scavenging machine guns and other military residue and was interned once again by the Russians. He escaped once more, but this time he was able to make his way to Munich, where he found work with the American Army as a laborer in a military warehouse. Here he was able to work at night and complete his interrupted schooling by day.

Two years later, with the assistance of some of his new American friends, Gerhard embarked for life in the United States. He promptly enlisted in the Army of his American friends and was almost immediately sent to the chaos of battle at the outbreak of war on the Korean Peninsula.

Following the war, Altmann completed a university degree under the GI Bill and he returned to the Army as a freshly commissioned lieutenant. He was just in time to become one of the earliest members of the Army's newly formed Special Forces. He met Charlie Beckwith during a tour in Vietnam, and he must have made quite an impression on the future commander of 1st Special Forces Operational Detachment—Delta, because Beckwith selected him to be one of his original staff officers when the unit was born.

On Friday afternoons back at the Ranch, Altmann delivered a worldwide intelligence update to the assembled membership of Delta Force. He found and brought out the humor in the most dismal world events, and his delivery of these dire reports of global mayhem was so hilarious that the weekly updates were known as the "Four O'clock Funnies." But one day, at the close of a briefing, he turned strangely serious and said to us, "Men, hope that you never have to go into combat with me. I have been in three wars... and lost them all. I fear that I am the worst of Jonahs in this regard and that perhaps I should have pursued some other calling in life."

Now we were assembled in a large suite in our Washington hotel, and Major Altmann was briefing us on the final phase of the Operators Training Course, appropriately termed the "Culmination Exercise."

"My young friends," said Altmann, striking an Il Duce pose with a lifted chin and a fist waving about in the air, "you have come far, very far indeed, and now you must demonstrate that you can apply the skills you have acquired by your persistence, diligence, and hard work. The task before you is not easy. And why should it be? The simple truth is that our mission is not easy. Were it otherwise, we would not be here now, for other men would have already shouldered the burden you now so nobly carry."

He dropped the Mussolini act and continued in his normal voice.

"But enough of that *Scheisse*. This is your final exam and I believe it to be one that will test your abilities to the fullest. I like to think of this as an exercise in resourcefulness, and before you are finished, I believe you will think of it that way too."

He pointed toward the back of the room.

"On the table there is a folder for each of you marked with your code name. Inside it you will find one thousand dollars in cash and a set of instructions. You will find an emergency contact phone number on the inside cover of the folder. Use that number only in the event of an emergency that requires you to come out of the play of the exercise. In all other situations, you are to rely on your designated covers for status and action. You do not have authority to break any national, state, or local laws. However, you may treat regulations according to your own discretion." He smiled in punctuation of that last remark.

"And, oh, by the way." He slapped his forehead with the heel of his hand. "I almost forgot. The FBI starts looking for you in about three hours." He lifted a wrist and consulted his watch. "Or less. I think it would be very unpleasant for you to be apprehended and interrogated by those most diligent and persuasive gentlemen.

"And since there are no questions—and I know that each of you has a pressing and diversified itinerary—my wish is that you all . . . have a good 'un."

He dismissed us with a flourish of the hand like a master of ceremonies gesturing for the start of a show.

Three hours, I thought, as I located my folder, counted the money inside, and signed for the package on the roster nearby. *Man, I've got to get cracking. But not in such a hurry that I start making mistakes. First I'll go back to my room, read my instructions, and make a plan that will get me through the next twenty-four hours.*

I left the briefing suite and ambled down the corridor to the elevator bank.

Guys are already acting in character, I thought as I waited for the elevator. The more excitable ones had taken off like quail flushed from a covey, but most of the men simply moved off like they were winding up an ordinary, boring day.

My method of preparing myself for the ordeal ahead was to

make haste slowly. To purposefully slow my movements and thoughts—at least until the adrenaline rush was over. That's how I had learned to impose self-discipline and keep from running off half-cocked.

Back in my room, I stashed the money and sat down to read my instructions. They directed me to a personal meeting and read as follows:

PERSONAL MEETING PLAN

1. <u>Purpose:</u> Conduct personal meeting with local agent.
2. <u>Date/Time:</u> 9 June 1979, 2200 hours.
3. <u>General Location:</u> The Embassy Row Hotel, 2105 Massachusetts Ave. NW, Washington, D.C. (See area map.)
4. <u>Specific Location:</u> Embassy Lounge on the 1st floor, adjacent to the "Le Consulat" Restaurant.
5. <u>Contact Procedures:</u>
   a. Enter lounge, spot agent, and join him at table or bar.
   b. Agent will give brief verbal instructions about recontact and pass written mission instructions by placing them inside newspaper or magazine which he will leave on the table upon departure.
   c. Team Member: Will retrieve the newspaper/magazine and depart a suitable time later.
6. <u>Recognition Signals:</u> (Bona Fides)
   a. Visual: Both Team Member and Contact Agent will make visible one (1) red and one (1) black felt-tip pen.
   b. Verbal:
   Team Member: "Have you been waiting long? We got hung up in traffic."
   Contact: "No, not too long. The traffic does get bad sometimes."
7. <u>Danger Signal:</u> Team Member or Agent upon recognizing danger or compromise will scratch side of the nose with finger.

My mother's twenty-first birthday. My sister Iris is four months old

My second grade photo, 1959.

My sister Iris and I playing at the old home place.

Basic training platoon, 1970. I'm in the top row, sixth from the right—seventeen years old.

```
                        DEPARTMENT OF THE ARMY
        HEADQUARTERS, 1ST BATTALION (RANGER), 75TH INFANTRY
              HUNTER ARMY AIRFIELD, GEORGIA  31409

AFZP-IB-CSM                                    27 November 1978

SUBJECT:  Letter of Appreciation


Staff Sergeant Eric Lamar Haney
254-███████
Company C, 1st Battalion (Ranger), 75th Infantry
Hunter Army Airfield, Georgia  31409
```

1. On your departure from the 1st Ranger Battalion, I would like to express my appreciation for your manner of performance and loyal support.

2. Your vast knowledge of Infantry weapons, tactics and your exceptional abilities as an instructor contributed greatly to the outstanding performance of your platoon in all phases of training. Your close supervision, attention to detail and devoted assistance to others in the unit was clearly demonstrated at all times. You always insured your squad and team leaders werekept well informed and ready to accomplish any mission assigned to you or in support of the company and Battalion. Your initiative, resourcefulness, and untiring efforts to achieve perfection in all phases of your duties resulted in increased morale and esprit de corps in your platoon.

3. Your military bearing, dedication, physical fitness and professionalism make you an asset to any organization. You could always be counted upon in any situation to give a hundred and ten percent and make the decisions necessary to excell in every area. I am certain you will continue to excell in all your endeavors and move on to the top of the Noncommissioned Officers Corp. Your high standards of appearance, military courtesy, cheerful and cooperative approach to all problems and task encountered have drawn many favorable comments from superiors and subordinates alike.

4. You can take great pride in the remarkable performance of duty rendered to this Battalion. I charge you to continue to lead the way. Your actions reflect great credit upon yourself, the 1st Ranger Battalion and the US Army.

```
            "RANGERS LEAD THE WAY"


                         Glen E. Morrell
                         GLEN E. MORRELL
                         CSM, IN
                         Command Sergeant Major
```

Letter from Command Sergeant Major Glenn Morrell on my departure from 1st Ranger Battalion.

Sergeant Major Walter J. Shumate shortly after retirement from active duty, but as he said, "You don't stop being a soldier just because you don't still wear a uniform."

My "after photo" of Selection, the morning after the Forty Miler. Another six men in the photo were cut by the commander's board. I'm in the second row, first on the left.

Wreckage of the C-130 and RH-53s in the Iranian desert. The helicopters
were burned by the Iranians because they thought they were booby-trapped.
Navy pilots fled so quickly, they forgot to destroy them even though each bird
had a destruction kit.

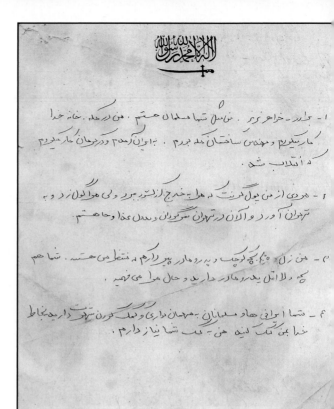

1. Brother - Sister. I am a Moslem like you. I was an engineer in Mecca to make the home of God then I came to Iran. I was in Kerman when revolution took place.

BARADAR - KHAHAR - MAN MESLE SHOMA MOSALMAN HAS TAM. MAN
MOHANDESE KHANEHE KHODA DAR MACCA BODAM. BE IRAN AMADAM.
DAR KERMAN BODAM KE ENGHELAB SHOD.

2. Amman took money from me to take me out of the country, but he brought me to Tehran. He deceived me. Now I am alone without a place and food.

2. YEK MARD AZ MAN POOL GEREFT KE MARA KHAREJ KONAD VALI OU
MARA GOOL ZAD VA BE TEHRAN AVARD. HALA TANHA VA BE DONE JA
VA GAZA HASTAM.

3. I have a wife, 5 kids, an old mother and father. They are waiting for me. You may have kids. You have father and mother and you know what I feel.

3. MAN ZAN. PANJ BACK CHE - MADAR VA PEDAR DARAM ANHA MON
TAZERE MAN HASTAND. SHOMA HAM BACH CHE - MADAR VA PEDAR DAREED
VA MIDANEED HALLE MARA.

4. You Iranian and Moslem are famous for hospitality. For the sake of God help me. I need your help.

4. SHOMA IRANI HA VA MOSALMAN HA BE MEHMAN NAVAZI MAAROOF
HAS TIED. BE KHA TERE KHODA BE MAN KOMAK KONEED. MAN KOMAK
MI KHAHAM.

"Pointy Talkies" carried into Iran for use in escape and evasion.

8. <u>Cover:</u> Embassy Lounge was recommended as a place to visit when in Washington, D.C.
9. <u>Security Considerations:</u> The Embassy Row Hotel is used by foreign dignitaries. Real agents are likely to be throughout the hotel. Smooth civilian clothing is most appropriate.
10. <u>Alternate Contact:</u> If scheduled meeting does not take place within ten minutes of time specified, or if meeting has to be terminated prematurely, attempt to reestablish contact exactly two (2) hours later at the same point.
11. <u>Instructions to Insure Continuity:</u> If neither the scheduled nor the alternate meeting takes place, attempt to make contact by calling telephone number *202-324-2805*. Identify yourself as *"Mr. Jones"* and ask when and where you could meet with *"Mr. Alden."*
12. <u>Props Required:</u>
    Contact Agent: Newspaper or magazine and red and black felt-tip pens.
    Team Member: Red and black felt-tip pens.

The last page of instructions consisted of an area map showing the street location of the hotel and a sketch of the hotel layout depicting the locations of the restaurant, the lounge, and the hotel's main entrance.

After reading the meeting instructions, I called the front desk and extended my stay in the hotel for two days. Then I got out the Yellow Pages and looked up the numbers of several van rental companies. I wrote the numbers down on a scrap of paper from my wallet instead of the pad from the nightstand—no need to leave behind any impressions of those phone numbers.

Then I went back to the "Hotel" section in the Yellow Pages and copied the numbers of six D.C.-area hotels to the phone pad. I called each number and inquired about room availability and price. When I finished, I pulled the page with the numbers off the phone pad, tore it into small pieces, and threw them in the wastebasket. All I wanted to do was leave just enough evidence of a trail to slow down any trackers. I knew the FBI would start here at the hotel, and I wanted to keep their attention focused here for at least one night. By then I would have put some distance between where they were look-ing and where I actually was. I needed to trade space for time.

I checked the room to make sure I hadn't left anything behind that I didn't intend to leave, and made my way out of the building. I was traveling light, with only a small suitcase and a suit bag, so luggage was not a burden. I walked a few blocks from the hotel, hailed a cab, and told the driver to take me to the train station. As soon as we pulled up to the station entrance I paid the driver, told him to keep the change, and hopped out.

I walked inside the station, wandered through the building, and came back out again through a side entrance where I caught a cab to the Greyhound bus station. I know Gerhard had said we had a three-hour window of grace before the hunt started, but I didn't be-lieve it, and felt it was better to get with the program right away.

At the bus station I changed clothes and stashed my luggage in a locker. I wouldn't leave it there very long, but I didn't want it with me for a while. At a pay phone outside, I called the van rental com-panies whose numbers I had written down in the hotel and selected the one that seemed to be the smallest company of all, one not affili-ated with any national chain.

"Yes, sir, that's right," I said to the manager. "Just a decent cargo van I can use to move to my new apartment. No, I don't have any-thing really heavy, mostly just my clothes and some other personal things. I don't have much in the way of furniture. Biggest thing I own is a television set and a bag of golf clubs. What's that? Okay, that's just what I need and the price is good. I'll be there by two o'clock. Thank you, sir. See you then."

With transportation taken care of, I decided to have a bite of lunch and do some planning. I thought about the rest of the day while I had a sandwich at a small diner near the bus station. *No need to make any plans for tomorrow because more than likely, I'll be responding to whatever instructions I receive at the meeting tonight.* For now I just needed to make the most of the time I had until the meeting at ten o'clock tonight. I finished my sandwich and went to collect my van.

The vehicle was just about perfect. Seven years old, no side or rear windows, cream colored with a few dents and scrapes here and there. Yep, she'd do just fine. I left a cash deposit instead of using a credit card and drove off to find a Kmart.

It didn't take long to find one. I bought just a few things I had calculated I would require: a sleeping bag and patio lounge-chair cushion, an assortment of pens, a couple of notepads, a box of white and a box of colored chalk, a small leather-covered address book, a pair of dark blue coveralls, a couple of baseball caps, a small pair of cheap binoculars, a Styrofoam cooler, a towel and a couple of washcloths, a roll of duct tape, a set of maps of D.C., Maryland, and Virginia, and a small toy water pistol.

Next stop was a grocery store where I picked up fruit, canned goods, saltine crackers, several jugs of water, and a bottle of household ammonia. Then I drove around to the back of the store and found the last items I needed at the Dumpsters: a couple of cardboard boxes to hold my "goods" and a five-gallon plastic bucket with a lid to serve as a chamber pot.

Then I drove two blocks away to another parking lot where I packed and rearranged my things in the van, and filled the water pistol with ammonia. To prevent it from leaking, I sealed the tip of its nozzle with a Band-Aid from my wallet.

Now I was set. I could live in the van for an extended period if necessary, and if I had to go to ground for a few days, I could safely hole up somewhere without having to come up for air. I had a means of self-protection, just in case of emergencies. The water pistol full of ammonia was a trick I learned from an old man I worked with as a young boy on a delivery truck. It would stop a vicious dog in its tracks and worked equally well on people, but it wouldn't cause lasting harm. And just as important, it wasn't a firearm, which would be about useless in this situation and could only serve to get me in trouble if a cop got a glimpse of it. But there was nothing wrong with a harmless water pistol.

When I was happy with my arrangements, I drove into town to have a look at the area around the hotel where the meeting would take place. I wanted to get a feel for the streets and traffic routing as well as find some easy-to-recognize landmarks on all four sides of the hotel. I chose several different options for places to park and ran getaway routes from them. I wanted to have several different ways to get completely out of the area as rapidly as possible or make a short run and dodge into some hiding spot.

After I had run the routes in the van, I went back and parked in each spot and walked around the areas to make sure I knew what the ground looked like and felt like when approached from different directions. I also found and noted on my mental map several spots I could duck into and elude a pursuer. I was pretty confident that if it came to a footrace, I could outdistance any FBI agent. But that would only be to lay a false trail and then get back to the van.

When I felt that I knew the area like it was my own neighborhood, I went back to the van and drove out to a marina on the Potomac River near National Airport. I spoke with the man running the fuel dock and told him I was there to meet my boss who was bringing his boat up from Virginia Beach. Boats are a passion of mine, so that gave me a cover for status that allowed me to be in the area without drawing much attention.

I could hang out in the lounge, use the showers, walk around the docks, and just generally blend into the scenery. Marinas are good transient places with people coming and going at all hours, but they are also abnormally crime free, and consequently cops and other investigative types seldom, if ever, venture into them.

In fact, whenever I've had occasion over the years to slip into and out of various "interesting" spots in the world, I prefer to do so by boat. It's like wearing a cloak of invisibility. You can come and go undetected and unmolested. Bus stations, train terminals, and airports are all crawling with surveillance, but the waterfront goes unobserved.

I had dinner in the marina restaurant, watched the evening news in the lounge, and showered. Back in the van, I changed into a dark blue suit and a pair of comfortable shoes I could run in if necessary. Then I made a mental review of where I was going and what *should* happen there while I placed one red-tipped and one black-tipped felt pen in the outer pocket of my new address book. When everything was ready, I sat for a few minutes to make sure I was master of myself and prepared for action.

My contact was the last person in the world I would have expected—which just proved the wisdom of my own adage to expect the unexpected.

He was an exquisitely dressed man in his sixties, with a head full of elaborately coiffed silver hair, and he was as drunk as a lord. He had the appropriate colored pens displayed, a red one tucked behind his left ear, a black one behind his right, and he was haranguing the bartender, who was doing his best to keep his distance. I slid onto the stool next to the guy, ordered a drink, and put my address book holding the colored pens on the bar between us.

After a few seconds, he felt my presence and turned in my direction. He squinted at me through a boozy fog and started to say something. Then he noticed the address book with the pens showing, gulped like a fish, stared at the pens for a minute longer as the cogs rumbled in his befuddled mind and then looked up at me with a conspiratorial grin splattered across his face.

"Hey! It's my buddy! How ya doin', buddy?" he slurred at me as he swiveled perilously around on his stool.

"I'm okay," I replied. "Have you been waiting long? We got hung up in traffic."

"Nah, I ain't been waitin' long—I ain't been waitin' long at all. But the traffic—the traffic," he belched, "the traffic does get pretty bad sometimes, don't it?" He gave me a leering wink and smiled hugely in self-satisfaction at getting the phrase right.

"You a Yankees fan, ain't you?" he suddenly yelled. "You seen what those nitwits did in Chicago yesterday?" He waved a folded newspaper in my face. "It's right here in the paper. Look for yaself. Jus' take a look at it, 'cause I don't even want to think about it no more. It's . . . it's . . . it's . . . jus'—*terrible!*" He put his head down on his folded arms, and I swear to God, he started weeping.

I put my address book down on top of the paper he had given me and then awkwardly patted the lunatic on the back while he rolled his head back and forth in the crooks of his arms, sobbing and wailing like the world was coming to an end. I could feel every eye in the lounge locked on us as I looked around in embarrassment. The people at the bar and nearby tables had given us a clear circle with a diameter of at least ten feet. It was like we were known carriers of the galloping pneumonic gonorrhea or some equally loathsome disease. I felt like I was in a bad dream, one of those where you suddenly realize you're standing naked in a crowded room. It was surreal; but I was trapped and would have to extricate myself as best I could from a damned uncomfortable situation.

So much for an unobtrusive and low-key contact.

"Hey, man, it's okay. They just had a bad day, they'll do better, I'm sure they will. You can't keep the ol' Yankees down," I said as I gripped him by the upper arm and rubbed his back like I was consoling a child grieving over a broken toy. "They just had a bad day was all, it happens to every team."

"You really think so?" he asked as he raised his head, gave me a hopeful look, and wiped the tears from his swollen eyes.

"Yeah, of course they will. Here." I handed him a paper napkin and motioned him to wipe the snot from his upper lip. *Damn,* I thought, *son of a bitch reminds me of some of my kinfolks.*

"Well, in that case, what say we have another drink!" he bawled as happiness shot across his face, clearing away the misery of his former anguish and woe.

"Why not," I said, motioning the bartender to give us a refill. He glanced at my partner and then gave me a raised eyebrow. When I silently mouthed, "It's okay," he shrugged his shoulders in exculpation and turned to make the drinks.

"Hey, look, buddy, I've got to make a trip to the men's room. You'll be okay till I get back, won't you?" I asked as I slid the newspaper and address book under my arm.

"Sure, I'll be okay, take your time. But just remember," he shouted at me across the lounge as I walked away, "shake it more than twice and you're playing with yourself!"

He started to laugh at his sophomoric joke, but instead, he collapsed into a choking, coughing fit that bent his head back to his folded arms on the bar, where he heaved and hacked and gasped for air like he was in the throes of congestive heart failure.

It took every atom of restraint and self-discipline I could muster to keep from breaking into a one-man stampede as I strolled through the lounge toward the men's room. *Jesus H. Christ,* I thought as I turned a corner, *was that for real?* If it wasn't, then it was without doubt the best acting job I've ever witnessed, and I'd seen some good ones during my years as a platoon sergeant. I went past the men's room, down the next corridor, and out the nearest exit. Time to make tracks.

I made an abrupt departure for a couple of reasons. One, we were drawing too much attention (which I could only believe was purposeful), and two, I wanted to start checking for surveillance right away. By making a sudden exit, I thought I might force a surveillance team to show itself. Once outside, I walked rapidly away from the hotel and across a side street. When a raft of traffic clogged the avenue, I jaywalked through the cars and doubled back on the other side. That would jam up any vehicle following me along on the street and would make a foot detail either walk on by me or scramble around a couple of corners to get back in formation. If I saw anyone on the street reverse himself or herself when I did the crossover, I intended to break into a run.

None of that happened, so I continued zigzagging around for a while. I circled the block where I had parked the van, walked ten meters past it, and then spun about and made a beeline straight to the van. I didn't see anyone behind me on either side of the street as I jumped in, cranked up, and pulled away.

There wasn't another vehicle on the street as I pulled away, but that didn't mean a lot. If I was the target of surveillance, a good team would have me bracketed on parallel streets and catch me at a corner. I made a couple of turns and timed two stoplights in succession so that I punched through the intersections mid-yellow. I checked the rearview mirror to see if anybody followed me through. Looked like my "six" was clear, so I headed back across the Potomac River as straight and fast as possible.

I cruised out toward Fort Meyer and pulled into the back lot of a hotel across from the fort's main entrance. I changed out of my suit and into jeans, sweatshirt, running shoes, and a ball cap. Now I was back in the guise of a normal working-class guy. Once I changed my costume, I turned on the van's lights, wedged down the brake pedal with a tire iron, and climbed out to check the vehicle. The best way to make a vehicle easy to follow at night is to punch a small hole in a taillight. That lets a small spot of white light shine in the middle of the red lens, making the vehicle stand out from all the others. It's a simple trick, but it's damn effective.

I was in luck—no holes. I checked all the lights and the blinkers; I didn't want a cop stopping me for a burned-out light. Next I took my flashlight and checked all around and under the van, especially on the sides. Back at the marina I had purposefully driven through several mudholes to throw a nice layer of muddy water and dirt on the sides of the van and underneath the chassis. Anybody screwing with it would wind up smearing or scuffing that faint dirt layer. No signs of that, either.

I knew there was only a small chance I would have been already targeted. The FBI would have only a limited number of agents they could throw into a training exercise like this. And having more than twenty of us wandering around Washington like tadpoles in a pond would make life difficult for even a large surveillance operation. But a healthy dose of paranoia isn't necessarily a bad thing, and I sure as hell didn't want to be apprehended and blow the final exercise.

I was satisfied both that no one had tampered with my vehicle and that I hadn't been followed to this location. And as long as I had freedom of movement, I didn't think anyone could latch on to me. The danger areas where things could start to go bad were those choke points—the specific places I had to go—such as that last meeting. Those are the spots where a would-be tail could fall in behind me or I could be nabbed. When you set up an ambush, that spot is known as the "kill zone." I was determined to head into those dangerous places with all the caution of a crippled antelope limping past a pride of lions.

Back in the van I pulled a manila envelope from the folds of the newspaper I had received from my drunken contact and read the contents. An index card clipped to a few sheets of paper read:

MISSION: UNLOAD DEAD LETTER DROP
(See attached Casing Report.)

I put the card back in the envelope and looked at the other papers.

CASING REPORT: DEAD LETTER DROP

1. <u>Location:</u> Richmond, Virginia.
2. <u>Description of Area:</u> Inner-city area frequented by people from all walks of life.
3. <u>Drop Site:</u> Middle telephone booth (#648-9587) in a bank of five in left rear of lobby of HOTEL JEFFERSON, 112 WEST MAIN STREET. (See sketch 2.)

4. <u>Specific Drop Location:</u> Underneath metal shelf inside booth. (See sketch 1.)

5. <u>Size and Type of Container:</u> Magnetic key box attached to underside of shelf.

6. <u>Servicing Time:</u> Between 0800 and 2200 hours only.

7. <u>Cover:</u> Making telephone call.

8. <u>Route:</u> When unloading, first check LOAD SIGNAL SITE (see sketch 2), park vehicle, and enter lobby of JEFFERSON HOTEL through main entrance. Service drop, exit, and place Unload Signal. (See sketch 2.) Depart at your discretion.

9. <u>Seasonal Limitations:</u> None.

10. <u>Security Considerations:</u> Avoid loitering in the lobby. Avoid using drop between 2200–0800 hours.

11. <u>Props Required:</u> Loader: Magnetic key box and white chalk. Unloader: White chalk.

12. <u>Date of Casing:</u> 14 May '79.

13. <u>Cased by:</u> EAGLE.

14. <u>Load Signal:</u> Small piece of white chalk crushed on sidewalk in front of main entrance (south) to JEFFERSON HOTEL on MAIN STREET. (See sketch 2.)

15. <u>Unload Signal:</u> Small piece of white chalk crushed on sidewalk in front of side entrance (west) to JEFFERSON HOTEL. (See sketch 2.)

The next page of the instructions included an area map of downtown Richmond and two sketches: one showing where the magnetic box was located on the telephone shelf, the other showing a diagram of the hotel layout and the adjacent streets.

Next morning I drove past the Jefferson Hotel at 0930. Sure enough, there was the load signal right out in front of the main entrance to the hotel, a half-dollar-size splatter of white chalk crushed on the sidewalk. I found a good place to park a few blocks away, snugged up my tie, slipped on my blazer, and made my way through the river of the people going about their lives that beautiful morning.

The Jefferson looked like it had been built sometime around the turn of the century: high ceilings, tall windows, worn carpets, and marble everywhere. Shabby gentility came to mind. She was one of those grand old Southern hotels that had been a social and cultural landmark in her day, but was now firmly in the dotage of her declining years. She probably would not be around much longer to grace the downtown scene.

I said good morning to several elderly couples in the lobby as I made my way to the rest room for a quick stop. I dragged out my visit a little longer than necessary to see if anyone would lose patience and come in after me, then popped back out and crossed unobserved to the bank of phones on the opposite wall.

I dropped a quarter in the phone slot and dialed the number I had memorized for the correct time. While leaning closely into the small phone cubicle, I slipped my free hand under the stainless-steel shelf, palmed the magnetic box that was right where the diagram had indicated it would be, and slipped it into a jacket pocket. I said thanks to the recorded voice that was still counting off the minutes, hung up the phone, and made my way to the Jefferson Street exit.

While walking back through the hotel lobby, I took a piece of chalk half the size of the last joint of my little finger from a jacket pocket and transferred it to the pocket of my slacks. I held it in my hand as I walked along. Outside the hotel, I stopped on the sidewalk directly in front of the door and quickly looked both ways up and down the sidewalk as if I was momentarily unsure about which direction to take.

In that little instant of seeming indecision, I dropped the chalk through a hole in my pocket I had made that morning, felt it rattle its way down my leg, and glanced down long enough to note the little white lump on the sidewalk next to my shoe. Then, pretending that I had made up my mind about direction, I put my foot on the chalk and spun on it as I turned to head down the street. Leaving the unload signal had taken every bit of two or three seconds. I jaywalked to the other side of the street, turned the next corner, took a circuitous route back to the van, and ran a few counter-surveillance moves as I left the area. So far, so good.

A few miles away, I pulled into the parking lot of a small restaurant, where I unfolded and read the three sheets of onionskin paper that were in the magnetic box (or magic box, as I often thought of it). The first page was a directive to survey a site for (1) a vehicular pickup, and (2) a dead letter drop, and write the casing reports for each site. The rest of the material was instructions for a personal meeting at 1500 hours that afternoon at the Iwo Jima, Marine Corps Memorial back in Arlington. At that meeting, I was to turn over my casing reports and receive additional information from my contact. We were to pass the material in a rolled newspaper or magazine. All very normal, but I was going to have to work fast if I was going to survey two sites, write the reports, and get back up to Arlington by 1500 hours. I jumped to it.

My contact turned out to be Major Altmann himself. He was sitting on a bench looking for all the world like a veteran lost in the contemplation of the memorial depicting that small band of heroic Marines raising the American colors on the summit of Mount Suribachi. I quietly took a seat beside him, and after a few moments of silent contemplation myself, we spoke as two strangers would and then went through the formalities of exchanging the recognition sentences. The verbal execution of a secret handshake.

"Let us walk as we converse," said Altmann. We rose to our feet and as we started to stroll, he put his arm through mine, as is the fashion among friends in Eastern Europe and the Middle East. It was a nice touch. Not only because it's a custom I enjoy, but because in those days, the Iwo Jima monument was known as a meeting place for gay men. Remember, in tradecraft, cover is everything.

"I must say that my friend in the bar the other night was most distressed by your abrupt departure. He wishes me to tell you he hopes he did or said nothing to cause you displeasure or consternation," said Altmann. "However, that technique for making your exit was very effective. It was so sudden and unexpected that the FBI's surveillance team was unable to keep pace and you had completely eluded them by the time you were on the street."

He chuckled at the pleasure of the memory.

So, my gut feeling had been correct—there had been surveillance of the meeting that night.

I wanted to ask if the contact had actually been drunk or if it was an act, but I kept silent. I preferred not knowing for certain. Some things in life just feel better when they are left as mysteries.

As we walked arm in arm, Gerhard held a rolled magazine in his free hand and occasionally used it to gesture toward the monument as though he were a historian giving a personally guided tour to a younger protégé.

"It has given me a great deal of satisfaction," he continued, "that not one of your comrades has yet been caught in, shall we say, flagrante delicto by the team the FBI has assembled to run you to ground. In fact, I suspect the team leader is making excuses to his superior, even as we speak, as to why he has been so conspicuously unsuccessful in the effort. This has a special appeal to me after having listened to his arrogant—and I should add, insolent—opinion that it would be an elementary task to round up a bunch of amateur practitioners of the art. I am certain your tradecraft instructor will be pleased by the results so far."

As he flourished his hand skyward for emphasis, he stumbled ever so slightly and dropped the magazine he was holding.

"Let me get that," I said. As I bent to retrieve the magazine from the ground at our feet, I exchanged it for the one I had been carrying.

"Thank you, my friend. Your young spine is more supple than the one I must contend with at this time of my life." He inclined his head in appreciation as he took the magazine I proffered. He stopped after another step or two and turned to face me.

"Do be alert," he said, looking into my face with twinkling eyes that had seen so much of the dark side of life. "The tempo of the operation is going to increase. You and your comrades will be gathering into cells, which makes for a greater chance of compromise. And though this exercise began with feelings of mutual affinity, I fear that due to their lack of success, the FBI may now take this as a personal confrontation. Therefore, if you should find yourself in a situation where physical force is used against you, I believe you would be justified in responding in kind."

He was smiling at the thought of that eventuality as we shook hands and departed for our separate destinations.

The instructions I found in the magazine directed me to conduct a vehicular pickup of a subject at the Washington mansion at Mount Vernon. I would find him in the visitors' parking lot just as the facility closed for the day. The contact would be someone I knew.

I cruised through the lot just as a stream of cars and buses was pulling out. I didn't see anyone familiar. But just as I had almost completed a circuit of the parking area, I saw a tall figure with a shock of long red hair dart from behind a small outbuilding into an edge of the parking lot where he was screened by a hedge of boxwoods.

It was John Yancy, and his timing was perfect. His path intercepted the edge of the pavement just as I rolled up. I stopped the van for a split second while John jumped in, and then we were on the move and headed for the exit. It was a smooth and natural-looking pickup that would have been difficult to observe.

I had felt neither interest in our passage nor a tail, either going in or coming out, but that meant little. So on the way back to town we made a few "shakes and scratches" just to see if any fleas fell off.

One of the best ways to do that is to cruise into a cul-de-sac in a residential neighborhood and see who follows you in. If it's a tail, they're "burned." This means that you know what they look like—along with the car they're using—so they have to be pulled from the surveillance team, all of which makes life just a little more difficult for the "trackers" and may cause them to make other mistakes. But we were clean.

John and I had first met during Selection and hit it off. He was a tall, muscular Texan with a long, loping stride, a narrow, foxlike face, and a sly sense of humor masking granite toughness. He had been a renowned recon man with Special Forces in Vietnam, and was considered one of the best men to be beside during a fight. He was absolutely unflappable no matter how bad things got.

He came to Selection from the Special Forces battalion in Panama but had badly twisted an ankle during the Eighteen Miler at the start of Selection and had to drop out of the course. Rather than go back to Panama, he stayed at Aberdeen Camp while his ankle healed and attended the Selection course that started as mine was finishing. The ankle continued to be a problem for him throughout Selection, and he told me the best thing about the Forty Miler was that when his legs finally went numb on him, he couldn't feel the pain of that ankle.

John was another of our comrades who would leave us too early. He was shot and killed just a few years later, only two weeks before he was to leave the unit for a "safer" assignment.

We compared notes as we rode along. John, too, had been servicing dead drops, casing various sites, and writing reports. In fact, he had unloaded a drop at Mount Vernon directing us to a pickup in Georgetown that evening. But first we retrieved John's gear from the flophouse where he had stashed it, and then we cruised Georgetown to ready ourselves for the pickup.

We plucked Pete Vandervoort from a bus stop just as he walked up and set his bags down by the bench. He was in such a hurry to get in the van that John had to remind him that it would probably be a good idea to bring his bags along for the ride. Pete agreed, and jumped back out to grab his bags and give them a toss into the back of the van.

If ever a human being was the spirit and image of a Viking, Pete was that man. Six feet four inches tall, wide shoulders, long muscled arms and legs, a thick chest, and a small waist. White-blond hair, a long, drooping mustache, a craggy brow overhanging deep-set glacier blue eyes fixed in a face that had been forged from steel. At rest, his visage was as fierce as a bird of prey. Animated, his face would set in a clenched-jaw, tight-lipped grin.

Pete carried his shoulders bunched up a bit, which made his arms hang perfectly straight by his side. He had a peculiar way of walking on the balls of his feet and his toes—never on his heels—and this combined with the set of his shoulders made him always look like he was ready to throw or take a punch. Pete was a very powerful man, but he was also a big kid. Something I suspect the Viking warriors were as well. Big, rowdy, fun-loving, deadly kids.

Pete was carrying information that pertained to all three of us. We would form a cell tasked with performing several collective tasks. He gave us the highlights and caught us up on his recent activities as we drove out of the city to a motel John and I had already earmarked for our base of operations. We needed a more "normal" place to hole up. Three men living out of a van were sure to attract attention we didn't want and couldn't afford. We took two adjoining rooms at the motel and settled in to study the papers Pete had retrieved from the dead drop he had serviced just before we picked him up.

We were charged with several missions—complicated missions—with the potential for hazard and compromise.

We were directed to get a roster of the cleaning personnel at the Naval Observatory, a list of the number and types of weapons at a specific National Guard Armory, and a copy of next month's operations schedule from Andrews Air Force Base.

We had two days to accomplish the assignments and prepare a detailed after-action report. The material, the reports, and two passport photos of each of us were to be turned over to a contact at a personal meeting. We would get the details of that meeting from a dead drop. The instructions for servicing the drop were on the last page of the instructions.

All well and good, but first we needed some nourishment and a plan. Pete folded up the sheets of onionskin and shoved them down the front of his pants. Unless he was strip-searched, they were undetectable and perfectly safe. Then we set out in search of a Korean restaurant. For some inexplicable reason, all three of us had a yen for kimchee that evening.

Over dinner we talked "man talk." Sports, fishing, hunting, women, politics—anything other than what we were actually doing. By now, the custom of watching what you said and where you said it had become such a habit with us that the only time we discussed "business" in an open setting was in the sanctuary of the Ranch. Back at the motel we determined a course of action.

We would have to divide and conquer. Time was short, the tasks were tricky, and cover for action was going to be critical with a capital C. If even two of us showed ourselves at any one place, it would only cause problems. We decided to draw lots for the missions. John drew the Naval Observatory, Pete got the National Guard Armory, and I received Andrews Air Force Base.

We were each going to need wheels. I figured that my van had reached the end of its useful life; if it wasn't burned yet, it would be soon, so it was time to turn it back in. John scouted the Yellow Pages for several "Rent a Wreck" places and a passport photo shop while Pete and I kicked around covers for status and action.

The next morning I dropped the guys off at two different lots to pick up cars and I drove back to turn in my van. It deserved a good rest. It had been a good vehicle and had given me yeoman's service.

Pete picked me up on the street two blocks away and took me to a lot where I rented a Ford Maverick. It was the best vehicle they had on the lot—which should tell you a lot about the place. Still, the little car was a V-8 with plenty of power left and she was relatively nondescript.

Before setting off on our individual tasks, we rendezvoused in a grocery parking lot and piled in one car to a little photography shop to have the passport photos taken. We were making small talk as the photographer's assistant trimmed the pictures and placed them in paper holders when, completely out of the blue, Pete launched into a world-class weird conversation. He spun the shop owner a yarn about how the three of us were heading to Amsterdam to visit a particular fountain where beautiful buxom young women gathered every day to frolic topless in the splashing waters of the fountain, all the while encouraging passing tourists to take their pictures. Mysteriously, inexplicably, only the most attractive women were drawn to the fountain—never the old, never the homely, and never the flatchested.

Pete's eyes had a wild, satyric gleam as he told his tale. He leaned into the man's face, holding him with thumb and forefinger by the point of his lapel, all the while extolling the wonders of this miraculous Dutch fountain. He delivered his travelogue with all the snickering glee of a young boy whispering his first dirty joke to his best buddy. The poor shop owner was struck mute by the blond giant and his unbelievable tale.

Pete finally finished his story, released the man, and patted his lapel. He gave him a sly wink and then stood up to his full and imposing height. The shop owner blinked once and the spell was broken. He looked around at the three of us, standing head and shoulders above him, and said in a small voice, "Well, wherever you gentlemen travel, I think you'll be able to take care of yourselves."

As we grabbed our photos and retreated for the door, Pete called over his shoulder, "I'll send you a postcard."

Pete's behavior—and his story—had been so bizarre I didn't know whether to laugh or curse. But John could barely wait to get outside, and jumped him the minute we hit the parking lot.

"Pete, what did you do that for? What was the purpose of that damn story about the Magic Titty Fountain in Amsterdam? What were you hoping to accomplish?" John's face was red with consternation, but he had himself under control and his voice was calm.

"Aw, John." Pete smiled back indulgently. "The guy seemed a

little fidgety with all of us standing around the shop and nobody saying much, so I decided to put him at ease with a little small talk. Why, you could see how it took the tension right out of him."

Pete nodded his head as if to acknowledge his own sagacity and amazing social skills. "But don't worry, John. There's no fountain like that in Amsterdam. I made the whole thing up." He slid into the backseat of the car and closed the door.

John looked at me across the top of the car and silently shook his head in disbelief. I looked back at him and shrugged my shoulders. From inside the car, Pete called to us. "C'mon, guys, let's go."

Yep, just a big kid.

It took every hour of those two days to accomplish our assigned tasks. The methods we used were simple, didn't require elaborate covers, and could be easily imitated by someone with sinister designs, which is why I won't explain how we did it. But the results were impressive.

John was able to obtain the roster of the people who worked on the housekeeping staff of the Naval Observatory. He also got their work histories, their addresses, and their home phone numbers.

I was able to gain the Operations Schedule for Andrews Air Force Base—and as a serendipitous bonus, the maintenance schedule for *Air Force One* for the rest of the year.

Pete made quite a haul. He not only got a copy of the weapons roster from the National Guard Armory but also found out that the bolts for the M-16s were stored in the unit safe, that four bayonets were missing, and that none of the organization's M-60 machine guns would work. Pete had made such a vivid impression on the unit commander that he returned with an autographed picture of the two of them shaking hands and an invitation to the armory for their next weekend drill. I would like to have been a fly on the wall to hear the tale Pete told that commander.

That afternoon we sat down in my motel room to go over everything we had acquired and put all the material into a reportable format. Later John went out to unload a dead drop while Pete and I worked on a draft of the report. He came back with instructions as to how we would turn over our material and a directive to case two more dead drop sites and a location for a personal meeting for the next morning. We decided that I would work on the report while my partners went out to case the sites.

Pete asked if there was anything they could bring me when they returned, and I said, "Yeah, bring us a six-pack of beer and we'll have a couple of cold ones while we go over the finished report." I was still working on the report when they returned.

John let himself into the room, closed the door behind him, and leaned against it as if barring further passage. He didn't say anything but just stood there looking at me. I glanced up from my work and asked, "What's up, John? Where's Pete?"

"He'll be along in a minute. He's got his hands full. But I want to ask you a question, Eric, before he comes in." He had a strained look on his face.

I put my pen down. "Sure, John. What is it?"

"If you were going to buy some beer, where would you go?"

There was a muffled knock on the door. John pressed his back against the door and barked, "Wait a minute!" He looked back at me with a strange intensity in his eyes. Something was up, but I didn't know what.

"Oh, I don't know, John. Where do you usually get beer? A convenience store. A package shop. A grocery store, I guess. Someplace like that."

There was another thud on the door, but John ignored it.

"That's right," he said. "Any of those places are where a *normal* person buys beer. But not... *our buddy*." He turned to throw open the door, revealing Pete standing there, delicately balancing a wobbling cardboard tray that held six large plastic cups of beer.

"Come on in," John announced as Pete walked through the door, his tongue sticking out from between his lips in concentration, his eyes focused on the tray he was holding at arm's length, trying to keep the beer from dribbling down the front of his shirt. "Come in, Pete, and tell Eric where *you* buy beer."

"At a bowling alley," Pete calmly replied as he set the dripping tray down on a lamp table. "You always get the best-tasting beer at a bowling alley. You ought to know that, John." He said it like a patient teacher speaking to a favorite student who was having a little trouble with a subject.

John threw up his hands in defeated exasperation.

"That's right," he said, turning to address me. "A bowling alley.

Not a 7-Eleven. Not a grocery store. Not a package store. Nothing else would do. It had to be draught beer from a bowling alley."

"Here, John, have a beer before it gets warm." Pete acted as if he'd never heard the retort and handed a cup to John before passing one to me.

"Cheers," he said with a contented smile as we touched the rims of our plastic chalices. "Here's to good friends and a mission well done."

The simplicity and heartfelt warmth of that toast took away the rancor that had been building in John's breast for our comrade. I saw it drain from his being as he relaxed, took a sip of beer, and smiled back at Pete. Then he lifted his cup and said, "Yep, cheers, boys."

We reviewed the reports as we finished our beer. Once we were satisfied with everything, I made a tight bundle of the papers and went out to load a drop confirming what we'd accomplished. Then we settled in for some sleep.

Pete went to the personal meeting at 0400 hours the next morning to turn over our report while John and I pulled counter-surveillance and overwatched him just in case things got sticky. The meeting went off all right, but Pete was pretty animated when we got back together at our motel.

"Guys, we've got to haul ass. We have to be at the train station in Hamlet, North Carolina, for a pickup at four o'clock this afternoon. And more than that, we can't go by rental car. We're going to have to make our way by some form of public transportation."

"Then we take the train," I said, and realized how stupid that was as soon as it came out of my mouth. "No, that won't do, will it? It's too obvious." I tried to think of another way.

"We fly," John announced.

"But it's a simple matter to watch the airports for anybody going to North Carolina today," said Pete. "We'll be picked up."

"We don't take a commercial flight," John countered. "We rent a plane and fly to Hamlet. There's a county airport right outside of town. I flew in there several times when I was taking my private pilot's license after I got back from Vietnam the first time. Then we take the airport courtesy car to the train station.

"From here it should be about a three-hour flight. We just find us a small flight operation at an airfield somewhere around here.

Tell 'em we want to rent a plane to fly to North Carolina and that we want one of their pilots to go with us and ferry the plane back. They'll be happy with that, and we'll arrive undetected in Hamlet. And with the three of us splitting the cost, it'll also be the cheapest way to go, even paying for the pilot to fly the plane back up here."

"That's brilliant, John," I said. "What kind of a plane should we get?"

"I think a Cessna 182 would be just about perfect. It can carry four people and our luggage. It should be able to make the trip in one jump and it's relatively fast for a single-engine plane." He picked up the telephone book. "I'll get on the phone and find us one as soon as business hours open. If we can be off the ground by ten o'clock, we should have plenty of time to make it to Hamlet before four o'clock."

I looked at my teammate with admiration. "That's perfect, John. A great idea. While you're arranging it, Pete and I will get the cars turned in and get us checked out of here."

"Sounds good to me," said Pete. "But first, let's go to breakfast. I'm starving."

That, too, was a good idea.

I love flying when I can see something outside, but in those days, I wasn't wild about landing. I was far more accustomed to coming back to earth by parachute.

In the Ranger battalion, I had gone for as much as eighteen months at a stretch without landing in an airplane I went up in. It had gotten to the point that I just didn't trust any reunion with Mother Earth that I wasn't in control of myself. John was a good pilot, our trip was uneventful, and the landing was smooth as silk. We said good-bye to the ferry pilot and ambled over to the main hangar and FBO (fixed base operator) to see about arranging transportation into town.

An airport courtesy car was available for our use, but since it was a little over an hour until our pickup time, we elected to have lunch and hang out at the airport before heading into town. Pete struck up a conversation with a young guy who seemed to be the airfield handyman, and he gladly agreed to drive us to the train station.

We arrived at the station with about ten minutes to spare. Just a few seconds past four o'clock, a white van with the appropriate markings pulled to the front of the station and came to a halt. The driver pulled his sunglasses down on the tip of his nose, looked at us over the tops of the lenses, and then pushed the glasses back up and adjusted the outside mirror.

That was the "safe" signal. We put our baggage in the back and climbed in. Our instructions had said that the driver would not speak to us, nor were we to speak to him—and it wasn't hard to do. I've never met such a quiet person. It was like the invisible man was driving the vehicle.

We drove down Highway 74 and through the small town of Laurinburg, North Carolina. A few miles outside of town, we turned onto a narrow gravel road that carried us a couple of hundred meters off the highway to a large building that looked like an abandoned trucking company terminal or warehouse. I looked over at the driver as we came to a halt. He returned my look and then very deliberately pointed to a door on the side of the building. I turned to tell my mates to wait in the van while I checked out the building, but the driver motioned for us all to dismount. *Screw that,* I thought, and told the guys not to let the van leave until I got back.

I got out and tried the door; it was locked. Before I could knock, someone inside threw it open. It was Jerry Knox.

"Come on, Eric. Get your guys and come inside. The driver has a tight schedule to keep."

I waved to Pete and John and motioned them to hop out. Jerry held the door as we grabbed our stuff and went inside. He then led us down a short corridor, past a few small office cubicles, through another door, and into a large open area the size of a small aircraft hangar. The place was hopping. Trucks were lined up along one wall of the building. Nearby, all of our individual and team equipment was arranged in rows. In the far corner of the bay, an operations center was in place. Guys from the signal section had radios set up, and wires ran out the high windows to the antennas outside.

Jerry sent us over to Ron Cardowski for a quick briefing. Ron told us that as part of the play of the Culmination Exercise, we were responding to an aircraft hijacking. Our OTC class would form the assault troop and field a couple of sniper teams. Ron would be the troop sergeant and Jim Day would be the troop commander. Jim Bush was in charge of the snipers and would run the

TOC. The plane, a Boeing 727, was on the ground now at the Laurinburg/Maxton Airport, which for the purposes of the exercise was to be considered in a somewhat friendly but very backward and corrupt foreign nation. Jim Day and a couple of snipers were at the airport now, working with the local authorities and trying to sort out a lot of conflicting and confusing information.

Ron told us to check the TOC status board for our team assignments and then move our equipment into the respective team areas we would find laid out on the floor in chalk. I moved over to the board for a look at our organization and found my slot.

Assault Troop: C Team
Team Leader: Haney
Assistant Team Leader: Masters
Benevides
Vandervoort

C Team. That meant that in an assault we would enter over the plane's wings through an emergency exit and move aft. It also meant we would probably form half of the emergency assault team in case things went suddenly bad and we didn't have time to mount a deliberate assault. But if it came to that point, it would only be an attempt to make the best of a bad situation and salvage something from the erupting disaster. Emergency assaults are executed only when terrorists start killing hostages.

This was the first of what would become full-blown hijacked aircraft exercises. During my many years' service in 1st SFOD—D, I would respond to a couple of dozen actual hijackings and almost the same number of aircraft exercises. But whether it was a real situation or training, we went at it with the same intensity and sense of urgency—but the training operations were always the more difficult of the two. And that was true of all our training.

About half of the OTC class was already here, so Pete and I found our gear and moved it to our designated team area. Neither Andres nor Jimmy was in yet, so we grabbed their equipment and brought it over, too. Then we went to take a look at the information board at the TOC. Not much there yet—just some generalizations about the flight, the estimated number of passengers, and some vague information about how many terrorists *may* be aboard. We went back to our team area and got out of the way of the guys at the TOC.

By nightfall almost everyone was in. We grabbed Jimmy and Andres as soon as they arrived and brought them up to date—which didn't take long because we had so little information. We grabbed ourselves a case of C rations and stepped out on the loading dock at the back of the building to heat up some supper and compare notes on our experiences over the last few days. Before long, I got a call to report to the TOC for a team leaders' meeting.

Ron had the floor. "We're having difficulties with the local authorities, which is why we haven't moved to the airfield yet, but we've been able to deploy two observation teams around the plane and we're going to send two emergency assault teams forward just in case things decide to go bad.

"Eric and J.T., your teams will initially comprise the emergency assault. I'll rotate the other teams through that position when we're able to move forward. As soon as we break up here, get everything you need to conduct an assault and also what you'll need to live on for three or four days. Load the stuff in the gray and blue vans and get ready to move to the airport. Don't worry about drivers; I'll provide them. Be ready to move out in ten minutes."

Ron then shifted his attention to the rest of the group. "As for the rest of you, consult the info board. I'll set up a schedule so that everyone will get a chance to work a rotating shift in the TOC. We're going to do our best to get everyone forward under one pretext or the other to at least have a look at the airfield and where the plane is situated.

"There's one final thing." Ron lowered his voice to a conspiratorial level as he continued, "Jim Day really has his hands full and he needs everybody's help. This exercise alone is a son of a bitch, but whether you know it or not, Jim isn't exactly one of Colonel Beckwith's favorites. If we don't pull this off and do a good job of it, the Old Man may well use it as an excuse to bounce Jim out of here.

"Officer business is an area I don't generally concern myself with—no NCO does. But Jim Day is one of the best young officers I've ever served with, and I'd like to keep serving with him. I think you all might agree with me when I say that he's a rare breed. He's worth protecting and we can do that best by making sure he shines. Pass the word to be extra-sharp and give Jim every assistance we can—but don't let the other officers know what's going on. They're good guys, too, but they're not under the gun right now.

"Okay, that's it. You can get back to your teams. J.T., Eric, let me know when you're ready to take off."

So that explains why Jim Day was made commander of the exercise, I thought, *even though he isn't the ranking captain in the class. Ol' Charlie's putting him under the microscope and having a real close look at him. Well, that isn't necessarily bad.*

But I agreed with Ron. Jim was a good man and I wanted to continue working with him. In reality, there was never any danger he would receive less than everyone's utmost and enthusiastic support. That's just the way we operate.

J.T. and I had a quick huddle before we loaded on the vans for the trip to the airport. We had a couple of things to coordinate in case we got a call en route to immediately execute an emergency assault. We agreed that J.T.'s team would enter over the right wing and clear aft, and that my team would enter over the left wing and clear forward. We would run the vans right up to the sides of the airplane and throw the ladders into place, and both teams would mount and enter the plane simultaneously. Speed would have to replace stealth. Once the plane was cleared of terrorists, we would pop all the emergency slides and send the passengers out through every exit. In the event of a fire or an explosion on board, we would open whatever doors we could reach and send people out through those.

Within my team, our order of entry into the plane went like this. The short guys would enter first—Jimmy followed by Andres—and clear down the aisle all the way to the cockpit. I would come in third and Pete would follow me. Since Pete and I were taller than Jimmy and Andres, we would be able to shoot over their heads as they cleared the aisle. Once they hit the forward bulkhead of the cabin, Pete and I would spring forward and clear the cockpit and forward lavatory.

The whole thing sounds tricky, but we knew we could get into the plane and clear our sector with a speed that looked like stomping toothpaste from a tube. Controlled mayhem would enter that plane from the middle and sweep in opposite directions. We loaded the vans. I got a radio check with the TOC, gave Ron the high sign, and we were away.

When we arrived at the airfield, we made contact with Jim Day and found a place to set up that was out of sight but still gave direct access to the taxiway leading to the plane. We never executed an emergency assault, but the preparation for one was always part of the choreography of Delta Force's response to an aircraft hijacking. A few hours later, our whole group moved to the airfield and we rotated the duty of the emergency assault teams.

For the next seventy-two hours we were put through the ringer. During a hijacking response, one of the things our side does is wage a war of fatigue against the hostage takers. The objective is to wear them down mentally, physically, and emotionally.

The job of the negotiator is to make sure everything has a price. If the terrorists want water—they have to give something in exchange. If they want the toilets pumped out—they have to give something in return. With every communication, the effort is made to throw the terrorists off their plan and loosen their hold on the initiative. If they can't be induced to give up, we want them to be at their lowest possible state when an assault is mounted. We want them to be tired, frazzled, and drained of confidence. But during this exercise, we were the ones being pushed to the edge.

Deadlines for demands would approach. Tension would build. We would stand to and get into assault position only to stand down and pull back. Then, while we were trying to get some rest, some kind of an emergency would come up and we'd stand to once again. This seemed to happen every few hours.

Jim and Ron had their hands full dealing with the "local authorities" and representatives from the "American embassy."

The ambassador demanded to be informed of every development in the situation, but instructions came from the National Command Authority in Washington to exclude him. The CIA chief of station (COS) showed up and said that all operational plans had to meet his approval. He was rebuffed and went away mumbling threats. The national minister of internal security demanded that our sniper/observers be pulled in; the U.S. embassy refused to intervene because the ambassador was miffed at being excluded from the information chain. We suspected that the COS had instigated the security minister's demand. Problem after problem arose and had to be dealt with.

The demands were draining to all of us, but particularly so with

Jim and Ron. During the second day of the ordeal, we grabbed Jim and Ron one at a time, took them to a hidden spot, and made them lie down and rest for a few hours. During those times, we team leaders rotated command duties and took the heat from all the competing interests. We built a psychic shell around our unit, adhered to our operational plan, and fought off the worst of the intrusions.

Twice during the second night we prepared to conduct an assault. The first time, we were in approach formation within twenty-five meters of the plane when we were called back. The second time, we were actually on the plane with our hands on the doors, ready to start the countdown, when we were recalled. That one took a lot of energy out of us, emotionally and tactically. It's a lot more difficult to back down from a target, without detection, than it is to make the approach in the first place. And every time we pulled back, we had to leave two teams in overwatch in case we were detected and had to launch an emergency assault.

But every difficulty we faced, every problem that surfaced during the course of these exercises, showed itself for real over the coming years. And whenever we encountered a new and novel irritant on an operation, we would incorporate it into a future training exercise. Subsequent OTC classes caught unmitigated hell because they received the accumulated experience of every operation that preceded their arrival.

Finally, just before dawn of the third day, we attacked.

At that point, for everyone involved, for the hostages, the hostage takers, and us, it felt real. We were all playing for keeps. And when I went through that emergency exit into the plane, I was shooting to kill—it's just a good thing it was blank fire.

The thing that hit me hardest on entering the plane (and the thing I never got used to, though in the future, I would be ready for it) was the overwhelming stench. One hundred people crammed into a small space for three days produce an almost unbearable smell. It hits you like a blow to the face—it's something you have to physically fight your way through when the doors open. The snipers said that as they closed on the plane to help us handle the passengers, they ran into a wall of foul odor pouring from the open doors as much as fifty meters away.

One other thing was always the same. Whether it was a training exercise or a real operation, if the ordeal lasted more than twenty-four hours, the hostages and the hostage takers always reacted the same way. Their sense of reality was restricted to the confines of the plane. The airplane was their planet (in fact, their universe) and everything outside it became alien to them. The group psychology that germinated and took root in that short period of time was always amazing.

Outside, the hostage handling was taking place according to plan. After the team leaders inside the plane met and talked out an initial report of actions during the assault, we called to Jim Day that we were ready to turn the scene over to the locals. We went through those formalities and climbed off the plane.

We pulled back to the hangar that had been our holding area and stowed our gear. Finally we were finished. And I, for one, was damned glad of it. I was so tired I was punch-drunk. Some guys were almost asleep on their feet, and to a man, we were glassy-eyed and weary. Then Ron called us all together.

"We have one thing left to do yet, guys," he told us. "Load all the equipment on the trucks but keep your pistols and your submachine gun. On the way back, we're going to stop at Range Nineteen and take a shooting test. We have to be there at 0830, so let's get moving. When the equipment is loaded, get on the vans. Team leaders, give me an 'up when you're ready to move.'"

I noticed two cadre members, Bill and Carlos, watching us intently as Ron gave us this last-minute information. But there was no bitching or grousing as we turned to load the equipment onto the trucks, and after seeing no outbursts, the two observers went to their own vehicle and departed.

Nothing goes unwatched and no action is too small to go unnoted, I thought as I watched Bill and Carlos walk away. We were tired, we were hungry, we were sleepy, and we thought we were finished when they hit us with the news of this next test. And taking one of our shooting tests in this condition was going to be a hell of a challenge.

But as I thought about it, it made perfect sense. The only thing that had not been tested during the assault on the aircraft was our actual shooting abilities. And when we had finally hit the plane, we were tired, hungry, sleepy, and frustrated—all of which would affect the accuracy of our shooting. It was imperative that the unit know how each man would perform in that condition. Once again, I had to marvel at the thoroughness of our trainers.

I slept all the way back to Fort Bragg, but it seemed that the nap only made me groggier. When we climbed out of the vans at Range 19, Sergeant Major Shumate was there to greet us.

"Okay, ladies," he purred. "There's nothing new here this morning; you've all done this shit before. The shooting stations are labeled with your current team designations. Start there and then as individuals, fill in where you see an opening. Move along with purpose. I don't want to screw around here all morning. And try not to shoot yourselves." He paused. "Unless, of course, it's absolutely necessary." He waved us away with a grin.

I felt like I was moving in slow motion and had a hangover to boot as I moved to the first point. I usually breezed through these shooting tests, but now it took all my powers of concentration to focus on the required task at each station.

The shooting itself wasn't hard; instinct seemed to take over and guide me on that part. But I had to *think* about what I had to do and then *tell myself* what I had decided. Fatigue is a powerful narcotic. But the shots went where they were supposed to go, and within the allowed time limits. I didn't realize I was finished until Donny took my scorecard and told me to go sit down.

Finished. Finally finished. Isn't that something? I cleared my weapons and put them in my bag. *It's June now and I started this ride last September. Not an awfully long time, but a lot has happened since then and I've changed a good bit.*

I had found some things inside myself that had never had a chance to show themselves before. I didn't feel different. I felt, well, *extended.* As if there was now a greater span to my reach. And I felt happy. I had come a long way from the hills of Floyd County, Georgia, in the last ten years. And so far, the value of the trip had been so much greater than the cost.

When everyone was finished, we picked up the brass, cleaned the range, and reconvened in the mess hall back at the Ranch for one of "White Water Willie's" fabulous full Army breakfasts. We were a hungry bunch and did some serious damage to his menu that morning.

Later we gathered in the OTC bay for further instructions. Gerhard Altmann spoke with us.

"Gentleman, it is apparent from your current state that it would be senseless to attempt an after-action review of the Culmination Exercise at this time. Few of you would be able to stay awake and those who did manage to maintain consciousness, I doubt would contribute much to the process. Therefore, let us gather tomorrow morning in this same location and at this same hour. Now take yourselves to a place of rest for some delayed, but well-earned, sleep. I will see you all on the morrow. Until then, I bid you adieu."

Common sense continues to rule, I thought, as I gathered my things and walked out to the parking lot. In the Ranger battalion, we always did it by the book and conducted the hot wash immediately following an exercise. Consequently, we usually gained little from it because we were so dead on our feet it was all anyone could do to stay awake—much less give the review the attention it deserved. Tomorrow we would all be fresh and mentally alert and able to glean everything possible from a detailed look at the Culmination Exercise.

I really liked being in a smart organization.

The after-action review lasted seven hours. Each man's actions were gone over in complete detail, and everything that had happened, from the time we left Fort Bragg until we returned, was brought out and discussed. Mistakes were analyzed and successful methods were noted.

But this was not intended as the equivalent of a Chinese self-criticism drill. No one was going to be remanded to a reeducation camp. The purpose of the review was to learn everything we possibly could about what we had just done—the good, the bad, and the ugly. We dissected problems and we came up with solutions—and the whole group profited from what we learned.

There is no better way for an organization to improve itself and move forward in a professional manner. But it is a process that must be fundamentally rooted in trust and mutual respect. The very instant it becomes a weapon rather than a lens for diagnostic analysis, the process is dead.

Finally it was over. OTC-3 had no further business to conduct. Jim Day sent a runner to Colonel Beckwith to let him know we had concluded the review, and the runner returned with a directive that we assemble in the mess hall in fifteen minutes.

The entire unit was gathered in the mess hall when Colonel Beckwith came through the doors with a crash.

"Si'down, si'down," he waved impatiently as he strode to the center of the room and leaned back against the empty salad bar.

"Well, looks like we got ourselves a bunch of new operators, Country," he said, addressing Sergeant Major Grimes. "Reckon now we gonna have to do sumpthin' with 'em. And it's high time they started earnin' their keep. 'Cause I swear, you boys have been 'bout to eat this unit outta house and home. Now you can start payin' back the cost of your board." He took us all in with a smile that swept the room from side to side.

"Mark this day down in your diaries, men," Beckwith thundered. And then he dropped his voice to a raspy, theatrical whisper. "This is the day we've been working towards. This is the day that 1st Special Forces Operational Detachment—Delta becomes an effective unit. We have now achieved critical mass. By the time we finish business this afternoon, we will be of a size and a configuration that gives us the means of accomplishing the tasks our great nation sets before us.

"Before I leave here today, I'm calling General Shy Meyer, the Army Chief of Staff, and telling him that Delta Force is formed. That Delta Force exists. Then I'm gonna beg him for just three more months to conduct unit training before he tells the Joint Chiefs we're ready to go. But I'm also going to tell him that if the bell rings tomorrow . . . we can come out fighting."

He turned to the unit adjutant.

"Now, Smith—call out the squadron assignments. And when that's finished, let's have a beer." As he concluded what for Colonel Beckwith was a short speech, the mess hall guys wheeled in several beer kegs nestled in trash cans filled with ice.

It was an exciting moment. I felt like a kid at Christmas as I listened to the names being called out and the squadron, troop, and team assignments being made. I had hoped for a posting to a sniper team, but wasn't disappointed in the least when I was called as a member of C Team, Troop One (an assault troop; Troop Two is the sniper troop), B Squadron.

Dave Donaldson had been designated as the leader of C Team,

and he waved me over to join him and the other two members of the team. Billy Oswalt was assistant team leader, and the other man was Chris Cable. I had seen Chris on many occasions—he had helped Dave on the range during our demolitions training—but so far, I'd never had the chance to speak with him. That was about to change. Over the years, I guess Chris and I came to know one another as well as any two men on earth can.

"Boys, first things first," Don rumbled around the chaw of tobacco he always kept tucked deep in his jaw. "Let's get at that beer before it's nothing but suds, and then we can talk."

Chris filled four large cups and passed them back to us. We stood close to each other and watched the animated crowd of our friends and comrades. The room rang with laughter and jovial voices, and as I looked around I realized—*this was a birthday party.*

We were celebrating the birth of our unit. Our conception had happened on paper over a year ago, and since that time, we had undergone a long and difficult gestation. Just as a cell divides itself, we had grown slowly at first and then with an increasing tempo as life multiplied life. With inexorable growth, we had eventually achieved viability and emerged as a new phenomenon: a fully grown and reasoning predator, armed with fangs and claws and intelligence, able to run and to fight.

We stayed that day and talked with one another long after the beer ran out. It was as if no one wanted to leave. Unconsciously, I guess, we knew that this was a golden day, a day that would never come again, and we were reluctant to let it go.

Now, as I write this, almost a quarter of a century later, I look back on that small place in time and I'm glad to be able to tell myself I was there at the beginning, and I know all the heroes who were gathered there, many of whom no longer walk the earth.

It was a rare privilege to be in that room, on that day, with those men. It was an honor to be one of the founding members of that brave band of warriors.

It was an honor and a privilege for which I am extremely grateful and eternally thankful.

For the rest of that summer we worked like men possessed. Beckwith had promised he would give us three months of unit training before he announced we were ready for action, but the generals in Washington were breathing down his neck. So we looked at every day like it was the last opportunity we would have for preparation.

We shot eight hours a day. B Squadron went to the range every morning while A Squadron was in the Shooting House. We changed over in the afternoon. The snipers stayed on the range all day every day, and often late into the night.

The Shooting House took such a pounding that we had to rebuild the interior walls every three weeks because the internal frames were completely shot out. Previously we had needed to rebuild the walls only every ten weeks.

I don't know how much ammunition we went through that summer. But in comparison, the following summer—when more than half the unit was scattered around the world on different missions—Colonel Beckwith called those of us not deployed into a classroom and chewed our asses for not shooting enough. He said we were screwing off, that he had checked the ammunition reports and we had expended only a million rounds during June and July. To Charlie, that was ample evidence of slothful behavior.

Each squadron ran a large exercise every two weeks. Always at night, always including at a minimum a coordinated assault and a sniper-initiated assault. Different teams were designated to design the situation and prepare the scenario for each exercise. The point was to test a different problem (and a different facet of the problem) every time.

Twice that summer, the entire unit flew out on no-notice exercises, each one replicating a different mission. The first one was an operation to recover a stolen nuclear device being held by a band of terrorists who were also holding a group of captured American scientists. We spent the week prior to that exercise at the Department of Energy's nuclear laboratories in Idaho Falls, Idaho, learning about reactors, nuclear materials, and atomic weapons.

While deployed on that exercise, we had our first opportunity to work with the Department of Energy's NEST Teams. "NEST" stands for "Nuclear Emergency Search Team." There are two of these teams, NEST East and NEST West, and they are positioned on either side of the Mississippi. These are teams of scientists whose

B Squadron—early winter 1982. I'm in the center row, fifth from the right.

Beirut street where I was
caught in shelling, far corner

Approach to the port crossing
through the Green Line.

The old Beirut embassy
several years before its
destruction by a suicide
truck bomb.

Beirut. The view of the Holiday Inn from the kitchen window of my
apartment in the Hotel Charles. Note the shell holes in the
upper walls.

Ambassador's motorcade in Beirut. Don Feeney in the lead car.

Don Feeney (kneeling, lower right) and some of the Beirut bodyguards mugging for the camera during an afternoon shooting session in the Shouf Mountains above Beirut.

Remnants of B Squadron at Grenada.

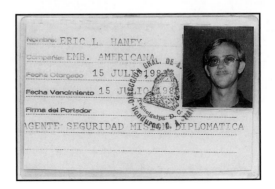

Embassy and local credentials used in Beirut, Honduras, and Haiti.

<table>
<tr><td>See Privacy Act Statement in AR 623-205, APPENDIX E.</td><td>ENLISTED EVALUATION REPORT
(AR 623-205)</td><td>Proponent agency for this form is the US Army Military Personnel Center.</td></tr>
</table>

PART I. ADMINISTRATIVE DATA

A. LAST NAME – FIRST NAME – MIDDLE INITIAL		B. SSN	C. RANK (ABBR)	D. DATE OF RANK
HANEY, ERIC L.		254-	MSG	830313

E. PRIMARY MOSC	F. SECONDARY MOSC	G. UNIT, ORGANIZATION, STATION, ZIP CODE/APO, MACOM
11B5V	19Z5C	1st Special Forces Operational Detachment-DELTA (Airborne) Fort Bragg, North Carolina 28307-5000 (DA)

H. CODE/TYPE OF REPORT	I. PERIOD OF REPORT						J. RATED MONTHS	K. NONRATED MONTHS	L. NONRATED CODES
3 Change of Rater	FROM	YEAR 85	MONTH 04	THRU	YEAR 85	MONTH 11	8	NONE	NA

PART II. DUTY DESCRIPTION

A. PRINCIPAL DUTY TITLE: Senior Instructor/Training   B. DUTY MOSC: 11B5P

C. DESCRIPTION OF DUTIES Primarily serves as a Senior Instructor/Trainer in the six month Operator Training Course. The course, conducted semi-annually, is designed to prepare operator designates for service in the unit's operational Sabre Squadrons. Serves as a principle in planning, preparing, conducting, and evaluating numerous special operations training programs. Performs LNO functions with DOD and other government agencies. Provides senior NCO leadership, management, and supervision in conducting special operations training.

PART III. EVALUATION OF PROFESSIONALISM AND PERFORMANCE

RATER	INDORSER	A. PROFESSIONAL COMPETENCE	SCORING SCALE	RATER	INDORSER	B. PROFESSIONAL STANDARDS
5	5	1. Demonstrates initiative.		5	5	1. Integrity.
5	5	2. Adapts to changes.	(High)	5	5	2. Loyalty.
5	5	3. Seeks self-improvement.	5	5	5	3. Moral courage.
5	5	4. Performs under pressure.		5	5	4. Self-discipline.
5	5	5. Attains results.	4	5	5	5. Military appearance.
5	5	6. Displays sound judgment.	3	5	5	6. Earns respect.
5	5	7. Communicates effectively.	2	5	5	7. Supports EO/EEO.
5	5	8. Develops subordinates.	1	35	35	SUBTOTALS
5	5	9. Demonstrates technical skills.				
5	5	10. Physical fitness.	0			
50	50	SUBTOTALS	(Low)			(Add the Rater's SUBTOTALS (A&B) and enter sum in the appropriate box in PART VI, SCORE SUMMARY. Do the same for Indorser.)

C. DEMONSTRATED PERFORMANCE OF PRESENT DUTY   8512/PASS   74/165   YES

1. Rater's Evaluation: During this period, MSG Haney has played a very important role in elevating the proficiency of newly assigned personnel to 1st SFOD-D's Operator Training course as well as the combat readiness of this unit. On a daily basis he proves himself to be highly skilled in all aspects of sensitive, low-visibility operations. He is always ready to deploy independently or as a team member to accomplish any mission, real world or training at a moments notice. His ability to communicate with the highest government officials on matters important to national security places him in high regard by everyone he comes in contact with. MSG Haney also plays a very important role in recruiting new personnel into this unit. His credibility within the elite units such as the rangers has brought many outstanding young NCO's to 1st SFOD-D. He is constantly striving to improve his education during off duty time.

2. Indorser's Evaluation: MSG Haney is an outstanding NCO and Operator. He was chosen as a senior instructor because of his leadership, ability to communicate, and technical skills as an Operator. He is tough, quiet, and exceptionally talented in all aspects of low-visibility operations. He is extremely competent in all means of low-visibility infiltration. His ability in an austere field environment is without equal. In his present capacity he is frequently chosen to represent this unit to other government agencies, private organizations, and to foreign governments. He is equally comfortable with superiors and subordinates alike. The new Operators readily respond to his positive, firm leadership. He is a strong, dynamic factor in the growth and development of this unit. I want to continue to serve with this fine NCO.

DA FORM OCT 81 2166-6   REPLACES DA FORM 2166-5A, OCT 79, WHICH IS OBSOLETE.

Annual Efficiency Report as Senior Instructor for OTC.

A critical commando task—baking bread.

job it is to track down and locate missing nuclear materials or a nuclear device that has been smuggled into the United States. They are phenomenally good at what they do. I can assure you that as unlikely as it is to happen in the first place, it is virtually impossible for a nuclear device to be brought into this country and hidden for terroristic purposes. NEST will find the culprits and find them quickly.

Working on this nuclear exercise, we got a bit of a start. We found out that our normal rules of engagement didn't necessarily apply to nuclear materials.

Delta's philosophy of operation was that we would go to any extremes to avoid harming a hostage. But national policy dictated that when nuclear materials were involved, hostage lives were of secondary importance. The mission was to recover the material—regardless of the cost in human lives. But national policy didn't change either our mind-set or how we went about an operation. We were confident that even in a nuclear incident, we could still save hostages. We hadn't worked as hard as we had just to revert to indiscriminately firing on a target. Any band of yahoos could do that.

The nuclear exercise was also tremendously valuable in that we started to build professional relationships with both the FBI and the Department of Justice. We needed very definitive answers to the legal questions we would encounter. It was vital to work out the mechanism for defining what would constitute a legitimate role for the deployment of Delta Force on a domestic terrorist incident. Especially since the Posse Comitatus Act forbids federal troops from being used for the purposes of law enforcement inside the United States. The President can, however, temporarily suspend the Act if doing so is overwhelmingly in the interest of national public safety. And it's up to the attorney general to determine when that criterion is met.

This was just the first of many exercises we would conduct over the course of the next few years accompanied by enough Justice Department lawyers to form another assault troop. The end result of our joint studies was the formation of the FBI's own counterterrorist unit, the HRT (Hostage Rescue Team). As the FBI had provided us with much-needed assistance during our formation, we reciprocated by providing the initial training for their HRT. From that point forward, we maintained an extremely close relationship with them, even conducting joint training and sharing information and techniques.

The next exercise that summer was a big one. It was conducted at a government facility in the desert Southwest and lasted more than a week. The FBI created the scenario and provided the terrorists—and I can tell you that those guys make for some formidable opponents. They gave us a hell of a time. For our country's sake, I just hope none of those guys ever really go bad.

That exercise culminated with Delta making a simultaneous daylight hit on a plane, a bus, and a building complex, an attack that was spread across forty miles and stretched us to the limits of our capacity. It also resulted in our blowing up one of our favorite FBI agents. While he was playing the part of the terrorist leader as the bus was being attacked, a flash-bang landed in his lap and detonated. He was left nude and smoldering, but thankfully, he wasn't seriously harmed and continued to work closely with us for many more years.

Early that autumn we faced a modified version of that simultaneous-attack exercise, which was considered our Validation Exercise. The test was administered by the National Command Authority to determine if we were ready to conduct operations if and when called upon by the President and the Chairman of the Joint Chiefs.

At almost the exact hour we finished the exercise and were packing to return to Fort Bragg, a bunch of young students half a world away in the city of Tehran were taking over the American embassy in Iran and taking hostage every man and woman inside.

That embassy and the people inside it, both American and Iranian, became the focus of our life in Delta for months to come.

INTO THE FRAY

WHEN THE MISSION ALERT FOR TEHRAN HAD BEEN GIVEN, MY squadron, B Squadron, was winter-mountain training in the western United States. A Squadron had already deployed to a secret CIA site to begin planning. We returned immediately to Fort Bragg and quickly followed our mates to the seclusion of the isolation site.

The most tense part of any mission is during the initial alert. That's when you're operating with half-assed information and surrounded by rumors. This time was no exception. Most of the news we received at first was so ludicrous it didn't deserve the dignity of the term "intelligence." The CIA had no usable assets in place and was proving incapable of providing us with the type of information we needed, and they made it clear they would not take the risks entailed to get us what we needed. (This turned out to be a long-term problem for us that has never been resolved.)

That's when Dick Meadows volunteered to lead a small undercover team into Tehran. Dick was a legend in Special Forces and the Rangers. He had been the ground commander on the 1970 Son Tay raid to liberate American POWs in North Vietnam. Now a retired major, he had been hired as a civilian consultant by Colonel Beckwith when we had formed the unit. Once Dick was on the ground inside Iran, a flow of usable information started to trickle in and we were able to start planning in earnest.

Until Colonel Beckwith slammed his foot down, we had the all-too-common phenomenon of a mission being planned by men who wouldn't be taking part in it and putting their own lives at risk.

Though SAS commandos had planned their own missions for years, it took Charlie Beckwith to sell the idea to the U.S. military. This was a sales job akin to administering a forced enema, and it didn't endear Charlie to any of the Pentagon armchair commandos who felt they should be running the operation. But it became a Delta Force mandate: those who actually *conduct* the mission will be the ones to plan *how* to do it. It also prevents the Rambo syndrome from coming into play: nothing is impossible for those who don't actually have to do it.

So, far away from Fort Bragg in the seclusion of our CIA hideaway, we dug in and started to figure out how to crack an egg without scrambling its insides. In effect, the embassy compound was now a prison complex. It was an egg we would have to break into, take, secure, hold, defend, evacuate hostages from, and last but not least, escape from ourselves.

We soon had a basic plan we were confident would work. The plan was refined and rehearsed and refined and rehearsed and refined again as new intelligence came in. The changes felt endless, but no one ever despaired, because that is just the nature of this kind of beast. A combat plan is an animal in a constant state of metamorphosis and is under continual revision right up until the first shot is fired—at which time it usually ceases to have relevance.

So each time we learned something new and important about the situation inside Iran and the captive embassy, we incorporated it into the developing plan. Eventually the parts started to come together until it felt smooth. At that point we finally knew exactly what to do when we got to the embassy. The hard part was getting there.

All during this time, the Air Force was playing a masterful shell game of gathering and staging aircraft from around the world, casually and randomly, so as not to alert the Soviets that we were up to something. Delta Force was playing a similar game. When the Soviet spy satellite window was open overhead, our rehearsal stage was dismantled and hidden and we slipped undercover.

Back at Fort Bragg, the unit's support troops were working double duty to cover their own demanding functions while also going to the range, shooting, blowing off explosives, and in general making it look like the Sabre Squadrons were all still at home, their focus a million miles away from Iran.

Our biggest unresolved problem was how to get into Tehran. The Air Force could carry us into and out of Iran with their workhorse C-130s. But we needed helicopters with long legs and a big lift capability to put us close to the city and later pluck us and the hostages back out again. And that's where some real problems started to show.

At the Joint Chiefs level, the decision had been made that the rotary wing of the operation would be naval. On the surface, it seemed a sensible decision. After all, the helos would have to launch from a carrier, and we wanted things to look as normal as possible.

But the helicopters were nothing but problems. They were maintenance beasts at a time when maintenance and spare parts were a low priority—shortly after Vietnam and during the shoe-string military budgets of the Carter administration. To put it bluntly, the birds stunk. The crews weren't ready, and more important, I believe the pilots had convinced themselves the mission would never go.

The question of the helicopters simply wouldn't go away. And this is where service parochialism reared its ugly head. Even as it became obvious that neither the naval air crews nor the Navy helicopters were capable of executing the mission, the edict came down: *no change*. The admirals would keep their piece of the pie no matter what the eventual cost.

My team was the last element scheduled to be lifted out of Tehran, and we were certain the helicopters would fail during the extraction phase. The plan called for us to lift out of a soccer stadium across the street from the embassy compound. While the stadium was a relatively defensible site (and a safe place for the hostages), it was a nightmare for helicopters—even the best of them.

After some really bad experiences with those birds, we were convinced at least one of the choppers would crash in the stadium. Since a crash like that would leave us to our own devices in Tehran, my team prepared a plan for that contingency.

We would clear out of the city in stolen cars, move north on foot into the remote Elburz Mountains, and then head across the border into the Soviet Union. Once there, we would turn ourselves in to the Russians. Not an ideal situation but better, we thought, than taking the obvious route to Turkey, where Khomeini's henchmen would be waiting.

To assist in that eventuality, we took along our car theft kits, "escape and evasion" packets with maps, satellite signaling panels, ten thousand dollars in rials and U.S. currency, some "pointy-talky" phrase sheets, and a letter written in Farsi on Royal Saudi letterhead. The letter asked the reader, as a good Muslim, to render assistance to us. We also had a phonetic English translation of the Farsi letter. The main problem we had with this "help me" letter was that we figured anyone stupid enough to believe what it said wouldn't be able to read!

By late January 1980, we felt confident in our plan. Given a little luck, we could pull this thing off. But we needed long, dark winter nights to cover us, and cold winter air to provide maximum lift for the aircraft. As the diplomatic effort crawled nowhere, the nights became shorter and warmer. If we were going, we needed to go soon.

The concept of the operation was this:

Delta would infiltrate by teams to a staging base in the United States. From there we would fly to a remote marshaling base (REMAB) on a Soviet-built airfield in Egypt, where we would rendezvous with other assets.

The other assets for the mission included: A Ranger company that was to seize an Iranian airfield at Mansariah for use during the extraction phase. A Ranger squad that would come with us to Desert One with the mission of providing security for the helicopters during their layup. A Special Forces team from Det-A, stationed in West Berlin, was to retrieve the Americans holed up at the chancery of the Canadian embassy. And a couple of former Iranian generals who were to provide some sort of assistance (I've never known what kind) once we were in country.

We were also supposed to take along a swaggering, loud-mouthed, smart-assed former member of SAVAK, the Iranian secret police. He supposedly was a man who knew the underside of Tehran, but when it came time to leave the United States, he developed what Colonel Beckwith called "intestinal problems" (lack of) and refused to board the plane. I guess he was fundamentally opposed to going into action against anyone other than unarmed civilians.

From Egypt we would relocate to an island airfield off the coast of Oman, lie low for a few hours, and then board the C-130 Combat Talon aircraft for the flight into Iran. The helicopters, with several of our signal squadron communicators aboard, would lift off from the carrier *Nimitz* in the Persian Gulf and fly to a spot in the desert code-named "Desert One" to refuel from the C-130 tanker aircraft.

From Desert One, we planned to board the helos and spring forward to a hidden canyon where the birds would be camouflaged and put to roost. At sundown that day, Dick Meadows and his team would meet us with covered trucks to transport us to a side street adjacent to the embassy. Then we would slip over the walls of the embassy and execute the recovery of the hostages, while AC-130 gunships orbited overhead to address the expected hordes of armed militants, and Navy fighters controlled the skies to ward off the Iranian air force.

My team's mission was to assault and clear the ambassador's residence and to recover the American women located there. I still have the door key to the kitchen entrance we planned to enter through. The cook brought the key out with him when he fled the country. The other teams were tasked to assault and clear their respective areas of the embassy compound and recover the hostages in those locations. Two machine gun teams were assigned to fight off the inevitable visitors at the front gates; they were burdened like pack mules with the more than one hundred pounds of ammo they carried.

Then the extraction phase would begin. Fast Eddie, the demo man, would blow a hole in the walls of the embassy—right across the street from the stadium. We would take the hostages out and across the street to the stadium through a corridor held open by the machine gun teams. Then we'd load the hostages and their accompanying security teams onto the first helicopters and fly them out to the Iranian airfield the Rangers had seized. The rest of us would follow as the other helos staged in. From there we would load onto C-141s for the flight out of country with Navy fighters providing protective coverage. An ambitious plan, but certainly workable.

It's a good thing we're not able to foretell our own future, otherwise most of us would never get out of bed in the morning. While we were still in the CIA isolation camp during the planning phase, the only outsider we saw other than our handler was the cook. He was an old CIA employee who had seen all sorts of characters come and go over the years. One evening after supper he stood around with a few of us, smoking and joking as he waited for his truck to be loaded. Suddenly he became quiet and looked around the area as if he was seeing it for the first time.

"Boys, I believe the last time we used this particular lodge was for the Bay of Pigs."

By the first of February, Delta was ready to give it a try. We weren't happy with the helos, but then again, we never would be. We were just going to trust that portion of the plan to luck and hope for the best.

As February slid into March, we continued to rehearse and fine-tune the plan. Several times during the winter, we leaned forward in the foxhole and readied ourselves for imminent departure, only to be disappointed by another delay.

March came and went. By the time April arrived, we were back home at Fort Bragg and more anxious than ever. The weather was warming and the nights were getting shorter.

When the execution order finally came, we simply loaded our gear on the planes and slipped away quietly. By this time, no one paid the least attention to our movements. Our first stop was the remote marshaling base at Wadi Kena, Egypt. A small advance party had preceded the main body to ready the site for the reception of the main unit.

The fortified Soviet-built aircraft hangars were covered inside with human excrement. The Egyptians had used them as huge communal outhouses. The advance team spent several days before our arrival scrubbing the hangars with disinfectant just to make them habitable. When we arrived, what had been a deserted airstrip was throbbing with activity. We linked up with our other assets and waited a few days for the final word to go.

Just prior to boarding the C-141 for the next phase of the journey, Colonel Beckwith asked us to pause for a prayer. Then, with the final amens still hanging in the air, we loaded up for the next stop on the journey—the airfield on the Omani island of Masirah.

Arriving there in midmorning we found—wonder of wonders—

tents set up for our shelter. Now, to most people that may seem like a small thing. But those who have ever been in the combat arms will recognize it for the true gift it was. Like any other band of nomads, we were accustomed to fending for ourselves. The idea that someone else would provide us with not just shelter from the sun but *cold sodas* was almost unthinkable. My comrades and I still thank the Air Force folks for that kind gesture.

If there is one thing that always sticks in my mind about how Delta Force goes about a mission, it is the utterly businesslike attitude of the men. There is none of that Hollywood crap. No posturing, no sloganeering, no high fives, no posing, no bluster, and no bombast. Just a quiet determination to get on with the job.

And in that fashion, late in the afternoon of 24 April 1980, we roused ourselves from siesta, made a final equipment check, test-fired our weapons, and climbed aboard the C-130s that would take us into Iran.

My squadron was aboard the lead plane. For the course of the mission we—along with our attached Ranger squad, the two Iranian generals, and some Farsi-speaking drivers—would be known as "White Team." We would land at Desert One about ten minutes ahead of the others and provide security for the rest of the unit as they came in.

I have been told that the command pilot of White Team's C-130 was an old lieutenant colonel with more C-130 flight hours than any living human being. That is probably true. And I have no doubts he sat in a specially constructed seat—one big enough to accommodate his huge brass balls.

Twisting and squirming, hugging the ground, flying nap-of-the-earth, the Combat Talon aircraft threaded their way through gaps in the Iranian radar coverage. Flying low enough, to borrow a phrase from *Dr. Strangelove,* "to fry chickens in the barnyard."

Even by Special Operations standards, that was a memorable flight. On the way in I had been lying under the Ranger squad's jeep at the edge of the ramp. But when the three-minute warning sounded and the loadmaster yelled, "Grab something and hang on!" I reconsidered my position and wrapped myself around the diagonal brace just aft of the ramp hinge.

We hit the ground hard—really hard—with no detectable change in speed or engine sound. The plane never bounced; the propellers just changed pitch, and we slowed so fast it felt like we had landed in a lake of molasses. I found out later that the pilot took her in at combat emergency landing speed so that if the plane broke through the desert crust, he would still have sufficient airspeed to wrestle her back into the air. Some pilot.

The ramp started to drop as soon as we had three wheels on the ground. Well before the plane had come to a halt, the Rangers had their motorcycles and the jeep unchained, and were ready to leap out into the desert. My team was positioned to hit the ground first, followed by the Rangers and the rest of White Team.

But as the back of the plane opened up and we could look outside, we saw headlights—right on top of us! We leaped off the plane like pouncing leopards. Three vehicles were almost on top of us. In the lead was a bus, followed by a gasoline tanker, and a small pickup truck that brought up the rear. My team went straight for the bus. We fired into the front of the vehicle, put a forty-millimeter high-explosive round from a grenade launcher in front of the bumper, and fired a volley of rounds low into the step cavity where the passengers mount the bus. The fire was close enough to the driver that he immediately brought his vehicle to a halt.

Bill shouldered the door open as our squadron commander, Major Logan Fitch, charged in and swept down the aisle as the lead man of the clearing team. Logan was never one to just stand back and give direction, he always led from the front—and this time he paid the price. As he barreled down the aisle to the rear of the bus, a young man in the back jumped up and punched Logan in the nose. A brave fellow. He was taken under control and Logan was the first to laugh about it as he dabbed the blood off his lip.

In the meantime, other things were happening there on God's Little Acre. The Rangers had gone after the tanker truck that was now trying to maneuver away. I knew all those men well—they were the third squad of my old platoon. Young Ricky Magee was now a team leader and Allie Jones was the squad leader. I also distinctly remember hearing someone shout, "Shoot that truck!" to a Ranger carrying an M-72 antitank rocket.

"Ba-woom!" The rocket launched, followed immediately by another, infinitely more spectacular *"Ba-woom!"* as the warhead missed low under the front bumper, hit the ground, skipped upward, and detonated in the belly of the tanker, setting off the gasoline it contained. The driver and his partner hurled themselves out of the cab and dove into the pickup following behind them. In a cloud of dust, the little truck then rocketed out of the area so fast the Ranger motorcycle couldn't catch up and was recalled before he got too far out.

While this was happening, we dismounted the bus passengers and searched them. For the most part, they were old men and women, with a few children and several young men thrown in for good measure. About forty very frightened people in all. And they had good reason to be frightened, for it looked like World War Three had erupted around them. There are few armies in the world that would not have killed them outright, but our feelings for those people were, but for the grace of God, they could be our own families or friends. By the time we had them searched and seated on the side of the road, the other planes were slashing in out of the darkness, and soon there were people all over the place.

We decided to kidnap the bus passengers. We would load them on one of the C-130s for back-haul out of the country that night and fly them back in for release after the mission was completed. Major Fitch detailed my team to stand guard over the passengers since we were the ones who had initially taken control of them.

I finished searching the prisoners by the light of the burning tanker. After we seated them on a low ridge of dirt edging the track, Bill Oswalt and I stepped to the end of the line to take a quick breather and compare notes.

We stood mesmerized in the desert night watching the flaming tanker in this remote part of an ancient world. The column of fire soaring some three hundred feet into the sky was absolutely biblical. I was certain the glow could be seen for a hundred miles across the Iranian desert.

"Bill, do you think this mission is compromised?" I asked.

Bill nodded toward the tanker. "Eric, I'll bet Ray Charles could see that damned thing." And then, glancing at the seated passengers-cum-prisoners, he said, "Just think of it, Eric. For a year, we worked like dogs to become America's counterterrorist outfit, and what do we do on our very first mission? We hijack a fucking bus."

Every group of human beings has a few members who stand out, and our guests were no exception. One was a little boy about five years old. He sat right next to his grandmother, and even though it was obvious he was scared, he put on a stern face and made it clear he was ready to defend his grandma if anyone threatened her. Another was the brave guy, now flex-cuffed, who had punched Logan in the nose. And last, but certainly not least, was the one we quickly dubbed the "Village Idiot."

In our very limited Farsi (we had learned about twenty phrases) we told the people to sit still and shut up. But there's always one person who doesn't get the message. Ours was a poor guy in his mid-twenties who was slightly, but obviously, limited in his mental faculties. He would lean over to talk to his neighbor in a loud whisper, and his cringing neighbor would lean away, gesturing to him to shut up—and surely telling the guy between gritted teeth that he would get them all killed. Twice I had walked over to the young man to tell him to be quiet. The second time, I stuck the muzzle of my CAR-15 under his nose to emphasize the point.

He was silent for at least a minute and then went at it again. This time as I charged over to him, his neighbors on either side rolled away in self-protection. He looked up with horror on his face when I jammed my weapon's muzzle under his left ear, heaved him up on tiptoes, and frog-marched him up the road away from the group. He was convinced he was being taken away for execution, and I'm sure his comrades thought the same.

As I led him away from the group of prisoners, he set up a kind of pitiable wailing it seems only Middle Easterners are capable of. He squalled and slobbered and begged and beseeched, all with upraised hands clasped in prayer as I marched him twenty meters away, turned him so his back was to his friends, pushed him to the ground . . . and left him to sit alone. I could hear him snuffling and mumbling what were probably prayers of thanksgiving (or curses) for his deliverance from certain death as I walked back to my position near the rest of his comrades.

In the glow of the fire, the faces of the passengers all looked relieved. Whether from the fact that their fellow traveler had not been killed or that he could no longer get the rest of them in trouble, I wasn't sure.

So there we all were. A nice fire to keep off the chill, some new friends to keep us company—but no helicopters. The tanker C-130s were arriving now, and the birds that had brought us in

needed to leave. But Colonel Kyle, the air commander, would keep
them with us until the helos arrived. Just in case.

Hours ticked by. We were burning precious darkness, and still
no choppers. Several times we thought we detected them, but it was
just our wishful thinking. Then suddenly, high in the sky—too
high, in fact—we saw one. He had his lights on and was making his
way to the flaming beacon we had lit. Close behind him came the
rest, but it turned out we were short one bird. One had developed
some sort of engine trouble as soon as it crossed the shoreline of the
Persian Gulf and had turned back for the carrier. The rest of the
flight had forged ahead, straight into a haboob—a storm of very
fine dust particles that can tower thousands of feet into the sky. This
was the undoing of the helicopter force.

The commander of the naval aviators was a badly shaken man
when he arrived. He was obviously rattled, and I heard him say that
he had never been through anything like that in his life. His demeanor was that of a man looking for a way out. He was led away
to a conference with Colonels Kyle and Beckwith.

While the powwow was going on, another pilot ran up to report
that his bird was showing transmission warning lights and was not
flyable. The plan called for six helos to go forward from Desert
One. We expected that at least one would fail to crank at the hide
site because they were notoriously difficult to start on their own
power. We were now down to five helicopters, with the expectation
of losing at least one more.

Things seemed to be steadily disintegrating, but we had come so
far and Tehran was now so close. A radio call was placed to Major
General James Vaught, the task force commander, to advise him of
the situation. He wisely left the decision-making to the commanders on the ground. Even under the best of circumstances, Charlie
Beckwith was not known for his patience, but he had controlled
himself pretty well up till now. But as he listened to the pilots talking themselves out of going forward, he had enough.

"Awright, goddamn it! Let's get the hell out! Scrub the mission
for tonight. We'll return to Masirah and the *Nimitz* while we still
have darkness. Reconfigure and come back tomorrow night. Radio
Dick Meadows about the situation and load up on the tanker
planes for the trip out. Okay, do it!"

The tanker we boarded was refueling three of the helicopters as we climbed inside. A C-130 tanker carries the fuel in huge flat rubber bladders that completely cover the floor of the aircraft, and these are what we sprawled out on. Think of it as sitting on a carpet made of twenty thousand pounds of jet fuel. But at least the outsides of the fuel bladders were dry. The interiors of the helicopters always ran with dripping fuel and hydraulic fluid, making it hard to even walk in them. The Air Force put up with no such sloppiness.

We scattered throughout the plane by teams. Our four-man team (Bill, Chris, Mike, and myself) settled against the fuselage just forward of the left wheel-well and relaxed a little. It was hot inside the plane, so we shucked off our black field jackets and put them behind our backs as padding between ourselves and the metal points and edges sticking out of the inner wall of the plane. We also wedged our CAR-15s between the edge of the bladders and the skin of the aircraft so they wouldn't rattle all over the place during takeoff. We would need both hands to hang on with. Getting off the ground was going to be a lot rougher than the landing.

Finally the helicopters were refueled and the plane was closed up and readied for takeoff. The whole time the C-130s were on the ground, their engines ran at full RPM but with the props feathered. So to those of us inside, there was really no difference in sound between a plane in flight and one on the ground.

A number of my mates were already asleep when we felt the plane start to move forward. But then something went terribly wrong. Just as we lurched forward, as if the brakes had been released, a storm of blue sparks exploded overhead and up front.

My first thought was that the bank of electronics between the flight deck and the cargo hold had shorted out—*and here we were sitting on all this jet fuel.* My initial frantic thought was—*where's the nearest fire extinguisher?* I glanced about for its location.

Then things started happening in fragments of seconds. The universe switched to slow motion, as it often appears to me when my life is in dire jeopardy.

While the sparks were still flying, the crew door of the plane blew in with an explosion and a wave of fire. Willy Corman was sitting in the hole of the stairwell to the flight deck, just in front of the crew door when it blew. But the flames turned upward instead of down, and he shot out of the hole like he'd been fired from a cannon. My teammate Chris jumped to his feet and yelled, "Haul ass!" At that instant, the flight deck erupted with a blast of fire and the ceiling over our heads in the forward part of the cabin was engulfed in roaring flames.

My first thought was that it was useless to even try to move. I was sitting on ten tons of jet fuel, I was a lifetime forward of the aft jump doors, and there was no way I'd ever make it out. My next thought was—*to hell with that! I've got to try!* So I took and held a deep breath I fully expected would be my last, and started moving.

It seems ironic now, but during the extensive psychological testing we underwent during Selection, I remember being asked the question, "What are you afraid of?" I didn't hesitate to answer: Fire. I fear it above anything else.

A quick glance aft showed that most of the squadron was already jammed up near the right rear jump door forty feet away. It wasn't open yet, but even if it were, I'd never get there before the flames poured over me. In the split second it had taken for me to get to my feet, the flames had burned through the top of the fuselage and were cascading down the walls.

I turned and ripped the blackout cover off a porthole midway down the left side. Nothing but fire outside! I continued down the left side of the plane just ahead of the cataract of flame. I was in a race for my life, and the fire matched me step for step. I made it to the back of the plane, just ahead of the flames, to the left jump door. I grabbed the handle and gave it a heave. When it cracked loose from the floor, a wide, flat sheet of flame gushed inside and Don Feeney yelled at me, "Close that fucking door!" I slammed it shut and momentarily denied entry to that torrent of fire.

While I was hurtling down the left side of the plane, our squadron sergeant major, Dell Rainey, quenched the initial confusion with a short command: "Fall in, boys, and hit the door like a jump." That's what everyone did, and that's what saved us.

The logjam at the door cleared immediately and the line moved with fire-hose urgency—just like we were jumping on a short drop zone. Dell's calmness and presence of mind saved many of us. I know it saved me.

When I turned from slamming the left door shut, the line on the other side had only three or four men in it, and they disappeared as I plunged straight across the plane and followed them through the hope of that open door. By the time I got there, it was ringed with fire down to the level of the floor. Fire was just starting to eat at the rubber fuel bladders, and I could see a frenzied hurricane of fire blowing outside that I still had to leap through.

But I was out. I hit the ground on top of someone who had fallen (it was "lucky" Willie) and together we scrambled away from that hellish inferno. Bounding to my feet, I released the breath I had been holding and sucked down a lungful of hot air. But I had to keep moving. I was being showered with burning fragments from the rapidly disintegrating C-130. I sprinted out about fifty meters, turned to face the plane, and flung myself down on the sand to view the catastrophe. It had probably only been thirty seconds since the initial explosion. A lifetime.

I saw a body lying in the jump door of the furiously burning plane. Just at the moment I saw him, the bird seemed to hiccup. It looked like the flames took a short, deep breath and then spat the man out onto the desert sand. Two other men ran up and dragged him away.

That man was Air Force Sergeant Joe Byers. He had fallen down from the burning flight deck, so terribly burned he was barely able to call for help. Jeff Houser and Paul Lowry heard Byers's faint cry. They threw their field jackets across their faces and ran back into the flames to drag him out. They had gotten him to the door, but he was deadweight and they had to drop him to save themselves. But it seemed the fire didn't like Joe's flavor and spit him out. What incredible luck.

One of our mates, Frank MacAlyster, was sound asleep when the plane detonated. He woke up to a furiously burning aircraft and people diving out the jump door. In his confusion, Frank thought we had taken off while he was asleep and had been hit by something in flight. His first thought had been "Where are the parachutes?" And his next thought, "Where are those fools going?" But he couldn't stay in the furnace of the plane so he launched himself out the door in a hard-arched skydiving position and, after a half-second of free fall, slammed into the ground. Several days later, I asked him what he'd thought he was going to do once he was out of the plane without a parachute. He answered, "One problem at a time, Sarge. One problem at a time."

By now the plane was almost consumed. The munitions inside

were cooking off and the two Redeye antiaircraft missiles we carried had launched themselves out into the night sky. I thought we were under ground attack and that the plane had been hit by rocket-propelled grenades. Trying my best to look dead, I was lying with the right side of my face in the dirt, watching with my left eye, with my right arm and .45-caliber pistol tucked underneath my body. I figured I'd wait like this for the ground assault force to come sweeping around the tail of the remains, let the first wave of troops go past me hoping they weren't shooting the dead, then kill the last one and take his rifle. With a bit of luck I might get a machine gunner.

While I was running this through my mind, out of the corner of my eye I saw my close friend, J. T. Robards, come running over. He dropped to the ground and threw an arm over me. "You all right?" he asked. "I thought you were dead."

"Yeah, J.T. I'm fine. Just playin' possum," and I told him my intention.

"Wrong answer, Bubba," he replied. "We aren't under attack. The damn chopper hit us. Look." He pointed to the wreckage. That's when I finally noticed what was left of the helicopter on top of the plane, just as the whole flaming mass started to collapse.

We got to our feet and started moving away. Other survivors of the collision were moving back toward where the other planes had been, calling, "Get aboard, the planes are taking off."

It was no joke. They were taking off.

"Should we destroy the helicopters?" The crews had abandoned them and were nowhere to be seen.

"No, they're going to call in an air strike to take care of them, just get on the planes!"

By now, a half-dozen of us had linked up and were chasing after a taxiing C-130. But as we drew nearer, it closed its ramp and picked up speed, blinding us in its dust as it rolled for takeoff. J.T. yelled and pointed, "That's the last one. We have to catch it!"

And then I could see it through the dust. Someone was shining a light off the back of the ramp, searching back and forth across the desert.

We ran to that light as hard as we could. The plane was picking up speed for takeoff. As we got close to the ramp of the moving plane, I saw Rodney Headman hanging off the back, held at the knees by Logan Fitch. He was sweeping the desert with his headlamp, looking for strays. I was the last man dragged aboard just as the ramp closed and the plane moved into takeoff position.

Damn. I was back aboard another fuel tanker! But anything was better than being left behind. On the takeoff run, we plowed straight across the dirt berm running along the roadway, bounced five feet into the air, smashed back down, but continued to gather speed until finally we were airborne.

But where were all our teammates? Bill and I were together.

"When did you last see Mike and Chris? Did they make it out?"

"I think so. They were both in front of me but I didn't see them outside."

"Did anyone else see them?"

Everyone was looking for missing teammates. The plane had been consumed in less than a minute and it had been impossible to know where everyone went. We got a list of those aboard our plane and gave it to the crew chief, asking that it be relayed to the other planes and that they do the same. He said he would do it when things settled down a bit.

Don Feeney and Keith Parsons were taking care of the injured air crewman. His hands had been burnt to claws and his face and head were charred and in pretty bad shape. To cool him down they poured canteens of water over his flight suit, which was so hot it steamed when the water hit it. But he survived. His worst injuries were to his lungs. Thanks to reconstructive surgery, a year later his hands looked fairly normal.

Jesus Hotel Christ! This had been some night. Things had come apart like a two-dollar shirt. Daylight was coming on rapidly and we were still a long way from friendly territory. How much worse was it going to get? Well, there was nothing I could do about any of it right now. I was just a passenger again, so like any good soldier, I curled up on top of the bladder and went to sleep.

I came awake to shouting.

"What the hell's going on now?" I asked.

"The loadmaster said we're low on fuel and may not make it back. We're going to lower the ramp and throw out pumps, hoses, and anything else we can shove out of the plane. Maybe we can at least make it to the Persian Gulf and ditch her near a Navy ship!"

That's just great. Really what we needed to top off this extravaganza. I couldn't remember anyone ever surviving a C-130 ditching. This last act was going to be a real crowd pleaser.

We threw out everything we didn't need to keep the plane in the air and hoped it would be enough. It was. We made it back to Masirah Island. I heard later that when the engines finally shut down, there was no measurable fuel in the tanks.

Once on the ground, we took stock. Everyone in the squadron was still alive—a real gift after what had happened. Most of us were scorched—Jeff and Paul more than anyone else—but none of us were terribly burned.

But what about the air crews?

Three Marines dead in the chopper. The pilot and the copilot had escaped unharmed. Five killed on the flight deck of the C-130. Only two had escaped from up front, both badly burned.

What the hell happened?

That's when we found out that as the last chopper finished refueling, she had lifted off to move away. But the pilot became disoriented in the dust cloud and drifted too far to the right, so the blades of the helicopter had slashed through the top of the C-130. This pulled the chopper on top of the plane at its left wing root. At the impact, the huge auxiliary fuel tank in the cargo bay of the chopper exploded, bathing the plane in burning fuel. The plane's spinning props spread fuel all over itself, assisting in its own immolation.

Beckwith gave the order to go aboard a C-141 that was waiting to carry us back to Egypt. From there we would make it back to the States and think of something else. It was a sad, quiet, introspective flight.

When we arrived in the States, we trans-loaded to a couple of C-130s for the short hop to our CIA site. All of B Squadron sat in the aft part of our plane for takeoff. The loadmaster waved his arms and yelled that half of us had to move forward, but we told him to go to hell. No one was about to budge from a seat near those life-saving jump doors.

Back at camp, we lounged in our hideaway while the controversy of the failed attempt raged on outside. This was the beginning of the frenetically dramatized news coverage that is now so much a part of our national being. And as we watched and listened to the television commentators endlessly chewing the event, I remarked to J.T., "Man, we were the ones who caused all this."

One Sunday morning, President Carter came to visit us. Up until then, he had been a remote figure, but following his visit, we became very fond of him and had a lot of respect and affection for the man. He told us he accepted full responsibility for what had happened and that there would be no witch-hunts as far as we were concerned.

But there was a funny little side note to the President's visit. Carter was accompanied on his trip by Zbigniew Brzezinski, the President's national security adviser. The President walked through our assembled ranks, speaking with us individually, and Brzezinski followed along in his wake. That's when we noticed that Brzezinski, though dressed in a business suit, was wearing a pair of bright green, high rubber boots, the kind you wear for mucking out stables or slopping hogs.

My mate, Branislav Urbanski, was on my immediate right, and as Carter stopped to speak with me I could hear Brzezinski and Branislav chatting in Polish. After the politicos had departed I asked Brani what he had said to his compatriot. He replied with delight, "I asked Brzezinski why he was wearing those stupid-looking boots, and he told me, 'The President called me just a few minutes before we left Washington and said, "I want you to come with me, we're going to the farm." And I thought...'" (The CIA site we were using is nicknamed "The Farm.")

When we finally returned to Fort Bragg, we were told to go away—to disappear for two weeks—and then call in for instructions. Until then, we were to lie low, avoid the press, and relax. And that's just what I did. With a fishing pole, a small boat, and nineteen fat Georgia bass the first day.

DEATHS AT DESERT ONE
25 April 1980

MARINE CORPS

Staff Sergeant Dewey L. Johnson,
Dublin, Georgia

Sergeant John D. Harvey,
Roanoke, Virginia

Corporal George N. Holmes,
Pine Bluff, Arkansas

AIR FORCE

Tech Sergeant Joel C. Mayo,
Roseville, Michigan

Major Richard L. Bakke,
Long Beach, California

Major Harold L. Lewis,
Fort Walton Beach, Florida

Captain Charles T. McMillan,
Coryton, Tennessee

Captain Lyn D. McIntosh,
Valdosta, Georgia

AFTERMATH

It's a terrible thing to be part of a failure. It doesn't matter if the failure wasn't due to anything you did or didn't do—you still didn't accomplish the mission and that's a wretched, bitter, hateful thing to bear. Fault? Fate and bad luck played their part, certainly.

But it is important to realize that we have the ability to manufacture our own fate when we want to. We can summon up intestinal fortitude and proceed when things look bad, or we can find plenty of reasons to quit if we don't want to go forward.

A sufficient number of the helicopter crews elected to quit, and that is what doomed the mission. Crashing a helicopter into the C-130 while B Squadron was aboard was just icing on the cake.

Colonel James H. Kyle, USAF (Retired), the Air Force commander for the operation, takes a close look at the Air portion of the mission in his superb book *The Guts to Try* (Orion Books, 1990).

His conclusion:

> It is my considered opinion that we came within a gnat's brow of success. Despite all the obstacles, frustrations and human failings and bad luck, despite all this, we were on the brink. We were there, we had the combat-savvy commandos of Delta Force within spitting distance of our objective. I knew Charlie [Beckwith] and his men—their attitudes, their skills, their competence, and their leadership—and I have no doubt that if we could have gotten them to Tehran, they would have pulled it off. There is also ample

evidence from former hostages interviewed that suggests that the
rescue attempt would have been successful. Think about it! All
that was lacking was the guts to try.

That's a pretty severe indictment, but one I also believe to be true.
So what was the outcome of all this?

Well, of course there was the inevitable blue-ribbon panel char-
tered to review the operation, to determine the reasons for its failure
and make recommendations to set those problems right.

This particular panel was called the Holloway Commission, in
honor of its chairman, retired Admiral James L. Holloway. And the
commission ably performed its primary mission: protecting the
active-duty admirals who had insisted that the helicopters *had* to be
Navy, and that there would be *no* changes even when it was clearly
known those Navy helicopters *weren't* working out.

But some positive things did grow out of the failed mission. One
was something Colonel Beckwith had been lobbying for all along: a
permanent Joint Special Operations Command (JSOC) that could
pull together and oversee the Special Operations efforts of the various services. JSOC was soon instituted, but its command only had
jurisdiction over counterterrorist operations.

The second positive outgrowth—and to us in Delta Force, the
most important one—was the formation of an Army Special Operations aviation group. That organization was initially known as Task
Force 160 and eventually evolved into the 160th Special Operations
Aviation Regiment—the "Night Stalkers" of today. They are one
badass aviation outfit, able to operate at night and under all weather
conditions anywhere in the world. They are a dedicated, highly proficient, and absolutely courageous bunch of flyers. They are to aviation what Delta Force is to commando operations.

A third result of the failed raid was that we started writing things
down. Up until then, Beckwith had been adamant that nothing
should be committed to paper. This meant that all lesson plans,
training documents, and materials pertaining to Selection and in-
house training consisted of nothing more than cryptic notes on
scattered scraps of paper.

But B Squadron—fully one half of the unit—had come within
an eyelash of perishing in the Iranian desert. And with it, one hell of
a lot of hard-won institutional knowledge would have died right

along with us. So we went to work to codify everything we knew and did, and how we did it, just in case we were all killed someday and our followers had to rebuild this thing from ashes.

Last but not least, we designed and had made fire-resistant assault suits. B Squadron had almost burned to death, and historical studies showed that about 30 percent of combat casualties were the result of burns. So ever afterward, we would wear our black suits on missions of the future. In fact, the suits we originally designed have become the ideal of SWAT teams around the world.

Delta men are a pretty resilient bunch, and though no one likes to fail, we cinched up our morale, dusted ourselves off, and got ready for another attempt. At the upper command level, there was a fainthearted effort to plan a second operation to go after the hostages, but it was obvious to us that no one in Washington had their heart in the idea. It was just a case of going through the motions.

I believe the one who felt the blow hardest of all was Colonel Beckwith. He was never the same. The failure of the operation seemed to completely deflate him. I never again saw a flicker of that fabulous internal fire of his. It fled his being, never to return.

Charlie was to suffer yet another disappointment before his day was done. He labored and lobbied hard for the formation of a joint headquarters that would coordinate and oversee the Special Operations forces of all services—and he made no secret of the fact that he wanted to command that organization. Measured against any and all rational criteria, Charlie was the hands-down logical choice for the command. But it was not to be.

Beckwith's mentor and protector, General Edwin "Shy" Meyer, was retiring, and Charlie had made too many powerful enemies at the two-, three-, and four-star level to go unpunished. Enemies who knew what to do with maverick colonels. This was their opportunity to click the buttons on their switchblades, wrap themselves in the cloak of bureaucratic invisibility, and cut his tendons. And they didn't waste any time striking their cowardly blows. Charlie was finished—gutted out and left twisting in the wind. From there he just faded off into retirement.

A lot of people have asked me what kind of man Charlie Beckwith was, and it's a question I've always had difficulty answering. Colonel Charlie Beckwith was both a very complex and simple man. He was a man of extremes who lived with, commanded, and held the respect of men of extremes. When I knew him, he was a large, blustery man with a mercurial temperament.

Around the men, Charlie tended to act more like a senior NCO than an officer. His most trusted confidants were his sergeant majors. That's not to say he was overly friendly with the troops, but he did have an affinity for his "boys" that was both obvious and genuine.

He was the only field-grade officer I've ever known who would provoke rough-and-tumble verbal exchanges with his subordinates and not fall back on the protection of rank if he found himself being bested. Charlie had no respect for a pushover. He liked a good tussle and he expected to get as good as he gave. But there was never any doubt as to who was in charge—he could chew ass like an old-time first sergeant. In fact, I believe I still have some of his teeth marks in my posterior.

Charlie wasn't a subtle man, but when the occasion called for the exercise of guile, he could be as cunning as the serpent. He was also quite emotional, as he readily admitted. He was easily moved to anger or joy, and he was incapable of hiding his feelings.

He admitted that he would never be confused with an intellectual, but he wasn't a dull man. Far from it. He went to great pains to select his staff and subordinates for their mental depth and thinking abilities. He liked having intelligent people around him, he admired great thinkers, and he was a voracious reader of classical literature and history.

The colonel was a staunch advocate of the philosophy "When in charge...charge!" and he acted on it. Hence his nickname of "Chargin' Charlie." He gained a reputation in Vietnam for getting troops killed needlessly because of his impatience and his reckless disregard for danger. A lot of men in the Special Forces community even used that as their excuse for not trying out for Delta Force. Odd, but I never saw any of those guys show up for Selection after Charlie was gone.

I don't know the truth about those rumors, but knowing Colonel Beckwith, there's probably a little something to them. I do know that he was keenly hurt by the whisperings. And I know from personal experience that Beckwith felt intense responsibility and concern for the men under his command. He never stopped learning how to exercise the responsibilities of a commander and always worked to improve his leadership methods and abilities. But Charlie was also a soldier, and mission accomplishment is the first priority of a combat leader.

Charlie Beckwith was a man who truly and deeply loved America and all she stands for. A man who would do anything he believed to be right to protect our nation and its citizens. He was a moral man and held human life as the most precious thing in existence. He was utterly selfless, never spared his person, and never shirked a duty or a danger. He was a commander who wouldn't send you where he wouldn't go himself and always acted on what he thought was in the best interests of the nation, the Army, and the unit...and damn the consequences to his career.

I do not believe there was any other officer in the United States Army who had the integrity, the perseverance, and the sheer guts to do the job Charlie Beckwith did in forming and breathing life into 1st Special Forces Operational Detachment—Delta.

And at the end of a life's season, that was one hell of a harvest to bring in.

Colonel Charles Alvin Beckwith was a great American, a great commander, and a great man. He passed from this life on 13 June 1994. He is highly revered and greatly missed by his comrades.

We didn't slow up after returning to Fort Bragg. If anything, the pace accelerated. Where previously the entire energies of the unit had been focused on the Iran mission, now we started to have people scattered around the world. Some men were off with the State Department protecting ambassadors in trouble spots. Others were surveying threatened American installations in dangerous regions of the globe.

I was assigned as a member of a presidentially mandated panel charged with gauging the security posture of our nuclear weapons production chain. It was a mission that also spun off into the chemical weapons field, and I would work in both areas for several months at a time over the next three years.

However, those of us at home that summer were tasked with participating in the Holloway Commission. Our part of the charade was to perform in a CAPEX, or capabilities exercise. This is something that all flag-rank officers love. In an artificial and elaborately choreographed performance, the units demonstrate their unique talents. The skills themselves are genuine, but the ways they are shown have little resemblance to reality.

For our part, we shot targets, blew things up, and executed building assaults. We also made free-fall parachute jumps with motorcycles and, upon landing, roared past the VIP stands firing our submachine guns.

I'm sure the Navy was also putting on some type of equally bogus show. Most of it, we felt, was a joke. But the brass loved the show so much that a few years later it became an annual affair with participation by the Rangers, the Air Force's 1st Special Operations Wing (1st SOW), and the newly formed Task Force 160. The event was always staged at a place called North Field, an abandoned World War Two airfield near Orangeburg, South Carolina.

The Army gave it some silly and completely forgettable code name, but we immediately dubbed the extravaganza the "Great North Field Dog and Pony Show." Naturally, we were cautioned never to say that phrase within earshot of anyone wearing stars on their collar. We merely considered these things an occasion for the generals and admirals and their invited guests to engage in a little relatively harmless mutual masturbation. We used it to make the most of the training time it afforded. You know there's always a silver lining if you look hard enough.

Within the unit, we were divided into two Sabre squadrons. In order to maintain one squadron ready for immediate deployment anywhere in the world in response to a terrorist incident, we instituted a program known as "Bowstring."

The squadrons rotated on and off Bowstring in roughly thirty-day cycles. While on Bowstring, the squadron stayed at Fort Bragg and worked on counterterrorist training tasks. The squadron on Bowstring had priority access to the Ranges and Shooting House, and could also borrow members of the other squadron if they were short on men with some critical skills.

The signal squadron provided a communications crew who stayed with the squadrons and received combat training so that they could fight if called upon to do so. When on Bowstring, you carried a beeper at all times and you couldn't travel any farther than twenty miles from Fort Bragg.

We always kicked off a Bowstring cycle by having a practice alert and a full load-out. We had a two-hour limit in which to assemble the Bowstring force, load all the equipment, weigh the loaded vehicles, and be positioned in the parking lot ready to move to Pope Air Force Base, the airfield adjacent to Fort Bragg. Everyone present for duty from the non-Bowstring squadron would come in to assist in any way possible, and be ready in case of a full deployment. It was a rare occasion if the Bowstring squadron wasn't ready to roll in seventy-five minutes.

We had a news service Teletype machine in the hallway up by headquarters, and it was monitored day and night. We never waited on notification from the powers on the Potomac but would initiate a load-out ourselves if we detected a potential incident somewhere in the world. For real incidents, we were always ready long before any decision regarding our deployment could be made in Washington.

And if a deployment wasn't ordered, at the least we had a good practice. We stayed on a "war-ready" footing around the clock, 365 days a year.

The squadron not on Bowstring picked up what we called the "Singleton" duties, taskings that required only one or two men sent out at a time. These included things such as those State Department and Department of Energy missions, or the deployment of a team on a foreign mission. We also used non-Bowstring time for troop or squadron training deployments such as arctic, or desert, or jungle training. The snipers would take advantage of the time to shoot in a rifle match somewhere or work with Secret Service or FBI snipers.

Simply put, on Bowstring you stayed close to home. When not on Bowstring, you traveled. Exceptions were long singleton missions or periods when men attended language school. But even for a language course, which could last for many months, we would hire an instructor and the men would take the course in a building we owned that was very near the Ranch. So if and when the balloon went up, those men were close at hand and could deploy with the unit.

It was a good system that met all needs. But the real meaning of an operator's existence was to be found on deployment; this was when we earned our pay. And one deployment that held much significance for me was my first trip to the ancient, historical, yet supremely dangerous city of Beirut. A place that held America's attention during the 1980s like a throbbing toothache.

Dan Simpson, our troop sergeant, caught me as I came in from the Shooting House one afternoon.

"Eric, soon as you get your weapons cleaned, go up and see Richards at the Intel shack and get a briefing," he said. "You'll be going to Beirut to replace Feeney on S.Y. [State Department term for security assignment]." He said it nonchalantly, as if he were telling me I would be driving the range truck next week, then shot at me before we parted, "But be quick about it. We've got a volleyball game at four o'clock."

"Wilco, Dan. I'll be there."

Conditions permitting, B Squadron played volleyball every afternoon. Even when we were deployed to some skunk-hole place in the world, we took a ball and a net and poles and engineer tape to mark out a court. It was a standard part of our Bowstring equipment.

Dan was a V-ball fanatic, and it rubbed off on everyone in the squadron. The brand of ball we played was a little more intense than the normal game. I am reminded of that by the two crooked fingers I'm using to write this. They were broken trying to block vicious smashes from one comrade or another. But the game was something we all enjoyed immensely and it was a great way to end the day.

I cleaned my weapons, locked them in my team's Ready Room, and ambled up the hallway to the Intelligence Section's offices, which were at the far end of the hall near the Headquarters area. As I passed the mess hall entrance, I remembered a little incident from a few weeks back.

I always ate breakfast in the mess hall and when I left, I'd get a cup of coffee to carry with me down to the troop bay. One morning I was walking down the hall with an overly full cup when I noticed I was dribbling coffee on the floor. Country Grimes, the unit sergeant major, had been fussing at us recently about the condition of the hallway. And being a skilled tracker myself, I knew that if I continued down the hall, I would be trailing evidence of sloth to my own area and Country would make us pay for it.

So I did the first thing that occurred to me. I increased the rate of dribble just a little bit and turned sharply into the A Squadron assault troop bay, leaving a faint trail all the way to their meeting area. I BS'd awhile with a few friends, talked about an upcoming shooting competition, and checked on their schedule to rebuild the Shooting House walls. Once I'd finished my coffee, I tossed the cup in the trash, said good-bye, and made my way to my own troop bay at the far end of the hallway.

That afternoon, I came across a team from A Squadron scrubbing the hallway floor. One of the charwomen was my buddy Jerry Knox. I stopped to talk to him.

"Damn, Jerry. What y'all scrubbing the floors for today? It's not Friday. And besides, my troop is supposed to have hall cleaning duty this week."

Jerry looked up from his mopping, and he wasn't a happy boy. "Aw hell, Eric. Somebody in the squadron dripped coffee down the hallway this morning and Country tracked him right to our troop bay. Whoever the bum was, he wouldn't own up to it so 'The Ratch' [Ratch Hanna, A Squadron's sergeant major] just picked the team whose area was closest to where the coffee trail ended and ordered them to clean the floor. Guess whose area that was?" he snarled. "If I can catch whoever did it, I'm gonna mop his ass like he was the hallway." He brandished his mop like a spear.

"Dang, Jerry. I don't blame you for being mad," I said with neighborly concern. "But I don't want to hold you up, 'cause I know it takes at least an hour to do this whole floor. I'll catch you later."

"Yeah," he growled, stabbing his mop back in the bucket and sloshing soapy water over the sides and onto the floor.

Ah, the pleasantries of a communal domestic life, I thought as I walked away. I know it was small of me, but I was really pleased with myself. In fact, I liked my little ploy so much that I did it at least a couple of times a year for the next five or six years—and always with the same results. I never told anyone about it and was never found out. Now you know who it was, A Squadron. But it was a long time ago and I hope you hold no grudges.

The briefing was perfunctory. I would be replacing Don Feeney as the B Squadron member assigned to the protective detail for the American ambassador in Beirut, Lebanon. Carl Eastman was currently the A Squadron member of the detail. I would be working

under the cover of a State Department security agent; only the ambassador and the embassy's security staff would know I was Delta
Force. State would provide all necessary backstopping and credentials.

While at the Intel office, I also had several photos taken and
filled out the paperwork for a diplomatic passport. I could carry my
own pistols with me to Beirut; they would be pouched when I got
to Washington, and I would carry the pouch with me as an agent
acting as a temporary diplomatic courier. Other weapons were
available at the embassy, but I was advised to carry plenty of ammunition because that was in short supply.

Richards apologized for the scant information and told me I
would get a more thorough, specific briefing when I reported in to
State Department. But he did have some maps for me, and an Area
Study that attempted a chronological explanation of the headlong
rush into violence and anarchy that had taken hold of Lebanon. I
took it with me to read back in my team area.

When I left the Intel shop, I stopped next door in Admin to update my Survivor's Assistance Packet and review my will—standard
procedure whenever we left the country on a mission. Then I went
by the Medic shack to update my inoculations and see if I needed to
take any special medical precautions for the trip.

By this point in my career, I was a firm believer in keeping my
shots up-to-date. If I saw a line formed at the medic's door, I got in
it just on the suspicion they were giving out shots. Better too many
than not enough. Same thing held true for malaria pills or any other
protective and preventative medicines. Nothing is worse than getting off in some remote, disease-ridden place in the world and
becoming sick. Except, perhaps, getting shot.

Back in my team cubicle, I settled in to read the area study. I remembered stories about Beirut from an old sergeant of mine. Platoon Sergeant Art Colville had been in the Marine Corps in the
early 1950s and spoke frequently of the wonderful liberties he spent
in Beirut while with the Mediterranean Fleet. For an infantryman,
Colville was an oddity: a rough-and-tumble soldier who enjoyed
culture, the arts, good cuisine, and a refined life. He had impressed
on me that Beirut was one of the most exquisite, cosmopolitan
cities in the world—a city well worth seeing. But that was years ago,
long before her society tore itself apart.

Now Beirut was the most dangerous city in the world. It had a violent death rate of over a thousand people a month, and it was a place where Americans were the most coveted of all targets.

I was excited. Art was right, Beirut was a must-see place.

The Middle East Airlines flight from Rome came in low and fast over the coast to make itself a more difficult target for anyone below who may have been afflicted with boredom and armed with a shoulder-fired missile.

I had never seen such a sight of utter destruction as the slums and refugee camps on the southern end of the city swept below my window. It was a city in absolute ruin. It looked like the old newsreels of Berlin immediately after the Soviets had assaulted and taken the city.

As we made our final approach, I could see dozens of Russian-built Syrian army tanks, dug into the ground and ringing the airport like the beads of a deadly necklace. It was a chilling welcome, but one that prepared me for the chaos and confusion in the airport terminal—and that was mild compared to life in the city.

Don Feeney and a couple of tough-looking locals were waiting for me when I stepped off the plane. "Hey, Bo Diddley, welcome to paradise," he said with a wicked grin as he gave me a hug.

"Yeah, hi, Don. It's good to be here," I replied as I returned the *abrazo* and shifted my attention to his henchmen. Each man carried a CAR-15, the shortened version of the M-16, slung around his neck with the muzzle pointed down, his right hand on the pistol grip. I could see that the safeties were in the "on" position, but they had their thumbs on the selector switch. They looked like men who knew what they were doing. They had looked at me at first but quickly shifted their attention back to the crowd swirling around us on all sides. Donny made the introductions.

"Eric, I want you to meet the Mokdad cousins, Ali and Maher. Guys, say hello to Eric Haney. He's the man I've been telling you about. Think of him as my brother."

I shifted the diplomatic pouch to my left hand and offered my right to Ali and Maher in turn. *"Sahlam Aleikum,"* I said as I shook hands with each man and then touched the joined fingers of my hand to the spot on my breast just over my heart. They barely raised an eyebrow at the Arabic greeting, but each warmly replied, *"Wah Aleikum es Sahlam."*

Donny laughed and announced in his Sunday-best Brooklynese, "Ah, you don't need dat stuff wit dese guys, Eric. Dey speak good English, nearly as good as you 'n' me.

He was referring to my accent, not his. Donny was always going on about my Georgia hill-country dialect, which I only allowed myself to use with family or close friends. But Donny always acted like I was the one with the funny accent.

"I'm glad of that, because that's just about the extent of my Arabic vocabulary," I returned.

"That will not be a problem, Mister Eric," said Maher as an immigration official came forward to stamp my passport. We picked up my baggage and were waved around the customs checkpoint. "I believe that you will learn rapidly; you have that look about you."

We stepped out of the terminal and into a day that felt like it had been conjured from Dante's *Inferno,* hot as hell and twice as grim. If chaos had been the theme inside the terminal building, bedlam reigned in the streets outside.

Cars and vans ran in all directions with all the order of a kicked beehive. No one seemed to think there was even the hint of traffic lanes. Vehicles just drove any old place, including the sidewalks and across would-be lane dividers.

In front of the terminal there was a mound of baggage, boxes, and bundles right in the middle of the roadway. Scrambling around it was what looked like a family of twenty people, all shouting and waving their arms and trying to load the stuff and themselves into an old Fiat taxi.

At a nearby two-way intersection, five cars sat nose-to-nose, drivers and passengers alike red in the face from the effort of screaming curses and shaking fists at one another. No one made the slightest effort to untangle the mess—especially the drivers. Not one of them wanted to be the one to back up and untangle the mess. There was enough room around the car-jam to drive a train through on both sides, so the other traffic just swept around them like water swirling around a boulder in the middle of a stream. It was a sergeant major's worst vision of hell.

Donny grabbed my arm, guided me to the left, and, as he led

the way to a stationary vehicle that presented the only visible place of calm in the midst of swirling turmoil, shouted, "Here's our car."

Our car was a big black, early 1970s Chevrolet Caprice that looked like a fugitive from *The Dukes of Hazzard*. Its front bumper had been fashioned from a railroad tie, and the body looked like it had been used in one of those high school football booster fund-raisers, where people pay a dollar to whack an old car three times with a sledgehammer. It was outfitted with what looked like truck tires, and there were bullet holes scattered down the right side and across the lid of the trunk. (There were also holes in the left side, but I didn't see those until later.) The glass in the side windows had been replaced with two-inch-thick Plexiglas with portholes cut in each one to shoot from. But in spite of her battered appearance, that old Chevy was clean and waxed and she shined in the bright Mediterranean sun like a diamond in a goat's ass.

The driver saw us coming. He stepped to the rear of the vehicle and gave the trunk a solid kick, then took one pace back and watched it pop open. The Mokdad cousins threw my stuff in the trunk, and the driver had to slam the lid twice to get it closed again. He looked up at me with a broad smile that gave a panoramic view of his gleaming white teeth. As I put out my hand and started to re-cite my one Arabic salutation, he slapped the palm of my out-stretched hand, snapped his fingers in the air between our faces, and said in clear, idiomatic English, "What it is, my man!"

I was so startled by the greeting that I almost took a step back-ward. Then I laughed, returned the "five," and asked, "What's your name and where are you from, brother?"

"Abdo's the name, bodyguard's the game," he laughed. "And I'm from right here in Beirut. But I'm also an L.A. man—and no, that's not for 'lower Alabama.' I lived in California for eight years. Worked in my uncle's business back there," he said as we got in the car and he began an aggressive entry into the maelstrom of hurtling motor vehicles.

Don talked and pointed as we made our way through the devas-tated city. "This is Chevy Circle, one of the main landmarks in this part of town. It has the only functioning traffic light in the city, but you can see how much attention anybody pays to it. It's as useless as tits on a boar hog."

I did, indeed, see the irrelevance of the light. The only way our passage through the intersection differed from that of the other cars was that our bodyguards brandished their weapons at the other motorists and thus won us a slight advantage in negotiating the vehicular shoals. Don continued his monologue as I took in the scenery.

"The city is divided between Christian East Beirut and Muslim West Beirut. The border between the two areas is called the Green Line—I don't know why, because there's nothing green anywhere near the line. It's just a strip of rubble between the two sides.

"There are three main crossing points between the different sides of town. Up north along the waterfront is the Port Crossing. Farther south is Sodeco and then Gallery Simone. The Port Crossing is almost always open, but the other two are usually blocked. The different militias that control the areas around the crossings use bulldozers to push up big mounds of sand and rubble to keep vehicles from getting through, and snipers shoot at anyone on foot. But don't take that part about 'snipers' too literally. They ain't snipers by our standards. They're just assholes who shoot at unarmed people. The people they kill most often are poor women out trying to buy food for their families.

"Every once in a while they announce that Sodeco or Simone will open on such and such a date, and the Syrian army comes in and clears the crossing. They stick around for the rest of the day, and the next day the shooting starts all over again. It's always innocent people who are hurt and killed." He shook his head in disgust at the stupidity of it all.

"The reason the crossings are important to us is that while the embassy is in West Beirut—which is also called Ras Beirut—the ambassador's residence is in the east, up in the hills of Yardze."

He saw my objection coming and waved it off.

"Yeah, yeah, I know. It doesn't make any sense, but that's the way it is. The Presidential Palace is just up the hill from the residence, and the ambassador thinks it's important to stay there. He wants to make the statement that the United States is impartial about the local squabble and that we *can* and *will* go wherever we please, when we please.

"As I said, the Port Crossing is almost always open. But even when it's iffy, we can usually force our way through. The militias that control the area around the port are fairly small and weak. But we get shot at every time we go through there—and that's at least twice a day."

"Yes," interjected Abdo with a laugh, "but the man who is usually on duty there has poor eyesight and is a very bad shot."

"That's true," Donny went on, "but we *have* been hit there a few times. At least they only use rifles. When Billy Oswalt was here, he was ambushed one morning near Yardze with machine guns and a rocket launcher."

"That was an interesting morning," said Abdo, nodding his head thoughtfully.

I had talked to Bill about that attack. The motorcade had been hit when it was at its slowest and most vulnerable point—a hairpin curve coming down the mountain. The limo's armor had stopped the machine gun rounds from penetrating to the inside, and fortunately, the guy firing the rocket launcher had flinched and fired low (just like the Ranger at Desert One). So the warhead hit the pavement under the body of the limo, skipped out the other side, and detonated in an olive grove. Also by good fortune, the shooters had targeted the limo and not the lead or follow cars; had they immobilized those two vehicles and blocked in the limo, they could have opened it up like a big steel barrel. You *can* penetrate an armored limousine, but first you have to bring it to a halt.

The perpetrators of the ambush were a Christian militia that was supposedly friendly with the United States. It was later rumored they were pissed with the CIA over some sort of funding or arming dispute, and decided not to bottle up their anger and run the risk of becoming depressed. An ambush is usually a pretty good tonic of catharsis.

Bill's postscript on the attack was "Allah was certainly most merciful and gracious that day."

Donny resumed his tour guide act.

"We never use any of the main crossings except the Port; the other two are just too dangerous. If everything is closed, the guys know some really back-street routes that some of their friends in the militias will crack open for a few minutes. But as you can see, in spite of all the rules of common sense, our movements are very restricted. And that's just in relation to the crossings over the Green Line. On either side of the Line—and in any part of the city—fights are always breaking out between neighboring militia groups.

Between militias and the Syrians. Between the Syrians and the Christians. And there are long-distance artillery and rocket contests between the Christians and the Muslims and the Syrians and sometimes, everybody.

"Then to add fuel to the fire, the Israelis bomb the place whenever they get bored. Just for shits and grins they'll put a party of Arab-speaking agents ashore to set up a roadblock, just like all the militias do, but in this case, they're checking papers for Palestinians. And when they find them, they haul 'em out and execute them. In fact, the last two times they did that they rented the cars they used from an agency just across the street from where we live. When the Palestinians found the agency, they burned the place out."

I had been taking in everything Donny said as we wound our way generally north by one helluva convoluted path. Sometimes we were on a wide, modern, multilane *autopista,* and sometimes Abdo would maneuver us through some of the most wretched urban trails I've ever seen. Donny and Abdo argued occasionally over which route to take, but the one constant, no matter where we were, was the destruction on every side. I had yet to see a building that was unscathed. The shops that were still functioning could be discerned by the multilayered sandbag walls and baffled entrances protecting their fronts. Other places were just gutted shells.

"We'll go by the embassy first and open your pouch," said Donny. "I've also got the rest of the bodyguards standing by there to meet you. You'll like the boys. They have an attitude that'll make you think they're from Georgia. You know what I mean, they like to take naps under a shade tree and shoot at things when they're awake."

He chuckled at his little cross-cultural joke. "After that, we'll go by the hotel and get you situated. If we still have time before it gets dark, we'll go up to Yardze so you can see the place and meet the guys on duty up there. Carl is there now, spending the night at the compound. We have an apartment on the grounds of the residence and one of us always stays there at night and on the weekends. You'll like that part of the duty. It's quiet up there, the air is clean, and you can use the pool. Now, here's the embassy."

Throughout the last part of our journey, we had been traveling along a wide boulevard fronting the Mediterranean. When we pulled into the front entrance of the embassy, it was very evident the building had originally been a luxury hotel. A wide portico covered the semicircular drive that brought traffic off the main street, named JFK Boulevard, and exited onto a large side street leading uphill past the French embassy to the main "downtown" thoroughfare, Hamra Street. I was aghast at the absence of security at the embassy's entrance. Any vehicle could just whip right in and pull up to the front of the building.

Donny saw my concern.

"Eric, I know what you're thinking: no barriers, no checkpoint, just a couple of doormen out front. Any old punk could just breeze right in here and wreak havoc. And you're right. And you can argue with the State Department until you're blue in the face about it, but their position is"—he pointed his nose and little finger in the air and parodied a blue blood accent—" 'An American embassy should have an open and inviting appearance that signifies the openness and inclusion of American society.' "

He dropped the phony accent and snorted in disgust. "But I don't shut up about it. I put it in a report to the RSO [regional security officer] and the ambassador every week, and I'm gonna put it in my report when I get back to the States and I expect you'll do the same thing. This ain't Paris or London, and not putting proper security in a place with the threat we got here is downright criminal. Sooner or later, somebody's gonna get killed."

That, unfortunately, turned out to be not just an accurate assessment of the situation but a terribly prophetic pronouncement.

After we plucked my "tools" out of the pouch, Donny gave me a tour of the building and showed me the Security offices and the three routes to the ambassador's suite of offices. Then we went to the basement to meet the ambassador's staff of local bodyguards. Or at least the Muslim staff. Because it was hard for Muslims to cross to the East Side and for Christians to cross to the West—and also because of some animosity on the staff—the local bodyguards were mostly segregated by religion. The Christian members of the force guarded the residence at Yardze and the Muslim members made up the bodyguard detail and embassy guards.

There was one notable exception to this division of labor, and he was a most notable man—an Armenian Christian named Cesar, who was both a bodyguard and motorcade driver. Armenians are ubiquitous throughout the Middle East, and Cesar, like so many of his countrymen, was not only a courageous man but one who didn't give a whit of thought to Christian/Muslim friction. Also, like so many of his countrymen, he had flaming red hair and blue eyes.

I've protected ambassadors, presidents, princes, princesses, CEOs, celebrity prisoners, and the offspring of all of the above, and the one constant in this line of work is that you must keep the relationship completely businesslike and at arm's length. If you become emotionally engaged with the Principal, you start making compromises that will eventually cause harm to the very person you are supposed to be protecting. I've never wanted to be buddies with the person I'm protecting. I don't require their friendship. The only thing I need or want is a civil and professional relationship.

But it's a different story with the local-national bodyguards on a protective detail. The relationship you have with these men is the same kind of relationship you'll find in a combat squad or team. Not only do you depend on these guys to get the job done, but more often than not, you depend on them for your very life. I probably would not have lived through that tour in Beirut if it had not been for those local bodyguards, and I came to love them.

When I first met my local comrades, they were lounging in the basement Ready Room. I have to say they were the most intimidating group of characters any potential foe could hope (or fear) to meet. I'm not saying they were piratical-looking or disfigured or even ugly—far from it. In fact, the Lebanese, both men and women, are one of the most handsome nationalities on earth, and these men were no exception. They had such an air of competence, determination, and self-confidence that they projected an almost visible aura of controlled, intelligent, and disciplined power.

These were sixteen tough, capable men who, day in and day out, had been handling an extremely hazardous undertaking in the most dangerous spot on the planet. You just didn't survive in that job unless you were very, very good. And as I was to find out, these men were very, very good.

I introduced myself around the room. I had already met Abdo and the Mokdad cousins, and as I circled the room and greeted each man, I knew I had fallen in with good company.

The two shift leaders were Mahmoud Boutari and Mustafa Kridieh, and they were about as different as any two Levantines can possibly be. Boutari was of medium height and built like an all-conference tackle. He had a bull-like voice and could wield it like a weapon when he needed to, but otherwise he was a rather professorial type of man. His appearance was European, his French was immaculate, and his English was very good. He took care of all the administrative needs for the detail and was the man who knew everybody who was anybody in the city. He also took his place in the protective detail every day.

Mustafa looked like a Bedouin and had a slender build and a sly, well-oiled sense of humor. But there was also an undeniable sense of authority about him, and his word was always the final one, no matter what the circumstance or the situation. His English was okay, and he made it a point to work with me every day on my Arabic. As he explained, one day I might find myself alone and have to depend on words to get out of a bad situation. And since half of the detail understood very little English, I needed to know how to give commands in Arabic during an emergency. Mustafa also had an infallible sixth sense, and when he smelled trouble, it was always just over the horizon.

Mohamed Al-Kurdi drove the advance vehicle, and by any standard, he was a bona fide character. It was his job to find us the safest and best routes through the city, and he was a master at it. Had Mohamed been in Hollywood during the 1930s, he would have been a natural as a swashbuckling matinee idol. He looked like a darker, more muscular, and slightly sinister version of Errol Flynn. He lived in a room in the basement of the embassy, where he composed poetry late into the night for the women he met during the day. He was as persistent as he was prolific. But in his basement sanctuary, he was fairly safe from irate husbands, fathers, and fiancés who didn't appreciate his style of verse. His radio call sign was "Eisenhower," and he thought of himself as the commander-in-chief.

Maher Mokdad became my right-hand man and was someone I depended on greatly. At twenty-two, he was the youngest man on the detail, but he demonstrated an uncanny maturity. He was very intelligent (he had taught himself English), well built, and had the startling amber eyes of a lion. He was from Baalbek in the Bekaa Valley, a place well known throughout the Middle East for courageous men, and Maher was a champion of his race. He taught me the small personal wisdom of picking a lime at the residence every morning and keeping it in my shirt pocket. Whenever the foul smell of the city became too much, I could squeeze the small green fruit and rub its oil on my nose and lips, where the sweet, clean scent would banish the stench of death for a while. To this day, my favorite scent is that of a small, freshly picked lime.

I became very close to Saleem Tamim. To use another Hollywood metaphor, if you were casting the handsome and dashing warrior sheik, Saleem would be your first pick. I could always count on him for wise counsel and pertinent guidance—often delivered via a talent he uniquely possessed. Saleem was perfectly able to communicate complex thought, give commands, and ask questions using only the movement of his eyebrows and facial expressions—and it worked across any language barrier. It was unreal, but seemed so natural that I only realized he was doing it after I had worked with him for several weeks.

A few of the guys stretched my leadership skills on occasion, and now and again we would all fall into some rip-roaring arguments. But that was only natural, and even when we disagreed among ourselves, or when someone questioned my methods in a particular situation, it was always about technique and not the principle of the matter. We all wanted the same thing—to do the best job we could to protect our ambassador—and stay alive while we did it. And if a man's not passionate about his work in that kind of job, then he has neither his heart nor his mind in the right place.

After introducing me to the bodyguards, Donny took me to our home in the Hotel Charles, which was located about six blocks from the embassy and less than half a block from the Green Line. The owner, a man named Charlie, wasn't in, so we went directly to our suite on the floor just below the penthouse. We could see a good portion of the northern part of the city from the apartment balcony, so Donny pointed out the sights. A couple of hundred meters to the east, right smack in the middle of the Green Line, was the old Holiday Inn.

If you remember any of the news footage of the civil war in Lebanon, you might recall scenes of the constant fighting for control of the Holiday Inn. It was the tallest structure in the area and sat on a strategically commanding spot, which made it a focal point of fighting, much like the Tractor Factory was in Stalingrad during the Second World War.

The building was shattered and riddled with holes caused by everything from rifles and machine guns to mortar and artillery fire. But it was still standing and it was still a hot spot. Donny warned me never to stand in front of the little window over our kitchen sink, because machine gun fire from the Holiday Inn would occasionally hit the wall on our side of the building and a "Seeing Eye Round" would come uninvited through the window and into the kitchen. They had actually lost two refrigerators to gunfire in the last month. He also told me with some relish that it would be a good idea to wash dishes crouched on the floor, especially for someone as tall as I am. He seemed to think the vision of that was hilarious.

From the apartment we could see downhill and along the shoreline to the Port, the nearby Hotel George, and the Syrian army positions along the northern part of the Green Line. I was warned to watch out for the Syrians; they tended to shoot first and not bother to ask questions. They weren't particularly vicious, but they were in the unenviable position of attempting to keep the peace in the city—and peace had fled this place years ago. By all accounts, the nearest place peace could be found was on the island of Cyprus, and even there it kept a low profile.

Then he pointed out the locations in the surrounding neighborhoods occupied by the different military and militia groups, and the corners where they usually set up their checkpoints. Just below us, between the hotel and the waterfront, was a small group known as the Nasserites who revered the late Egyptian President Gamal Abdel Nasser. They even had a statue of him on a street corner.

Right next to the Hotel George was the "Garbage Dump Gang," which controlled the approaches to the port and the garbage dump that had formed on a spit of land next to the hotel. Donny said they sort of reminded him of the sanitation workers' union back home in New York. Back to the west and just up from the waterfront was a group called the Morabi Tuun, a small group that made up for their lack of size by sheer viciousness.

At the approaches to the Green Line were first the Syrians and then the Lebanese army checkpoints. In the Green Line itself were refugees who had fled the fighting in other parts of the country and had homesteaded the rubble of no-man's-land. If you elected to live in the Green Line, the ground zero of fighting in Beirut, it had to be really bad where you came from. The Green Line militia didn't bother anyone; they just tried to keep out other squatters and claim-jumpers.

On the other side of the line was the monolithic Christian militia, the Falange, the strongest of all the different groups. The Falange were supplied, equipped, and funded by the Israelis. For some unknown reason—perhaps just the arrogance of power—they were the only ones who liked to screw with our freedom of movement. They could be downright hostile and often tried to cause trouble with the ambassador's motorcade.

Closer to home was the local militia, which controlled the neighborhood surrounding the Hotel Charles and the area extending to the United States embassy. In English they were known as the PSP, which stood for the "People's Socialist Party." Even though they were generally a pretty quiet bunch, they went unmolested by the adjacent militias and didn't allow the Syrians to operate in the neighborhood, which was quite a feat in itself. The headquarters for the group was at a coffeehouse on the Corniche (waterfront boulevard).

Donny told me that Abdo lived in the neighborhood and that I should get him to introduce me to the leaders of the PSP group. From the way he talked (as well as the things he didn't say) I got the impression Donny may have had some type of run-in with the PSP. Not unusual. Donny usually inspired strong feelings in the people he met, and those feelings weren't always affectionate. But it wasn't anything he worried about, and whenever he had a negative reaction from someone, he brushed it off with an appropriate Brooklyn street saying—something along the lines of "Fuck 'em if they can't take a joke!"

We called the embassy, and Abdo and the Mokdads came to pick us up for the trip to the ambassador's residence. From our hotel we swung downhill to the waterfront, and in just a few minutes, we were negotiating the passage of the Green Line. First we went through a Syrian army checkpoint, where they recognized the car and waved us through. Next was the Lebanese army position. The soldiers there stayed within their sandbagged position as one guy stuck an arm out of the bunker's aperture and motioned us to continue on.

Then we were into the Port itself.

On the left was the harbor and its wharves with sunken cargo ships that had been caught in the fighting, rendering the facility unusable. To the right were huge stacks and jumbled heaps of old shipping containers, where Maher said the shooting generally came from. Abdo floored the old Chevy just as the road we were on headed through the middle of a large warehouse, and we punched in one side and straight out the other. As it penetrated the warehouse, the flanks of the roadway were hedged in by containers stacked from the floor to the ceiling, making passage through the building feel like hurtling down a narrow canyon. Emerging into the sunlight on the other side, we flew past another Lebanese army position and then we were in Christian East Beirut.

"Get ready," Donny said. "If there's going to be any shit, it will be here."

At this point, the road was hemmed in on each side by a triple row of oil barrels filled with sand. This barrel channel took us through a tight S-turn that brought us to the first barricade manned by the Falangistas.

It was an impressive series of mutually supporting positions. There was the checkpoint itself, where vehicles were stopped and given a look-see, backed up by sandbagged positions on either side of the roadway that were just out of hand grenade range. Fifty meters farther, there was a sandbagged .50-caliber machine gun position mounted on the roof of a two-story building.

Each spot was manned by four men armed with M-16s. The men in the positions were fully uniformed and wore steel helmets with the chin straps in place—they were on full alert. The troops manning the checkpoint itself wore armored vests. We weren't stopped, but the men were deliberately slow about swinging the barrier and letting us through. I nodded to the man at the steel gate, and he returned my nod of acknowledgment with a curled-lip sneer.

In contrast to the militia checkpoints on the West Side, with all their yelling and carrying on, it was quiet as we made our way through, but the cold eyes of the Falange soldiers never left us. Nor did the muzzle of that .50-caliber machine gun. I didn't like the feeling of the place at all, but I could admire the discipline, structure, organization, and depth of force evident here. A firm, intelligent leadership was demonstrably in charge on this side of the city.

We all relaxed after we made it through the Christian check-point, and the spirit in the car lightened noticeably. Abdo started singing as we rocketed down a wide, clean boulevard, and the Mok-dads joined in with him.

That's one of the things I enjoy whenever I work with Arabs. They love music and like to sing whenever the mood strikes. Within a month I knew several of the songs and could join in even though I knew very little of the meaning of the words. But I did know the joy of life and living that was expressed in the songs, and that was the important thing.

Soon we started to climb into the foothills of the Shouf Moun-tains. Donny pointed out the "kiss-your-ass" curve where the motor-cade had been ambushed. It was the perfect spot for an attack, one I would have selected myself.

At an intersection, we turned uphill again and followed a sweep-ing curve around the crest of a hill that took us past the Presidential Palace. Abdo stopped the car, and we surveyed the scenery below and in front of us.

Just down the hill were the grounds of the ambassador's resi-dence. The surrounding area was rural and mostly open country, with scattered pockets of brush and the occasional small grove of olive trees. The terrain in front of us sloped down to the bottom of a wide valley five or six hundred meters to the west. From there the landscape became urban again and marched in a stair-step series of terraces up the next hill where the tortured scar of the Green Line could be seen, snaking its way north to south along the crest of the high ground about two miles in the distance.

Behind us the ground rose toward the east until it climbed into the mountain chain that separated the coastal region of Lebanon from the Bekaa Valley. After my general orientation, we got back into the car and, two minutes later, pulled into the gates of the resi-dential compound.

I caught up with Carl while Donny and the guys went to the kitchen to find their friend Josephine, the cook, to see if they could sweet-talk her into cooking us something to eat.

"It's good to see you, Carl," I said as we greeted one another, "but damn, brother, you've lost some weight since you've been here, haven't you?"

"Man, tell me about it. I got a case of the Beirut Belly last month and it damn near did me in. Lost over twenty pounds, all showered out my posterior aperture. And, buddy, I can tell you it just ain't fun.

"I caught it from drinking a glass of tap water in our apartment," he said. "I usually know better, but I woke up one night with a terrible thirst and before I thought about what I was doing, I went to the kitchen and downed a glassful from the sink."

He shifted in his chair as if the memory still hurt him.

"The city has been pounded so hard that the sewer lines and the water lines are broken and the stuff from one gets into the other. In essence, I drank a glass of shit that night, and by the next day, it was ripping my guts apart. Horrible cramps, championship diarrhea, chills and spiking fevers, night sweats, fatigue that made me feel like a sack of Jell-O. I had days when I would've had to get better to feel good enough to die—and I had to work through it all. But I'm okay now, even if my clothes don't fit.

"But my advice to you, my friend, is: 'Never drink the water!'" We laughed as we said the refrain at the same time.

As we walked the grounds, Carl filled me in on the work schedule. "The guy who stays the night up here is the detail leader the next day. The limo and the follow cars spend the night here, and the lead and advance cars take the guys and go back to the embassy. They return with the detail the next morning, and the show starts all over again.

"Both of us work the detail all day, every day, and we rotate duties as shift leader and detail leader. As you know, the detail leader works the Old Man and the shift leader handles the guys and the cars."

"How about the State Department guys?" I asked him. "What are they doing?"

Carl thought a few seconds before he answered.

"Eric, the RSO and the two ARSOs [assistant RSOs] pretty much leave us alone to run the protection. They're all good guys but they aren't really keen on this whole thing. And besides, that's why we're here. Mike and William, the ARSOs, take their turns staying the night here at Yardze. When it's a big diplomatic function somewhere, they'll step in and run the detail.

"Charles, the RSO, handles the administrative side of the house and lies low. You may see him once a week and you may not. He'll show up if there is something really big going on and the news cameras are around, but other than that, he's the Invisible Man."

I started to make a smart comment, but before I could say anything, Carl held up a restraining hand. "Eric, before you get all steamed up about the division of labor, reflect on a few things. First of all, their training or background hasn't really prepared them for the situation here—but ours has. Second, they're here for a one-year tour of duty and that will wear anybody down. We're each here for seventy-five days at a time, and as the saying goes, I could stand on my head in a bucket of shit for that long—as long as I don't have to drink it." He grinned at me.

"But most important, we know how to fight when we have to and how to avoid a fight when we can. We know how to lead the locals and we like doing it, and they like working with us. It works out for everyone and all hands are happy. So be ready to work straight through for the next two and a half months. No breaks and no days off. When nothing is going on and the Old Man stays in for the day, we can each have a few hours of downtime. But one of us is always locked and loaded and ready to roll—sort of like being on Bowstring."

"Carl, I think you've just answered all my questions."

"Good," he replied, "but there's one other thing I haven't told you. When you stay up here, you have the pool all to yourself. The Old Man hates the water and only uses it for the rare barbecue and diplomatic pool party, so it's usually all ours. Come on, let me show you."

"Lead the way, my man."

How do I describe those next eleven weeks? Each day, each event, each incident, seemed a disjointed, fleeting glimpse into some sort of kaleidoscopic and Kafkaesque vision of life:

Dawn each morning, first chore of the day: sweeping spent bullets that had fallen during the night off the balcony's edge and listening to them patter into the street below.

Scrawny feral cats stalking giant rodents through mounds of garbage heaped twenty feet high on the street corners; garbage spilling into the streets, fouling whole neighborhoods with a miasmic stench.

Little boys kicking a ball, using the shell of a bombed-out house as a make-do soccer field.

Other little boys fishing with hand grenades from the water's edge in front of the embassy. Muffled explosions, geysers of water, young screams. Pulling from the water the limp and lifeless body of a ten-year-old who had dived in too close to the fishermen.

Another grenade hurled from around a street corner, skittering under our passing motorcade. A shout over the radio, a burst of speed, an explosion in the street behind us—*thank God he didn't know how to cook one off.*

Being shot at—every single day. Sometimes randomly, sometimes by mistake, sometimes by intent. Coming to be concerned only with rocket, mortar, and artillery fire. Don't sweat the small stuff.

Car tire blows out with a bang and a lurch. Heart momentarily in throat. Blowout mistaken for rocket attack. Relieved laughter all around.

Syrian soldier shows a girl that he really *can* fire the artillery piece. Round lands on beach in Christian town of Juniya. Dozens killed and wounded—mostly women and children.

Next day, retaliation. In Ras Beirut. Rockets slam into Summer Land amusement park. Dozens killed—mostly women and children. An eye for an eye. A tragedy for a tragedy.

Happy father firing AK-47 into the air in celebration of son's wedding. Hits and kills the bridegroom just as he appears on balcony with his new bride. Father kills himself in despair.

Courageous man braving sniper fire to pull wounded women out of the street. Hit in the spine and paralyzed for his effort. No one will go to his aid and the fighting swirls around him as he tries to drag his shattered body to safety.

About to shoot a carload of men waving guns and trying to pass our speeding motorcade on the shoulder of the road. Stopped at last second when Mustafa yells, "They are taking wounded men to the hospital."

American-built Israeli jets streaking in low over the water. Thundering explosions. Smoking holes where moments before, living men had manned anti-aircraft positions.

More bombs, more explosions. Nine-story apartment complex dropped like a child's Tinkertoy building. Jets standing on their tails hurtling straight up into the sky while spitting missile-confusing flares. Others continue bombing. Flak bursting in the sky making small, random patterns of angry black clouds. Anti-air missiles flash through the sky, futilely chasing the deceitful flares.

Finally, silence.

Seconds later, the first low, keening wail of grief.

A father in mindless agony, face contorted in anguish, rushing about carrying the body of his dead child in his arms. There is no place to go. There is no one who can help. He collapses in sorrow and sobs his incomprehensible torment into the crushed remains of his darling five-year-old daughter.

Long, boring days spent standing outside while meetings take place in foreign embassies. Arranging meal and comfort breaks for the men. Rotating guard positions, some in the sun, some in the shade. Maintaining vigilance. Hopeful for quiet, always ready for the worst. Radio checks with the embassy. A welcome drink of cool water poured Bedouin-style directly into the mouth from the spout of a communal pitcher.

A favorite meal: bread, hummus, olives, mint, *Shish-Daoul,* Bekaa Valley peach. Eaten with comrades late at night from the hood of a car while standing guard outside a diplomatic function.

End of uneventful day, stopping in town on small errand for the Old Man. Caught in open on street corner in surprise artillery barrage. Shells bursting high on buildings and in the street with chest-shaking *kaa-rumps.* Shrapnel, masonry, flying glass, rend the air. Screams, running people. Fifty meters to frantic friends in engine-revving car. Oh shit, *oh shit, OH SHIT!* Doorway to doorway. "Hurry up! Hurry up!" Knocked flat by explosion—feel it, never hear it. Burning car behind me—*I was just there! Don't leave me!* Dive into backseat across the laps of friends. Car launches forward and away. Fifty meters farther, around a corner, and escape from hell.

Check self for damage. Covered in dirt, clothes torn and shredded, scraped knees and elbows, ringing ears. Feel drunk. But no broken bones, no real blood. No injuries in the car. Huge relief, rollicking laughter. "Eric, you should have seen yourself! You looked so funny running side to side with explosions all around. Then that one knocked you down and we were so scared, but you jump up again, fast like the rabbit."

Whose artillery? What difference does it make. Luck held out once again. Almost to the embassy. A loud, happy song bursts forth. The sweet, rich joy of being alive. "Goodnight, goodnight. See you tomorrow. *Baa' Salahmah.*"

Sudden gunfire at night. The pulsing red pop-pop-pop of muzzle flashes in the darkness. The crack-crack-crack of angry bullets. Lead and follow cars unleashing a storm of return fire. Motorcade blasts into seat-pressing dash of acceleration. "Is the Old Man okay? Is anyone hurt? All okay. Don't stop for nothing till we get to the embassy."

Ambassador in bed with the "Belly." A day off! Picnic in the mountains. Rich carpets over luxurious grass in the cool shade of an olive grove. Friends seated around a spread of food. Eating. Quiet laughter. Special treat—a jug of water from the sacred spring of Zam-Zam brought back from the Haj—a drink for everyone! *"Shukrahn Habibi."* Afternoon nap under an ancient tree. Contented snores. The brief illusion of normal life. Enjoyment of the moment. The city and the sea soft and hazy in the distance far below.

"It looks so peaceful and beautiful from here." If only that were true.

Time to go. Farewells. Hugs. Kisses. "Stay safe. Take care. *Alhahmdulilah.* Be well. You too. I will. We will. See you again. *In'shala.* Good-bye! Good-bye! *Baa' Sahlamah.*"

Airport pandemonium. No lines. Crowds of would-be passengers crush around the departure counter, shouting and waving tickets in the air. Sidestep to the diplomatic lounge. *Thank God for that black passport.* On the plane. Wheels up. Ground receding. "Scotch and water, thank you very much."

Overnight in Athens. Taxi ride to hotel. Puzzlement. Something peculiar? Realization: no holes in the buildings, no destruction of combat.

Sit back and relax.

Home soon.

TWO YEARS LATER

At 1300 hours on 18 April 1983, eleven Lebanese bodyguards led by Delta Force operator Terry Gilden were waiting in front of the American embassy in Beirut to take the ambassador to an appointment, when an explosive-laden truck piloted by a suicide driver careened off the adjacent side street and slammed into the embassy. The men under the portico were instantly atomized in a horrific explosion that took the face off the building.

Rick Downing, the other Delta operator, was upstairs waiting to escort the ambassador to the motorcade. He was blown from his chair, through an open doorway in the Security office, and into the hallway behind. He came to lying in the hall with his feet dangling off into open space. The office he had been sitting in was gone—along with the front half of the building.

Rick clawed his way upstairs to the ambassador. He dragged him down the back stairs to an emergency vehicle stationed in the back parking lot and whisked him to a nearby safe-haven apartment the Security section maintained.

In the resulting confusion, it took a while to determine exactly what had happened. But the first order of business was to evacuate the wounded and rescue the trapped. Rick organized and led the effort.

The final death toll of the bombing was sixty-four human souls.

The wounded and maimed were numbered by the score.

No one on either side has ever been held accountable.

SECURITY DETAIL KILLED IN THE BOMBING OF THE AMERICAN EMBASSY IN BEIRUT

18 April 1983

Cesar Bathiard, bodyguard

Sergeant First Class Terry Gilden, A Squadron, 1st SFOD—D

Ghassan Hammoud, bodyguard

Mohamed Hobeikah, bodyguard

Mustafa Kreidieh, bodyguard

Abbed Kronfol, bodyguard

Mohamed Mehio, bodyguard

Hassan Moula, bodyguard

Ali Mourad, bodyguard

Ali Najem, bodyguard

Taher Sleiman, bodyguard

Saleem Tamim, bodyguard

For many years, Beirut was to become a sort of second home for the operators of Delta Force. We chased, and sometimes we caught up with, hijacked airplanes that had started out in (or found their way to) a temporary resting spot on the tarmac of the Beirut airport. We prowled the slums and the underbelly of the city in search of kidnap victims.

But the outcome of those missions was always the same. Just as we had everything in place and a trap ready to be sprung, the "Indecision Makers" back on the Potomac would collapse into a last-second—but prolonged—case of the dithers that would inevitably prove fatal to the operation.

The plane would fly to a new location or the kidnappers would move their victims to a new hiding place, and the hunt would have to commence anew. I came to genuinely appreciate those training exercises where we had been poised in the breach position only to be called off the target just as the countdown was initiated. In the real world, it happened that way more often than not.

Beirut was a city of frustrated hopes for almost everyone intimate with the place. But at least one of our experiences with that volatile spot was 100 percent homegrown absurdity.

One morning at Fort Bragg the squadron sergeant major caught me in the hallway after lunch.

"Haney, you and Ansley report to the DCO [deputy commanding officer]. He's waiting in his office, has something for you two."

"Okay, Dan. You got any idea what it's about?"

"Something to do with Beirut, I think. Anyway you've been needing a vacation, haven't you?" Simpson was now the B Squadron sergeant major, and it was no exaggeration to say that he was the bedrock we were founded upon.

"Yeah," I replied. "But I was hoping for a quiet fishing trip on the Outer Banks."

"Well, see me when you get back—if you get back—and we'll get you squared away," he grinned.

"All right, Dan, catch you later."

The DCO, Jesse Anderson, was standing under the walkway canopy just outside the front entrance, looking at the rose garden we had planted when we formed the unit. He pulled his ubiquitous cigar from his mouth when we joined him.

"Guys, have you ever seen flowers grow the way these have?" he asked as he waved his cigar at the serrated, multihued ranks of the flower garden.

"I was on the detail that made the garden," I replied. "And I happen to know those roses were well fertilized when we planted them."

"That must have been some fertilizer y'all used."

"Yes, sir, it was."

I didn't tell him the flower bed was filled with five truckloads of muck we had hauled in from the sewage treatment plant, and that in the four years since then, those roses had never needed to be refertilized. Some things are best left unsaid.

Jesse turned his attention from the flower garden to us. "Guys, head on up to JSOC [Joint Special Operations Command] and report to the J-3 [operations officer]. He needs a couple of men who have been in Beirut recently and who know their way around.

"JSOC will provide all the coordination and support you need, but give me a call if you run into anything that gives you a headache bigger than normal."

He took a long pull on his cigar and squinted at us as he blew the smoke from the downwind corner of his mouth. "But as always—and I'm sure I don't need to tell you two this—how you handle the mission is your call."

"Right, jefe," I said as we turned to leave.

"And one other thing, men."

We stopped and waited while he took another pull on his cigar, his eyes studying our faces.

"What's that, sir?"

"Don't take no shit," he said with a quiet voice and a nod of dismissal.

"We never do," said Steve as we turned and headed for the parking lot.

"What do you think that's all about?" I asked Mustafa (my pet name for Steve) as we got in my pickup.

"Who the hell knows," he said. "But we'll find out soon enough."

We showed our badges at the front gate to the JSOC compound and then again to gain admittance into the building. A sergeant escorted us upstairs to the Operations Center briefing room. We sat kicking our heels and studying a world map on the wall for a few minutes before the J-3 arrived.

The "3" was a boyish-looking Army colonel, and when he entered the room he was practically rubbing his hands in glee. We stood and greeted him when he came in, but he sat down on the edge of a desk, motioned for us to take our seats, and looked at us with a conspiratorial smile on his face. He continued to just sit there and look at us for a few more seconds, and I had the impression that his silence was for calculated effect.

"Guys," he said, leaning forward and speaking in a theatrical whisper. "Do you think you're up for a quick trip to Beirut?"

"Yes, sir. We are. What's the mission?"

"You know that even as we speak, the Israelis are sweeping into Lebanon on a mission to crush the Palestinians." It was a statement, not a question.

"Things are rapidly heating up and we need to get a satellite communications radio into the embassy immediately, but the Beirut airport is currently unusable."

He swept on now without pause.

"So here's how we're going to do it."

I always love that *"we"* part from a staff officer.

"Tonight, you men will take the radio and your mission equipment and fly by C-141 to Sigonella Airbase in Italy. The following night, you will board a C-130 for the flight to Lebanon, where you will HALO [high-altitude, low-opening free-fall parachute jump] into the Mediterranean a few miles offshore from the embassy. You will jump from 28,000 feet—with oxygen, wearing your scuba equipment, and carrying the radio. You will swim subsurface until you run out of air and then surface swim to the shoreline in front of the embassy. Then you just climb ashore and walk right in the front entrance of the embassy like you were arriving for a party. It's as simple as that."

I had the feeling he expected us to applaud. In the Army, there's a feeling among the officers that if the mission is your idea, that's as good as actually performing it yourself.

Steve and I sat still for a few seconds pondering the matter. Then we looked at one another.

"Steve, you want me to tell him, or do you want to?"

"Allow me, Eric."

Steve shifted around in his chair. He put an elbow on his knee and a fist under his chin, and leaned forward until his face was only about a foot away from the colonel's.

Very politely, Steve said, "Sir, we're not going to do that."

The colonel jumped like he had been struck by a cattle prod. The smile vanished and so did the false familiarity.

"What the hell do you mean, you aren't gonna do that? You two will do as you're told, Sergeant!" The colonel stood up, the better to shout at Steve down the length of his imperious nose.

I stood up to leave. I'd seen this guy's type many times before. He'd happily send an entire rifle company to its death if he thought there was a Silver Star in it for him. "Come on, Steve," I said. "Let's go back to the unit. We'll get nowhere here."

The colonel rapidly resumed the mask of comradeship that had momentarily slipped from his face. "Wait a minute, guys, wait just a minute. What is it you object to? We can work something out. We can get something done."

"Colonel, look, it's the whole concept," I explained. "First of all, we do our own mission planning. Give us a tasking and *we'll* figure out how to do it. Second, everything you've proposed on the 'how-to' side of the thing sounds cool in theory but gets really complicated in real life. Night HALO drops into uncharted areas are almost always a problem. You don't know the velocity or direction of the winds and the plane almost always puts you out in the wrong place. And last but not least, the Israelis have sent too many commando and assassination teams into Beirut from boats at night. The local militias are wary and they'll shoot anything they see along the waterfront at night. And if they catch you in the water, they'll grenade hell out of you. I'm telling you, Colonel, a grenade can take all the fun out of your day."

"Well, just how would *you two* go about doing it?" He allowed contempt to come into his voice.

Steve answered immediately. "Go to D.C. and put the radio in a diplomatic pouch. Fly to Amman, Jordan, as diplomatic couriers. Take a car and driver from the embassy in Amman to the Lebanese border, where we meet a car and driver from the embassy in Beirut. Change cars and drive to Beirut. Turn the radio over to whoever wants it. Reverse the process and return to Fort Bragg. It's cheaper and faster than your proposal, and I might add, a helluva lot safer."

The colonel couldn't pass up the opening Steve had given him for one last dig at us.

"So, it's personal safety you're most concerned with. Is that it?"

Now it was my turn and I jumped in ahead of Steve. "Colonel, I'll make you a deal. You fall off the back of that C-130 ramp and swim ashore with us and we'll do it your way. Then you'll be a real hero."

He was still sputtering threats at us as we left the briefing room. Steve and I didn't talk until we were in my truck and out the gate. I was more than a little annoyed. I was upset that a full-grown colonel, a War College graduate, a man who should know better, would come up with such a harebrained scheme and expect us to be dazzled by the brilliance of it.

Steve spoke first, shaking his head and slapping the dashboard. "Too many movies, Eric. The man has watched too many movies and read too many superhero novels."

"Yeah, I know, Mustafa. But look at it from his point of view. The poor guy's only in the job for one year and he's got to make a mark of some kind. And if the only cost is the lives of a couple of jive-ass master sergeants—well, so be it. I bet he'd even have some kind words for us at our memorial service.

"I mean, after all—we're talking about something vitally important here. About a man's career and whether or not he makes brigadier general." I shouted with a whoop. "And compared to that, what are a couple of easily replaced yahoos like us? I mean, where is your sense of proportion, man?" We had a good laugh on the ride back to the Ranch, but knew we would have to pay the piper.

Jesse was expecting us when we stopped by his office to report in. He took his feet from his desk and gave us a smile that narrowed his eyes to reptilian slits in his face.

"Well, I had an interesting call from General Shukman just a few minutes ago—want to guess what it was about? Seems like somebody up at JSOC would like to see you two put against a wall and shot. You boys really know how to make enemies in medium places, don't you?"

"Yes, sir. We always do our best," I answered. I could tell Jesse was enjoying this.

He kept his eyes on us as he leaned to the side and spat a loose flake of tobacco more or less in the general direction of the trash can. "I know you do, Eric, I know you do, and that's why I sent you up there. And the general says for y'all to go ahead and do it your way and not to worry about what anybody else might think.

"But you've got to get to crackin'. You leave this afternoon. Check with Admin; they'll make arrangements for your transportation and you can draw any funds you'll need from Finance. Signal Squadron has your package ready to go. And if you need anything en route, just give us a shout. Hell, you've got a radio."

"Will do, sir. Hope we didn't cause you too much trouble with the general."

"No. Hell, boys, you made my day. Now y'all git on and I'll see you when you return." He was lighting another cigar and chuckling to himself as we headed down the hallway.

Steve and I did it our way, and it came off without a hitch. But the fishing when I got back was pretty crummy. Must have been the wrong time of the year on the Outer Banks. But it was an important peaceful interlude. All too soon, I would find myself back in Beirut on a mission that was anything but peaceful.

"The shooters don't seem to have any set schedule. Sometimes they appear several days in succession and then we won't see them again for a day or two. The only consistent facts are that they always show up in the afternoons in the same general area and always in a crowd of kids and teenagers."

I looked around at the other, drawn faces crowded into the mildew-smelling bunker as the Marine major continued his briefing.

"That last fact is what has made it so difficult for us to deal with them. When it was just lone shooters, our own snipers could handle the problem. But these guys seem to have discovered the limiting factors of our ROE [rules of engagement] and they've been taking advantage of it. They know we can't afford to cause unnecessary civilian casualties. So by firing on us from the protection of a surrounding body of children, they have us stymied.

"We can't shoot back. Our snipers have told me that even though they can probably pick each shooter out of the crowd, it's almost a certainty that the round will go completely through him and hit at least one other person. That other person is going to be a child, and that's a price we're not willing to pay.

"To this point, we've had several men wounded—fortunately none have been killed. But if this keeps up, it's just a matter of time until we lose some Marines. And I'm sure I don't have to tell you the effect this has had on morale. We were told you men had an answer for the problem. If you do, we'd be much obliged for the assistance."

The Marine major finished his soliloquy and quietly waited for an answer.

Andres and I had gotten the heads-up just a couple of days earlier about the problem facing the Marines in Beirut. At first we had been told that the Marines were having trouble with random shooters firing into their positions around the Beirut airport. That sounded screwy because the Marines have always fielded top-notch snipers. In contrast to the Army, the Marine Corps units maintain well-trained sniper teams and the Marine commanders know how to employ them. We had shot with the Marines on a number of occasions and found them to be the cream of the crop. But then we got the rest of the story, and the problem fell into place.

The Marine snipers couldn't shoot because the solid, hard-jacketed, 173-grain, military-issued round used by the Marine snipers was made for stability, accuracy—and penetration.

It was one of the first problems we had confronted when determining how to shoot into a crowded counterterrorist environment:

How do you kill one person out of a group at long range without harming anyone else? It was the principal dilemma of the "open-air assault," an attack conducted in the open when the terrorist is surrounded by, and shielding himself with, his hostages. It was a technique that had been successfully used on at least one occasion by Carlos the Jackal, the great terrorist mastermind, to transit from a building, to a bus, and then eventually to an airplane for his getaway. But we had cracked that code years ago.

The answer came in the form of a bullet that was accurate and powerful, but would stay in a human body upon impact. We had done some experimentation during our first year and had come up with rifle loads that solved the problem.

By hand-loading a round with a lightweight, lightly constructed bullet driven at a very high velocity, we got an accurate round that would dump its energy on impact so rapidly and violently, the bullet would stay in the body of the victim without exiting the other side. The trade-off with the round was that its range was somewhat limited.

Even though the bullet left the barrel at a very high speed, the same lightness that caused it to dump energy rapidly on impact also caused it to lose velocity rapidly. It performed admirably on shots to about four hundred meters or so. How did we know? After making our calculations and some preliminary studies, we conducted empirical tests at various ranges on live goats. Nobody enjoyed shooting the animals, but since the testing was done to avoid killing innocent fellow humans, it seemed to carry a lesser weight in the great balance of things.

When Andres and I were tapped for the mission, we first spent a few hours in the Reloading Room making our ammunition, then a couple more hours on the range to reconfirm the sight settings for our rifle scopes using this ammo. Then we climbed aboard the Air Force transport plane for the long flight to Beirut.

I knew the Marines weren't happy about asking for help in this matter. No service likes to send to another service or agency for help. But I also knew something about the Marines that wasn't common knowledge: they are a savvy bunch. In contrast to its rough-and-tumble public persona, the Marines are a service that uses its head. They believe in the application of violence when it's called for, but they believe in applying it with intelligence. I am convinced that's because they are led by selfless, high-quality officers. I've always liked working with the Marines.

I asked for and received the loan of a platoon during our stay here. I wanted a rifle squad standing by on a twenty-four-hour basis. The platoon would stay out of sight, but with one squad suited up and ready to go while the rest of the outfit lounged in place and rested. It was nice to have a little muscle backing us up, ready to provide assistance in case we stirred up a hornet's nest. You could never tell what might happen around this place.

After briefing the platoon leader and his squad leaders, Andres and I got out our spotting scopes and spent the rest of the afternoon looking over the area habituated by the shooters. We identified several potential hide positions and made a detailed sketch of the area. We stayed in our observation spot and watched for two hours after it was full dark. We wanted to get to know the landscape both as the light faded and as darkness came on.

Then we pulled back to the Marine TOC for a C ration and a last coordination briefing with the major. When we finally went out, we didn't want anyone acting out of the ordinary. We didn't want anyone to overwatch our movement or trot out any assistance unless we called for it. Radio silence was an imperative. If we needed any help, we'd call for it. As long as the "ready squad" was awake, in full equipment, and ready to go, the rest of the reaction platoon could stay asleep. In fact, we preferred it that way.

We were prepared to stay in position four days. If the mission was unresolved at the end of those four days, we would pull back, resupply, and go back into position. We would come and go only at night, and would always make a radio call first. We marked our probable positions on the map and asked the major to make sure no one fired any flares at night. If we needed to move around at all, it would be while it was dark, and we didn't want our position compromised. It was a simple plan requiring very little coordination, and we wanted everyone to stay loose until the task was accomplished.

We made a last equipment check, told the platoon leader who owned the sector we were going out, and crept out into the darkness between the Marines and the people who were shooting at them.

We made our nest in a large scattered heap of rubble and

garbage. The place looked like it had been used to dispose of materials from demolished buildings, and God knows, there was enough of that stuff around here. Once we were satisfied with our position, we took turns crawling outside and forward to check it out from the enemy side through our night-vision goggles. It wasn't the perfect way to check a hide site, but it was the best we could do under the circumstances.

Next we measured off distances and angles to several nearby objects. Tomorrow we would take sightings on possible target locations and then, using the trigonometric tables in our sniper data books, we would calculate ranges to targets. Even though we had brought our brand-new laser rangefinder with us, we didn't quite trust it yet, so we wanted to compare its findings with the old tried-and-true method.

Finally we settled into our position and both drifted off into "field sleep" for the remaining hours of darkness. Old combat soldiers know what I'm talking about.

When you're in the field on a mission, there is always someone awake and on guard. But with just the two of us out there, we couldn't split the guard duty. Instead, during the nights we would trust in the concealment of our position. That and the fact that we were both trained to sleep and gain rest and still keep a part of our minds on alert. You're asleep, but you're also awake. Your mind is resting, but if anything moves nearby, or something makes a sound that registers as a danger, you are instantly and completely awake.

Field sleep wasn't the only mind-over-body skill possessed by Delta Force snipers. We were also trained to consciously slow our heart rates. This enabled us to literally shoot between heartbeats—critical once you realize that the thump of a heartbeat can throw a shot as much as several feet off course at long range. This also gave us the ability to direct warmth to different parts of the body so we could selectively warm a trigger finger, or feet that had gotten too cold. We could also lie perfectly still for hours on end, letting the body rest even though the mind was staying active. Doing so made it possible to intently watch a target for many hours without losing interest (or the mind wandering), and still be ready for immediate action. Think of it as having the patience of a reptile.

These invaluable skills were attributable to the biofeedback training we received from the unit psychologist.

Day one was quiet. We spent the daylight hours rotating on and off the spotting scope thirty minutes at a time, to minimize eye fatigue. We took ranging shots with the laser rangefinder and found it to be perfectly accurate when we compared its results with our mathematical range calculations.

The range to the shantytown slum that was our target area was roughly 250 to 350 meters. The ground from our position to the target sloped gently uphill with a few scattered heaps of junk and abandoned buildings in the intervening space. There were no trees of significance, just a sparse ground covering of scraggly weeds and dry brush where an old donkey ambled aimlessly in search of grazing. On the extreme right of the area was a series of partially destroyed greenhouses, derelict reminders of more prosperous days.

We could see quite a few people going about their daily affairs, and as always when we viewed them through high-power lenses, we soon came to know the people we observed. Several small boys came out into the scrub between us and the village, and I watched as they ran back and forth yelling and slapping the ground with sticks. *What the hell are they doing?* I wondered. Then one of them held up a trophy and the other boys ran up to admire his kill. They were hunting lizards.

I hoped their hunt wouldn't bring them near our hide site. They would just about have to step on us to discover our location, but then, young boys have a habit of poking into all sorts of places. If the kids detected us, we would just walk away and try the mission again later. But it would certainly complicate matters. The only time we would shoot in self-defense was if an armed person stumbled right on top of us. Then we would use our silenced pistols— but only if we were certain we'd been detected and had no other choice.

But nothing happened. The day passed without incident and soon the afternoon sun gradually slid down behind us and extinguished itself in the blue Mediterranean. The night air carried voices easily, and we could hear conversations and family activity in the little finger of Beirut sticking out in front of us. Being a sniper is the same as being a voyeur, but you often see things you wish you hadn't.

I watched a man give his young son a beating that night and I positively ached to put a bullet through the hand wielding that stick. I know more than a little about beatings like that, and no child could possibly deserve that kind of a whipping. I also know discipline when I see it, and this wasn't discipline—it was pure meanness for meanness' sake. I hoped the bastard was one of the shooters, but I knew he wouldn't be. This man was a coward. He would never take the risk of shooting at U.S. Marines, even from the safety of a crowd of children. No, the shooters we were looking for might be a lot of things, but they weren't cowards. Deluded, perhaps. Stupid, maybe. Doomed, certainly.

Day two was basically a repeat of day one. Lazy, quiet, somnolent. That night we took turns watching a John Wayne movie playing on television in one of the houses. It was one of my favorite films, *The Searchers*.

The Marines had been great so far. I had been a little worried that in their eagerness to help, they might give us away by some act of attentiveness. But it hadn't happened.

I remembered all too vividly one time when it had, on a night jump into Twenty-nine Palms Marine Corps Base some years before. The Marines wanted to help us because they just couldn't imagine anybody having to parachute into the desert in the middle of the night. So a bunch of the guys had ringed themselves around the drop zone waiting for us, and when they heard the planes overhead, fired flares into the sky.

Worst jump of my life. Night vision destroyed, blinded by the flares, and in the grip of high winds, I crashed into the ground like a sack of shit, wrenching a hip on impact. Then the flares went out and I was blind again. But one Ranger had it much worse. I found him draped over his rucksack, unconscious, with a bone sticking out of his lower leg.

Save us from the help of the well-meaning, I thought as my partner and I lay in our cramped, but homey, position. Which brings to mind something some of you have probably wondered about—how snipers take care of bodily functions in position like that for such a long time. The answer is: Liquids go in a bottle and solids go in a plastic bag. And while you're putting them in there, your buddy gives you a little extra room and some friendly encouragement. When it's his turn, you do the same for him. And when you leave the location, you take the filled containers, and everything else you brought in with you, right back out again.

We were now on day three and the hours were passing quietly. I had just glanced at my watch—5:35—and when I looked back again, a group of people was starting to gather at a spot we had labeled "Position Four." It was at the end of a narrow alley and was bordered on the right by a high wall of concrete blocks.

"Action at Four, Andres," I said as I rolled from behind the spotting scope and we both took position behind our rifles. I brought the scope on to Point Four and quickly adjusted the sights for a range of 320 meters. Then I fully lowered the handle of the bolt, securely locking the round in the chamber. I let my finger find its place on the trigger and picked up a breathing rhythm that would cause the least movement to my sights. I adjusted for the shot by sliding my right knee back and away from my heart. I knew Andres was doing the same sorts of things.

In contrast to the last three days of inactivity, things now moved with an uncanny speed. There was an ominous feeling to the view before me. Seconds ago the mouth of the alley had been an empty, dusty spot. Then four or five teenagers appeared from nowhere. Now there must be twenty or twenty-five kids in the spot, all laughing, jeering, and pointing at the Marine position in the distance. They were calling and waving to someone behind them, someone hidden behind the concrete wall.

"Here it comes, Eric," Andres breathed.

"Ready," I whispered as the first shooter stepped out. I slipped him into the hairs of my sights. He was carrying an AK and glad-handing the crowd. "Call it when yours is out," I said softly, "and you have a shot."

My man was now facing in my direction. He started to lift his rifle. I knew Andres had his man in sight as well when just a split second later, he intoned, "Snipers...Ready...fire."

Thwoomp!

The two rifles spat their venom at the same instant. I was holding my sights on the upper lip of the young man when my rifle coughed, and as I rocked back with the recoil, he disappeared. A killing shot drops a man so fast it seems like the earth just gulps him down. When I came back to rest again, the only hint that just an instant before a man had been standing there was a faint pink halo of atomized blood and tissue momentarily suspended in the air. The chimera dissolved almost as soon as I saw it, and faded to nothing in the hot afternoon sun.

"Dead," I said as I chambered a fresh round.

"Dead," Andres replied as he did the same.

We watched as the crowd erupted. The bodies of the two men had been hurled to the ground before the sound of the shots reached the group.

Some people in the crowd ran. Some seemed to want to help but they clearly didn't know what to do. Others stooped over the bodies, horror on their faces. A few of the more experienced ones hurled themselves out of sight and screamed at the rest to move to cover.

Andres and I scanned from the center out. I searched in an arc to the left; Andres took the arc to the right. We had to make sure no one had figured out where the shots came from. When I looked back at the target area, I saw a few faces peering around the corner of the wall and others at the corner of a building. On my next sweep, I saw some of the braver lads move in and drag their friends' bodies out of sight.

It was done.

We didn't have much to say the rest of the afternoon. But I could read Andres's mood, and I was sure he could read mine. We had accomplished our mission, but it was nothing we could take pride in. I felt soiled and slightly guilty—as if I had stolen something and nobody knew it but me. When the action is hot and you know you're saving innocent lives with your shooting prowess, there is a certain elation to sniping. But this one didn't feel that way. It had been a necessary act, but an unpalatable one. And the only thing that remained was a vague, nasty taste in the back of my throat that refused to go away.

We stayed in our lair until darkness covered the land and then we slithered back to the relative safety of the American position.

In the spring of 1981, Delta started work on a mission that spanned more than two years—yet never took place.

That lost mission haunts me to this day. In fact, it bothers me more and more as time goes by. I've given a great deal of thought as to whether or not to write about this. Once I decided to do so, I wrestled with *how* to write about it. I've come to the conclusion that there is only one way: hard and fast.

In 1981 we (elements of the United States government) knew that approximately 125 American prisoners of war were still alive and in the hands of the government of North Vietnam. The men were being held in secret camps located in Laos, so when North Vietnam would periodically say, "There are no American prisoners alive in Vietnam," they were technically telling the truth.

Immediately an intelligence effort was mounted to pinpoint the exact location of the prisoners. At the same time, Delta Force initiated planning to conduct a rescue operation. We worked very rapidly and had gotten as far as completing a full-scale dress rehearsal of the proposed raid when the mission started to unravel. It was eventually scuttled.

"Scuttled" is probably the wrong word to use. The rescue effort was methodically pulled apart, piece by piece, until the only thing left was the unpleasant rumor of live POWs.

I do not claim to know the full story behind this tale. I know only the small portion Delta was involved in, along with other bits and pieces of information I've gleaned in the years since. From first to last, the mission was so highly compartmentalized that I'm sure only a handful of people know the whole story.

But from what I know firsthand and have learned from individuals I trust, I believe some of those who were in the know made a desperate, and ultimately successful, attempt to make sure no live Americans would emerge from captivity in Vietnam.

And yes. That is a painful thing to even contemplate.

By the summer of 1981 we were ready to launch. We had just conducted a final rehearsal successfully duplicating mission intricacies such as nighttime in-flight helicopter refueling (by tanker C-130s) while flying nap-of-the-earth through mountain passes for long distances.

Since this was only about a year after Iran, B Squadron in particular didn't relish that aspect of the mission. But in stark contrast to the Iran raid, this time we would use Air Force helicopters flown by Air Force crews—most of whom had flown search-and-rescue missions in Vietnam. These men could be trusted not to quit.

To make our rehearsal as realistic as possible, we actually "rescued" a class of Air Force pilots undergoing POW training. We wanted men who would really act like prisoners—and anyone who had ever undergone SERE (survival evasion resistance escape) training will tell you that within twelve hours of being in camp, you *believe* you are a prisoner of war. SERE is brutally real because it has to be. It is intended to prepare men for capture and interrogation.

We fought our way into the "POW" camp and sure enough, the pilots behaved like actual prisoners. The fifty men in the bunker my team hit were all cowering in fear in the farthermost corner of their dark, dank prison. They were so afraid of their captors, we had to literally drag them outside to the waiting choppers. The team hitting the other bunker had just the opposite problem. When the men realized they were being rescued, they were so ecstatic they had to be restrained from killing their jailers.

We rapidly loaded the recovered "prisoners" on the waiting helicopters and got the hell out of Dodge. It was a good rehearsal. Everything worked perfectly, and we were confident that the real rescue mission would succeed. All we needed was the word to go when one of the most bizarre things imaginable happened.

Retired Special Forces Lieutenant Colonel Bo Gritz popped up on national television announcing his intent to rescue a group of U.S. POWs being held in Southeast Asia. Gritz said that he had concrete information as to the location of the prisoners and was putting together a team to effect their rescue. During the interview, he trotted out the members of his supposed rescue team and the handful of weapons that constituted their arsenal. They were not impressive. He went on to say that his team had just completed rehearsals at their "secret Florida base of operations" and that they would be launching the mission within days.

We were absolutely and utterly stunned.

The only thing Gritz could possibly accomplish by a stunt like that was the compromise of a mission. His and ours. It was *unbelievable* that a former Special Forces officer could do such a thing. What could possibly explain Gritz's reckless behavior? Was he being manipulated or was he simply chasing self-promotion?

There were several men in our unit who had served with Gritz in other assignments, and they said he was entirely capable of the self-promotion part of the equation.

But I didn't completely buy it. I just could not, and would not, believe that a professional American soldier—even one who was, as rumor had it, a legend in his own mind—would purposefully do something that would cause harm to his former comrades. It just didn't add up.

I came to believe that Gritz was being used by people who were well aware of his personal propensities.

The day after that terrible news conference, we gathered at a remote drop zone on Fort Bragg, where we were spending the day free-fall parachuting. Our new commander assembled the operators in the shade of some nearby pines and we talked about the situation. He told us something we already figured: that the timing of the news release meant the mission had to go on hold for a while. The only thing we could do now, he told us, was put the operation on the back burner, lie low, let it all blow over, and come back to it again when the moment was right. In the meantime, we had a lot to do, so we got on with other things.

A little more than a year later, we brushed the dust off the POW mission once again. And once again, just as things were getting under way, Gritz surfaced on national television. This time he was in Bangkok, Thailand, holding a televised news conference about his recent extensive reconnaissance in the jungles of Laos where he had personally verified the whereabouts of the American POWs. He concluded the news conference by announcing he was launching an immediate rescue attempt.

When that second news conference hit the air, we were forced once more to drop the idea of a rescue attempt. And ultimately, we never picked it up again. I am firmly convinced that the American prisoners who were still alive at that time were subsequently executed, their remains scattered, and any evidence of their existence was obliterated.

Even now, some twenty years later, I am still stunned every time I think about it. I can only believe that some very powerful elements and people, both in and outside of the government, worked strenuously to scuttle the mission once it was learned that a rescue operation was under way. And when information about American POWs being left behind began to trickle out, those same people and elements later worked hard to discredit it.

To most of us, it is incomprehensible that any American would act in such a way. But sadly and reluctantly, I have come to believe it is true.

The question then becomes, who could do that and why? What could they hope to gain? I think the issue wasn't so much what could be *gained,* as it was what could be *lost.*

Years later, I spoke at length with a former highly placed member of the North Vietnamese diplomatic corps, and this person asked me point-blank: "Why did the Americans never attempt to recover their remaining POWs after the conclusion of the war?"

We compared notes on what we both knew, what we had heard, what seemed credible, and what we therefore believed. We came to conclusions that were very similar, differing only in the amount of money involved and the number of prisoners left behind.

This is what I came to believe happened:

In its hurried desire to conclude a treaty ending the war with Vietnam, the Nixon administration took the best, most expedient deal they could get and came back from Paris in 1973 declaring we had achieved "peace with honor."

The Vietnamese *knew that we knew* they were still holding prisoners, and they regarded this as the trump card to be used in later negotiations over the payment of reparations. (Why not? They had used the same ploy successfully on the French two decades before.) My diplomat friend tells me the sum of the secret provision for reconstruction aid was eleven billion dollars. I have heard a similar number from other individuals.

But then came Watergate. And when the Nixon administration imploded, there were no players left the Vietnamese could use the POW card on.

Furthermore, by that time the American public was so sick of the war they didn't want to hear about anything having to do with Vietnam. The country desperately wanted to forget it. And the politicos who had condemned American prisoners to a living death were equally desperate to forget the foul, dishonorable thing they had done.

So if it had come to light just eight years after we left Vietnam that American prisoners had been left behind for *the sake of political expediency*—well, the effect would have been devastating to a number of careers and reputations. And at the highest levels of power, nothing is more important than those two things: careers and reputations.

So the effort to locate and rescue those prisoners had to be squashed at all costs. It was imperative.

It is my personal and professional opinion that the CIA was the lead agency in wielding its power to thwart any recovery operations. Among other considerations, it is the only entity with sufficient contacts to do so. The first pressure to kill the operation was brought to bear against senior military commanders who knew about it, so the military intelligence collection effort was called off—but the cat was already out of the bag.

Several obstinate and courageous men relentlessly pressed for a continuation of the POW rescue effort but were told to shut up about it or face court-martial. Major Mark Smith and Master Sergeant Melvin McIntyre, two of the men who had been instrumental in pinpointing the whereabouts of the prisoners, did the unthinkable for military men: They brought suit against the United States government.

In September of 1985, Smith and McIntyre took the extreme step of going to federal court and suing the U.S. government for the release of evidence showing that elements of our government *knew* U.S. prisoners were alive in Southeast Asia and *knew* where they were located.

The government responded that the material was "highly classified," and its lapdog of a trial judge refused to force the government to disclose the information. Smith and McIntyre were publicly excoriated and their careers were ruined. These two brave soldiers paid a high price for trying to do the right thing, but they knew it was nothing compared to the price paid by those forgotten Americans in their wretched camps.

The squelching of the mission to rescue the POWs and the corresponding suppression of the information that live POWs had been left in Southeast Asia is one of the sorriest affairs I've ever been personally touched by. It is only in recent years that I have been able to piece together the few facts I have. But sadly, I have to conclude that nothing will ever come of it. Worse, the people who *knowingly* left those men behind and *deliberately* prevented their repatriation will never answer for what they did.

Not on earth, at any rate.

The abandonment of those men dropped like a stone in the waters of the Special Operations community, and the ripples spread out for miles. The message was clear. It told me and my comrades that our government couldn't be counted on to come and get us if we were captured on a mission in a foreign country. If it was expedient that we be denied, disavowed, and left to rot, so what? We in Delta Force didn't have an official existence anyway. The government would have an even easier way out with us than it had with POWs.

This experience also taught me to evaluate every mission by my own innate standards of what was just and right. I came to realize that there was no such thing as a monolithic government always striving to do the right thing, even if it did sometimes make mistakes. I understood all too well that a government was made up of many people with different—and sometimes venal—agendas. And sometimes those kinds of people hold high office and wield enormous power, simply to further their own ends.

Still, I knew that I was so far down the chain from the decision-makers that I would never be able to make an informed judgment regarding their intent. I could only try to deduce the real reason for an operation I was conducting and then evaluate its impact.

When those American POWs were lost to us, something of me was lost with them. Many times in the years to come, I would wish for the earlier, simpler days of my blissful ignorance. Days when I could believe our leaders without reservation. But none of those people had changed. It was me.

Life continued. Alerts, missions, and rumors of missions came and went. In the middle of a slack period between deployments, I was in the mess hall one morning, enjoying breakfast with Larry Freedman, when Walt Shumate sat down and joined us. Walt had retired only a few months earlier, but had stayed on with the unit in a civilian capacity as the safety officer. I guess it made perfect sense. Walt knew as much about how to be unsafe as anyone I'd ever met, so the issue of safety was pretty easy for him.

When Walt joined us, Larry had been telling me a story from his days as a young troop in the 82nd Airborne Division. Shumate listened intently as he ate his SOS, and when Larry finished, Walt launched into a tale of his own.

"You know I was in the 82nd myself. I was a buck sergeant in those days, right after I came back from Korea. And I remember this old first sergeant we had, First Sergeant Harold Jenkins, we called him Lord Harold, and I'm telling you, he was one rough old customer.

"When I knew him, he was just about to retire after thirty years' service—that would have been about 1953, I guess—and he wasn't very happy about having to go. That whole last year he was a pain in the ass, always getting drunk and wanting to fight. Then he'd go on a crying jag afterwards, hanging all over you and blubbering and shit.

"Then one night, it was a payday Friday, Lord Harold had made all of us stay with him at the NCO Club till the place closed and they finally threw us out. He'd been on good behavior that night but he was drunk as a rat, so me and a couple of other sergeants drove him home. He lived over in Bastogne, in your neighborhood, Haney.

"Mrs. Jenkins was a piece of work. She was a schoolteacher, a stern, hard woman, but a genuine lady—you know the kind—and I'm sure old Harold just embarrassed the shit out of her sometimes. So anyway, we pull up to the house and drag Lord Harold out of the backseat. With one of us under each arm, we walk him up the steps and lean him against the door frame. Then we ring the bell and jump off the porch into the bushes to watch the fireworks.

"The porch light comes on and Mrs. Jenkins hauls open the door and sees Harold sort of propped up there. The light is hurting his eyes so he's got one hand covering them while he's holding on to the door frame with the other hand, trying to keep from falling down. Me and my buddy are peeking over the edge of the porch because this is too good to miss.

"Mrs. Jenkins looks at him with disgust all over her face and says, 'Drunk again, aren't you, Harold?'

" 'Yeah . . . I am,' he says. And just leans there while she gives him the old stink-eye.

"Finally she says, 'Harold, how much money did you spend tonight?'

"He fumbles for his wallet, gives it a long look inside, and says, 'Oh, about a hundred dollars, I reckon.'

"She yells, 'A hundred dollars? You spent a hundred dollars in one night? Do you have any idea just how long a hundred dollars would last me?'

"Old Harold, he thought about that for a while and then he looks at her and says, 'Well, let's see, woman. You don't smoke.... You don't drink.... You've got your own damn pussy. Why, I reckon a hundred dollars ought to just about last you forever.'"

My laughter hit me so unexpectedly I blew a mouthful of eggs across the table. Larry put his head down on the table and laughed till he was gasping for air. At our outburst, the mess hall got quiet for a second, but when everyone saw that Shumate was at the table, they figured out what was going on and went back to their breakfast.

I looked across the table at Walt. He always laughed at his own stories, but in a peculiar fashion all his own. His smile stretched across the width of his face and his eyes almost closed, splashing laugh lines all the way to his ears. His shoulders bunched up and his upper body bounced up and down as the waves of laughter shook him—but he made not a sound.

And then it hit me. It was a recon man's laugh. The kind of laugh you make when you're on patrol in Indian Country and can't afford to laugh out loud, so you just choke off the sound but carry through with the rest of it. Walt had probably learned the habit as a young soldier during the Korean War and it had been with him ever since.

Walter J. Shumate was a hell of a man, as was his friend and contemporary, Country Grimes. They retired within months of each other, both with thirty years' service, and we were fortunate to keep both of them on with the unit—Walt as the unit safety officer and Country as the facility manager for our new Selection site.

Country had recruited me for Delta, and as its command sergeant major, he had become a great friend and counselor. I remember one day I had committed a serious screwup and spent the rest of the afternoon waiting for the word to see Country. When it came, I was so anxious to get it over with that I almost ran to his office. When I reported in, Country just looked at me a second and then said, quietly, "Haney, you've had your one chance." He delivered the lesson without anger or rancor, but the message could not have been more clear: Country would underwrite one mistake for a man he cared about, but after that, you'd have to pay full price for a dumb-attack. It was something I always remembered and acted on when I became a sergeant major.

When it finally came time for them to take leave of us, Walt and Country died within a week of each other. Both men succumbed to cancer, probably brought on by long exposure to Agent Orange in the early days of Vietnam. We had a joint memorial service for them, and people came from around the world to say their good-byes to those two extraordinary men. As is customary in our Tribe, they both left an endowment of sorts in their wills—a thousand dollars each to host an open bar for their friends and comrades at the Green Beret Parachute Club on Fort Bragg.

And Walt—as only Walt would—went one step further. He willed his famous mustache to the unit. It is framed under glass and conspicuously displayed in a place of honor in the Hall of Heroes at the Ranch, where it has become something close to a holy shrine.

These were two of Delta's fathers—good, strong men who did their utmost to form and guide us. We venerate their memory, and I'm proud to say I knew them both.

It was the mid-eighties and the years were passing so rapidly, and we were so busy, it was hard to keep up with where my mates were in the world. Some guys were off by themselves, some were in two-man elements, and some were in four-man teams deployed in different spots of the globe plying our trade. New men came into the unit, and older ones fell away.

I had the great opportunity to attend Spanish-language school, and what a boon that was. My street Spanish had always been just good enough to get me into trouble. And you can imagine the content of the phrases I had learned from my Puerto Rican and Chicano friends.

Instead of sending us to the Defense Language Institute (DLI) in Monterey, California, the unit hired an instructor and a dozen of us took the DLI course at Fort Bragg. By the second month, I was starting to dream in Spanish, and after that, class was a pure delight. After graduating from the six-month course, I had a pretty good handle on the language, and Latin America became my primary area of responsibility, with the Middle East as my secondary.

It was just in time, too, because Central America had become one of our main stomping grounds. In fact, I had the good luck to have a wonderfully boring, and successful, mission down there.

I led a double team—two four-man teams—to Guatemala on a mission to prevent one of the local guerrilla groups from blowing up the American embassy in Guatemala City. We had learned that the group wanted to commemorate their upcoming anniversary in a spectacular manner—one that would simultaneously bring them great prestige and enhance their recruiting effort. Naturally, the guerrillas believed the most festive way to celebrate the occasion was to blast the U.S. embassy into the stratosphere.

I made certain that the guerrilla surveillance teams saw us and that they could also see the preparations we were making to greet them, and make their lives even more exciting should they choose to follow though with their plans.

When we had positively identified the guerrilla observation points, we held up signs in Spanish telling them we intended to give them a warm welcome if they visited us, and that in addition to the unpleasantries they could see, there was a lot here that they couldn't. Then we posted politely worded signs telling them we would appreciate it if they would celebrate their fiesta somewhere else. After a couple of days, we became friendly enough with the guerrilla observation teams to exchange comradely waves to one another—we from our rooftop positions and they from their observation points around the embassy.

A day later, the guerrilla surveillance disappeared. We stayed at the embassy for an additional week after their anniversary had passed, and then posted a sign on the embassy roof saying, "Thanks for the hospitality." We said our good-byes to the ambassador and the RSO and returned to Fort Bragg.

The worst part of the mission had been standing on the roof of the embassy all night, every night. Not only was it cold up there, but right next door, on the upwind side of the embassy, was the most fabulous steak house in the world. Every night, the delicious aroma of grass-fed, Guatemalan beef grilled over charcoal on the restaurant front porch wafted in the night breeze straight to our flaring nostrils in our rooftop outpost.

So close, yet so far away. Now that's torture.

The mission was a success. Not one that makes for a hair-raising story, but the type of counterterrorist operation that I call a real success—a preventive success.

No one was hurt, no lives or property were lost, and now, a couple of decades later, guerrillas and Delta alike are able to realize there was nothing really so important about blowing up that embassy anyway.

GUERRILLA GROUPS ARE INDIGENOUS, NOT ONLY TO LATIN America, but to other parts of the world as well. And we had been busy in those other places, too. Quietly busy, busy in small ways, but busy nonetheless.

A few years earlier than my Guatemalan vacation, Don Feeney had been busy in one of those other places. He and his team had been sent on a very hush-hush mission to train a counterterrorist force for the Sudanese army. Then, as now, Sudan was a country we wouldn't admit to having direct dealings with. But someone in the State Department or CIA thought that if we gave them a little secret training assistance, it might open the door slightly for some sort of cozy back-porch socializing. So Donny and his mates were dispatched to build and train a Sudanese CT force—never mind that common sense said that such a unit would probably be used as a tool of oppression by the military government of Sudan.

The Sudanese had nothing. No ranges, no equipment, and no ammo. Feeney and his guys had to start from the ground up, but within a few months, they had created a pretty good little force. Of course, you have to remember one thing—"good" is a relative term.

One of the team members, Fred Brandy, was in charge of constructing the Range and the Shooting House, and by the very nature of the project, he had been forced to learn Arabic. He came back from the mission with a handwritten dictionary and an Arabic vocabulary of over one thousand words. Fred went on to attend the

Arabic course at DLI and is one of the few gringos I've ever known who is perfectly fluent in the language.

Almost as soon as the team returned from their little vacation in the desert, they were put on alert. A group of American missionaries had been captured by a separatist guerrilla group and were being held in a village near the southern border with Uganda. The U.S. embassy demanded help, but Washington said the rescue force had to be small—we didn't want to let on that we were having any sort of relationship with the government of Sudan. So, much like the old Texas Ranger saw of "One riot, one Ranger," we sent one operator. "Feeney, you trained 'em, now go lead 'em."

Don was dispatched to help get the Americans back. When he arrived in country he was pleased and surprised to see that the CT force was still intact. When we built the same type of force for the Egyptians, someone in power convinced President Mubarak that the group was more of a threat than anything else, and the members we trained were scattered throughout the Egyptian military. That decision was to bear some bitter fruit just a few years later.

Donny's main problem was centered in the American embassy. For some reason or another, the CIA chief of station and his two henchmen were trying to convince the ambassador that their clients, a certain brigade in the Sudanese army, should be the ones to rescue the missionaries. Donny told the ambassador that if the regular army made the attempt, at best the operation would be exceedingly slow, and at worst the guerrillas would probably kill their captives and slip across the border. If the CT force was used instead, Donny believed they stood a good chance of getting the prisoners back alive.

The ambassador made his decision: "Feeney, go get them and bring them back." From that point forward, the little CIA clan did everything it possibly could to foul the mission. They muddied the command relationship within the Sudanese army and tried to block the CT force from gaining use of the one airplane in the military that was capable of reaching the crisis area. But if there's one thing Don Feeney knows, it's street fighting, and he was able to push aside the obstacles the chief of station tried to put in his path.

The rescue force was able to get their hands on the one C-130 in the Sudanese air force. Fortunately, there was an airstrip less than half a mile from the small village where the captives were being held. Donny knew the area well, and so did the members of the CT force. Since they wanted to make the hit the next morning, the forty members of the assault force weren't able to conduct full-scale rehearsals, so Donny led them through walk-throughs of the attack drawn with chalk on the runway of the airfield.

Once he was satisfied everyone knew his place and his task in the mission, Donny was ready to go. He loaded his force, some food and water, some rudimentary medical supplies he had scrounged up, and three jeeps mounting .50-caliber machine guns aboard the C-130 for the thousand-mile flight to a staging base less than twenty miles from the crisis point. They would hit the guerrilla camp just as daylight was breaking, a time of the day known in military parlance as "BMNT," beginning of morning nautical twilight. In commonspeak, this is known as that time of the morning when you can just start to see stuff.

The C-130 hit the runway just as daylight spread across the dusty African landscape. The three gun jeeps absolutely covered with Sudanese commandos roared out of the plane and up the dusty track to a small hill about 150 meters to the west of the guerrilla camp. The machine guns opened fire on the camp's main buildings while Donny led the ground force on a sweep of the southern half of the village.

The handful of guerrillas who were awake fired just a few shots before they threw down their weapons and fled into the bush. The rest of the outfit woke up to the fusillade of those three .50-caliber machine guns and quickly decided to follow their buddies in search of a safer place.

The machine guns continued to fire for a few more minutes, just to let the guerrillas know the commandos were really serious about the affair, and then displaced forward and occupied the buildings the guerrillas had so hastily deserted. Donny and his maneuver element found the missionaries alive and well in a hut in the southern quarter of the village.

The assault had gone perfectly—easier, in fact, than the walk-through the day before. The CT force took no casualties, and the guerrillas had been so fleet of foot they had lost only four men.

While Donny and the Sudanese commander were rounding up the unit and the hostages for the flight back out, the boys from the CIA arrived by plane to have a look at what had taken place.

As soon as he saw them, Donny said, he knew what was up. Since they didn't have to fool with troops or hostages—and they had a faster plane to boot—the CIA boys were going to hustle back to Khartoum and spin the tale to grab as much credit as possible for themselves.

The only reason I knew about the operation is that I had been talking to Donny throughout the mission on our new satellite radio system. We stayed in contact just in case something went wrong and we had to go find Don. That way, we would at least know his last location and have a place to begin the search.

But my old buddy the Artful Dodger survived once again and returned home to a regular nonwelcome. He was told to never say anything about being in Sudan and that was the end of that.

He did have one important souvenir of the rescue. The missionaries gave him a Bible with their signatures and their thanks, and as Donny says, that's better than any kind of official recognition.

As I have said previously, Central America was a place of overwhelming political turmoil, and no spot was more volatile than the small country of El Salvador. That's especially ironic when you realize that the country's name means "The Savior."

El Salvador has a centuries-old tradition of political violence and civil war. It has a population density greater than that of India, and traditionally has been ruled by a small handful of families who believed that the only way they could stay at the top of the heap was to keep a firm and, when necessary, brutal foot on the neck of the "lesser beings" of the population. In the 1980s Delta Force was hip-deep in that bellicose little nation as our country tried to help put a lid on the discontent with the status quo.

It was a difficult job. The army of El Salvador was poorly equipped, poorly organized, and poorly led. The officer corps was about as corrupt as they could possibly be. They had convinced themselves that if they just stalled long enough, President Reagan would commit U.S. ground troops and do their job for them. And though they were reluctant in taking on the main revolutionary group, the FMLN (Farabundo Marti National Liberation), they had no qualms when it came to murdering priests, nuns, and poor villagers. As I said, it would prove to be a difficult job.

Some of us trained their Special Operations forces, doing our best to teach them that the indiscriminate killing of campesinos only *creates* guerrillas. To this day, I've met only four officers of Latin American armies who genuinely understood that concept.

Other operators were involved in leading weapons interdiction missions along the borders. Working in cooperation with the Honduran authorities, we had been fairly successful in choking off the supply of arms coming overland from Nicaragua, and that had forced the Nicaraguans to take to the water in an effort to keep their Salvadoran comrades supplied with the necessities of insurrection.

If you look at a map of the Pacific coast of Central America, you will see the Gulf of Fonseca, a beautiful stretch of water bordered by El Salvador on the west, Honduras on the north, and Nicaragua to the east. Centered in the northern portion of the gulf is the ancient volcanic mountain that constitutes Tiger Island. We had a "look and listen" station atop the mountain peak of the island, and from that vantage point, we were able to watch the entire Gulf of Fonseca and the surrounding land with a keen and critical eye. And at night, with assistance provided by the watchers on Tiger Island, we swept the waters of the gulf clean of gun-smuggling boat traffic.

My old compadre Andres Benevides was in charge of the countersmuggling operation. If you're wondering why an American headed the program instead of one of the locals, the answer is simple. The Salvadorans couldn't trust their own people not to confiscate a boatload of weapons, kill the smugglers, and then sell the guns and the boat that carried them. But with an American present to stay on top of things, the locals would do a pretty good job.

Andres's fleet of interceptors consisted of three twenty-seven-foot Boston Whalers, each one mounting an M-60 machine gun and carrying a crew of four men. Andres had trained his small navy quite well. They were able to navigate in formation at night wearing night-vision goggles, could fire their weapons accurately, and could communicate by radio without babbling like a bunch of old maids (no mean feat in itself). And once they put to sea, they did a land-slide business.

For two weeks they had a marvelous time. Following naviga-tional directions from the outpost on Tiger Island, they picked up arms-laden boats almost every night. Andres devised a simple and effective tactic that worked like a Swiss watch. When the radar sta-tion picked up a target, Andres would position his fleet in an open V formation in front of the approaching boat. When the smuggler was in the jaws of the V, the three boats would hit him simultane-ously with their spotlights and Andres would announce over the bullhorn that the pleasure cruise was over. Surrounded on all sides, the boat captains surrendered every time. Except one.

It was a pitch-black night and the Gulf was kicking up her heels. The water was very choppy, with waves running about four to five feet. Shortly after midnight, they got a call from Tiger Island that a target was approaching. Andres positioned his group and set the trap. Before long, they could see the boat snaking his way through the waves, oblivious to the net strung in front of him.

When everything was perfect, Andres called "now" over the ra-dio and the spotlights from his three boats pinned the interloper from three converging directions. This particular smuggler then did the unthinkable—he spun his boat around in an evasive maneuver, hit the throttle, and tried to peel those damn lights off his back. Andres yelled one time for the boat to halt and then he let him have a burst of machine-gun fire.

The stream of bullets hit the boat at the waterline and walked up its side just in front of the pilot. At the blast from the machine gun, the engine went dead and the pilot toppled over into the bottom of the boat. Andres and his small fleet closed in to take possession of the smuggler's craft before it could sink.

The boat was an oceangoing *cayuco,* a thirty-foot vessel made from a giant tropical hardwood log, carefully hollowed out and pre-cisely shaped. These kinds of boats have been in use for centuries and, until fairly recent times, were propelled only with oars and sails. Now most *cayucos* mounted outboard motors. Some of the larger ones, like the one Andres encountered, even boast a small in-board diesel engine.

Andres raced up alongside the *cayuco.* Just as the two boats came gunwale to gunwale, the smuggler popped up from the bottom of the boat like a jack-in-the-box, spitting mad. "Why did you shoot me?" he shouted at Andres.

Andres was so surprised, he snapped back just as quickly, "Why didn't you stop when I told you to?"

The smuggler, a weather-beaten old man, answered, "I thought you were pirates. I'm carrying a valuable commodity."

Andres quickly checked the *cayuco* to see how much water she was taking on. He was amazed to see that the bullets he had fired at a range of less than thirty meters had not even penetrated the hull of the boat. After verifying that the boat was indeed carrying a load of weapons and ammunition, he attempted a serious talk with the composed and quite nonchalant captain.

"*Abuelo*, why are you doing this thing? Why do you put yourself at such risk to carry weapons to a people you do not even know? Do you not realize that what you are doing is very dangerous?"

The old man eyed Andres calmly for a few seconds before he answered. "Young gentleman, do you not know what is going on in my country? The times, they are bad. And they were bad before, during the years of the Somozas. But at least then if you were quiet, and you did not meddle in politics, and you voted the way the village *alcalde* [mayor] told you to vote, you could live relatively unmolested. But today everything is politics in Nicaragua. One is no longer allowed the luxury to be quiet. Now one must be militant. One must be a revolutionary. One must strike a blow against imperialism. One must *act* to show solidarity with the revolution. It is required of us.

"So when an important and powerful man from Managua comes to my village and says, 'Citizens, you are fishermen and you know these waters. Now you will have the glorious opportunity to aid our valiant comrades in El Salvador in their struggles against the forces of the capitalist imperialists. Your village will be allowed to make five voyages to carry liberation supplies to our friends across the bay.' Someone had to do it and do it without question.

"So I volunteered to be the one to make the trips. I did not want my sons, or the sons of my brothers, or any of the other young men in my village, to make such a dangerous trip. If someone is to perish or be captured and sent to prison—then let it be me. I am an old man. My wife is dead and there is no longer anyone who depends on me for food or a father's protection. My loss would account for little and I would soon be forgotten. And that, young man, is why I am doing this thing."

Andres asked the old man how many trips he had made and was surprised to hear that this was the fifth and final trip. He had elected a direct crossing this time because it was a moonless night. On the other occasions, he had stood well out to sea and made a looping, roundabout approach to the Salvadoran coast. That accounted for his previous ability to avoid Andres and his men.

Now Andres was in a quandary. This was the first civilian they had captured and Andres really didn't want to turn him over to the Salvadorans—they were notoriously brutal with prisoners. But if he confiscated and brought in the old man's weapons, Andres would have to account for the boat and the captain. Andres had a huddle with the crewmen of his little fleet. After an extended conversation with his men, he turned back to the old fisherman.

"*Viejo,* if I return you to your home, will you and your village have to do this again? Will you have to make other trips like this?"

The old man answered slowly, "I cannot say either yes or no with certainty. The man from Managua says that with these five trips, our village will have met its quota. Our *alcalde* seems to think this is true. But we are dealing with a government, and there is little truth in any government—only appetite for the things it wants. So, will I have to do this again? . . . I do not know."

Andres made his decision. "Father, we are going to throw this stuff overboard and then you are going to go home. Travel slowly so that you return to your village at the usual hour. Tell no one of our encounter. If you are asked, just say that you made your delivery as ordered. If you are told that the people on the Salvadoran side never received the material, you are to reply that they are notorious thieves and they are probably keeping the shipment to sell for themselves. Now return to your people and when these bad times are over, I will come to visit you in your village. Go, and God go with you."

The old man nodded to Andres and his men in thankful farewell, cranked the engine of his boat, and disappeared into the darkness. Andres bought the silence of his crew members with a generous bribe and that was that. Or so he hoped, because he ran the risk of almost certain court-martial if the tale of what really happened ever leaked out.

But the secret held, and just a few years after the demise of the Sandinista regime, Andres kept his promise to the old fisherman. During a trip to Central America, he made a side tour to the old man's village on the Nicaraguan coast. He found a quiet, sleepy fishing village full of the old captain's descendants and relatives. But alas, the old man had died some years before.

Andres told the people of the village who he was and how he had met their kinsman. They were amazed at the tale, but not at the actions of that remarkable old man. He had been known for his quiet courage, they said, and he had protected his people and his village all his life. They were not surprised that a stranger, even one he had met as an enemy, at night on the waters of the gulf, would recognize what a special man he was, and wish to visit him again. Andres stayed for two days with those good and kind people. He visited the old man's grave and was happier than ever for his decision that night so long ago to send that good man home.

Nicaragua still isn't doing too well, but at least these days, she has a government that pretty much leaves her people unmolested to pursue their own lives without having to actively demonstrate their loyalty to an incomprehensible cause. And make no mistake about it—that, in itself, is a hell of a blessing.

Honduras had become a somewhat reluctant ally of the United States during the tumultuous decade of the 1980s. The poorest country on the mainland of the Americas, she was taking her first real, but faltering, steps toward democracy—and she was doing it between a rock and a hard spot. To the south was the ongoing mayhem of El Salvador that had sent several waves of refugees washing across the border. On the east she shared a long, sparsely populated, and porous border with Nicaragua that lent itself to cross-border raids by the American-supported Contras and retaliatory incursions by the Sandinistas.

The Hondurans wanted nothing more than for it all to go away. But that wasn't about to happen as long as Uncle Sam was determined to make the world safe for oligarchic fruit growers. And as

long as the Yankees were fixated on Nicaragua and needed potential
bases in Honduras . . . well, why not take the millions of gringo dollars being tossed around and make the best of an uncomfortable
situation?

Honduras already had a rather substantial and relatively well
trained army, but when she started having problems with political
kidnappings, assassinations, and cross-border raids, the decision was
made to ask for American assistance in forming a small specialized
unit that could counter those problems. The request was received
with favor in Washington and ultimately, Master Sergeant Santos
Matos was sent to fulfill the promise of assistance.

Santos had come to us in 1981 after many years of renowned
service in Special Forces and in the old Ranger reconnaissance companies. The superb reputation he had earned in Vietnam and elsewhere just wasn't sufficient to describe what a genuinely fine man
he was.

He was a native of Puerto Rico, but somehow or other, he
looked more like a Polynesian than a man from the Spanish An-
tilles. He was a tall, strong man with a quiet confidence that made
other people feel good just to be around him. He had a remarkably
intuitive tactical sense, but he was also a very detail-minded operational planner. In contrast to a lot of other so-called expert plan-
ners, Santos had an uncanny grasp of what *would* work in a fight
and what was a waste of effort.

His real strength, however, was in leading men. Whether he was
leading crack American troops or a tribe of indigenous warriors,
Santos could always get the job done and bring his own troops
home again.

It was a Herculean task, but within the ten weeks allotted for
training, Santos put together a pretty credible forty-man force. One
that could shoot, move, and communicate. Their operational planning skills weren't very good, but that would improve with practice.
But Santos didn't have any illusions as to the shelf life of the new
unit. They would not be capable of self-sustainment—and that was
a cultural fact.

The Honduran army doesn't have an NCO corps. No Latin
American army does. They have sergeants in the ranks but not in
the capacity of sergeants as we know them. In a Latin American
army, a sergeant is more or less his officer's servant or driver. At best,

he is a senior private soldier. But he has practically no authority and little, if any, responsibility, and is not required to do much more than say "yes" to his commander. The officer corps is responsible for all functions, no matter how small, and since mundane tasks such as training, maintenance of equipment, and caring for the troops are beneath the dignity of an officer...well, you get the picture.

So, Santos gave his little force about a year before the natural weight of entropy would exert itself and his boys reverted once again into a band of relatively well armed but marginally effective rabble. The shame of it all is that when given decent leadership, these guys make damn fine soldiers. But Santos didn't have to wait a year to test his theory. Within a few months of his return home, he was sent back to Honduras to lead the force on their first mission.

The adult daughter of a very prominent citizen of El Salvador, a man who was a genuine friend of the United States, had been kidnapped. Intelligence sources had pinpointed the location where the woman was being held. A Honduran guerrilla group, in a fit of solidarity with their comrades in El Salvador, was holding the young woman in a specially constructed house in a suburb of the largest city in Honduras, San Pedro Sula. The Hondurans wanted to make the recovery themselves, but they needed Santos Matos to give them the confidence to attempt the undertaking. Washington agreed to the request.

Santos climbed on an Air Force plane and headed south once more, carrying with him one limiting order straight from the banks of the Potomac: He could take his Honduran CT force right up to the house where the captive was being held, but he could not lead the men on the assault. That part they would have to do themselves. Santos didn't agree with the decision, but he would comply with it. Orders are orders, even stupid ones.

Once in Honduras, he got under way rapidly. The CT force moved to San Pedro Sula and started planning. Snipers were deployed to place surveillance on the house while the assault force started rehearsing. A rapid attack wasn't a tactically pressing requirement, but Santos knew that to dally around was dangerous. His snipers might be compromised, operational security might be broken, or his boys might start to doubt themselves, so he had to keep things flowing. The CT force didn't have night-vision goggles, so Santos elected for a dawn assault.

Fortunately, the windows of the house had been boarded up. Even though the snipers couldn't see inside, the kidnappers couldn't see out. That would help Santos get the force into an assault position right against the walls of the house without having to make a long and potentially compromising approach. Santos put his guys through one last rehearsal, designated the rotation of the emergency assault teams, and then put his outfit to sleep. They would roll in the predawn darkness of the following morning.

Their approach was neither high-tech nor splashy, just effective: Santos mounted his men in two flatbed trucks and away they went. They stopped about two blocks from the targeted house, got into team formation, and were led to the crisis point by the sniper leader.

Everything was looking good as the men moved into position. They seemed confident and capable. The teams put their explosive breaching charges on the doors, and as daylight gathered Santos told the *teniente* (lieutenant) to give the signal to commence the assault.

The *teniente* looked his men over one last time and then gave them the high sign.

Blaauuw!

The doors blew in with a blinding flash of light and a clap of man-made thunder. The assault teams poured inside like water from a fire hose. Santos and the *teniente* rushed up to the smoldering door and stood there listening to the first burst of fire from inside. But something was going wrong. It all should have been over in seconds, but after that initial blast of gunfire, the shooting was settling into something that sounded like a sustained firefight. And then a grenade came bouncing out the door!

Santos and the *teniente* dove into a nearby drainage ditch just as the grenade detonated and pelted the area with its deadly fragments. Enough was enough. Santos bounded out of the ditch, drew his .45, and leapt through the door and inside the building. He saw what he had expected—his guys had lost their nerve and failed to continue the assault. Now they had gone to cover in the building and were shooting it out with the kidnappers.

Then suddenly, like something from a Road Runner cartoon, a rope-bound and blindfolded figure popped out of a side room and went hopping across the floor—right through the middle of the close-range shoot-out.

It was the young woman they had come to rescue, trying to escape under her own power. But she was going to get killed if something didn't happen. Santos hurled himself into the middle of the room, right through the epicenter of the converging fire, and knocked the woman to the floor. While covering her with his body, he shot and killed two of the kidnappers—and that was enough to give his troops back their courage. They resumed the stalled assault and killed the remaining three kidnappers in short order.

Remarkably, the woman was unhurt and the assault team had taken no casualties. The police, Honduran Intelligence, and the CIA moved in and took over the scene. The freed captive was hustled away and taken to a hospital. The CT force reassembled and returned without fanfare to their base in Tegucigalpa. That afternoon Santos said good-bye to his friends and climbed aboard an Air Force plane for the flight back to Fort Bragg. A few hours later, he was back home and returned to the unit where a couple of days later he received his just deserts: an ass-chewing.

The Hondurans were so impressed with the operation and with Santos's bravery that they had immediately sent a message to Washington detailing the extraordinary performance of the American sergeant. It got even worse when the president of El Salvador sent his thanks and told the State Department he was going to award Sergeant Matos his nation's highest award for bravery.

The Potomac River Water Drinkers were not pleased that a sacred order from on high had been disobeyed. And their displeasure grew in volume and strength as it flowed downhill to Fort Bragg.

At that particular time, Delta was blessed with a man who, to put it kindly, was not the strongest commander we ever had. To curry favor with his political masters, upon whom he was counting for good things to come, he ripped Santos a new asshole for disobeying orders.

And so, for performing a necessary and courageous act, one that would have earned the Distinguished Service Cross or a Silver Star for a captain or major, Santos got the rough side of his commander's tongue and a piece of paper in his personnel file calling him a bad boy.

But Santos was not disturbed by the treatment he received. He wasn't overly concerned with the outcome because he knew he had done the right thing. And to get mad about the actions of a career-climbing colonel was like getting mad at the night because it is dark.

Santos was a remarkable, wonderful man. And as seems too common with men of his stature, he left us all too soon. Sergeant Major Santos Alfred Matos was killed in a parachuting accident in 1991. Like others of our Tribe, he left money in his will for a wake at the Green Beret Parachute Club.

But even among such an extraordinary group, Santos was an extraordinary man. He was so beloved by his friends that they erected a stone monument, dedicated to his memory, on the sidewalk by the front entrance of the Green Beret Parachute Club.

If you ever find yourself traveling on I-95 near Fort Bragg, stop in at the Parachute Club and pay your respects to Santos. And if you are lucky enough to get a stool next to a gray and grizzled retired Special Operations veteran, mention Santos's name.

It'll be good for a free beer and an interesting conversation.

It was the heart of the Reagan era and Honduras, much like Beirut, continued to be a second home for us. It seemed we spent an inordinate amount of time and energy focused on that poor but strategically important nation. And even though we usually operated there in small teams, that didn't mean that was the way we always did things. Like a carpenter planning a job, bigger lumber calls for bigger nails and bigger nails call for a bigger hammer. And sometimes, things would pop up that called for a larger force. Several times a year the entire Bowstring force would be called out for an operation that required a little muscle.

A Bowstring alert was usually the result of an airplane hijacking, and most of the time that meant a trip to the eastern Mediterranean. It happened so often that it became something of a summertime sport. We spent so much time in the region that it was seriously suggested we position a squadron in Italy or Cyprus from May until September. We chased a lot of planes around the Middle East but were never allowed to put our hands on them—we could look but not touch. Touching was reserved for the rare odd hijackings in offbeat places such as eastern Asia or South America.

We deployed on one particular chase and were pretty close to pulling the trigger when word came down that since the hijacked plane was an Egyptian airliner, the Egyptians would be the ones to take it down. And it just so happened that the Egyptians had a brand new CT force, all trained and ready, courtesy of their good American friends in 1st SFOD—D.

I was sent down by Navy fighter to join up with our Egyptian comrades and go with them as an *"adviser."* But when I arrived in Egypt and linked up with the force, there wasn't a single familiar face still in the unit. This is the example I spoke of earlier. The Egyptian government had concluded that a capable CT force was more of a domestic threat than anything else, and so had scattered to the four winds the soldiers we had trained, and had refilled the outfit with their own "political reliables."

I got on the radio and called our commander back in Italy to let him know about the situation. He told me he would send a plane and that I was to quietly slip back to the airfield and get the hell out of there. I caught a ride back to the airbase, met the plane that had been sent for me, and returned to Italy.

The Egyptians subsequently made an assault on the plane. The method they chose to get inside the aircraft was to place a fifty-pound charge of C-4 on the belly of the plane and detonate it. No one has ever figured out why they did that. After all, it's relatively common knowledge that high explosives and airplanes don't mix. The resulting explosion and fire killed more than sixty people.

So much for political reliability.

After that, we got out of the business of training foreign CT forces. It didn't help anybody and was a waste of our time and resources. Our special gift was hijacking—and we soon got the opportunity to add a beauty to our trophy case.

One lazy afternoon, just a few days before we were to relinquish Bowstring to A Squadron, we got a call to a hijacking in Honduras. The plane had been taken on the ground and was sitting on the tarmac in Tegucigalpa. And this time, Washington wanted to kick a little ass just to impress everybody in the region. There was only one problem: it was an airplane we didn't have in our playbook—a DeHavilland DH-7, a four-engine turboprop that carried about fifty passengers.

So while the squadron loaded on a C-130 for the flight to Honduras, I headed for Virginia Beach to get my hands on a Dash-7, as they are called, and take its measurements. A small charter outfit based in New England flew the Dash-7s, and they were happy to make one available for me that night.

I met the plane at the Virginia Beach airport and spent about two hours going over it, making notes, taking measurements, and drawing sketches. This one was going to be a snap. We wouldn't need ladders—all the doors and hatches were at ground level and opened to the outside. It was all coach seating with no partitions dividing the fuselage into separate compartments—you could shoot the entire length of the cabin with a pistol. When I had all the information I needed, I headed south to join my mates in beautiful Honduras.

I arrived in Tegucigalpa about 1000 hours the following morning on a flight from Panama. Our plane taxied to the military side of the airport and when it shut down its engines, I climbed out and set out to find my compatriots. After a short search I found one of our folks, Guy Harmon, sitting on an upturned bucket, meditating and smoking one of his trademark bad cigars.

Guy's call sign is "Oso," Spanish for "Bear," and it suits him perfectly. He has a furry look about him, speaks in a slow, deep growl, and walks with a padding gait. But he has some of the other physical characteristics of the bear as well. He can move with lightning speed when the need arises. He has phenomenal physical strength and unshakable resolve, and is fearless and deadly in a fight.

He didn't say anything when we made eye contact, just continued languidly smoking his cigar and watched me as I walked toward him. I didn't call out to him; he was obviously thinking about something and I didn't want to break his concentration. When I stopped in front of him, he blew a smoke ring at me and said, "Hey, gringo, where'd you come from?"

"From going to and fro over the face of the earth, and walking back and forth upon it," I answered.

Guy smiled. "Well, you've probably found the right place, Lucifer," he said, looking around the area. "If you're looking for the rest of the gang, follow this road on over the rise. You'll find Dan and the team leaders behind that gaggle of maintenance buildings and heavy equipment. They've got a Headquarters hooch set up between the Bowstring vans. Can't miss it."

"What's going on, Guy? What's on your mind? Something's not right here. You've got that look on your face."

"I'm not sure, Eric. But there's something's definitely uncool going on here. You know how at a hijacking site it's usually just us and a few representatives from the local authorities?"

"Yeah."

"Well, this place is absolutely crawling with people—and they aren't locals. It looks like every secret agent in the American inventory is gathered here—CIA, NSA, DIA, you name 'em. Why, you can't sling a dead cat by the tail without slapping at least three double-naught agents upside the head.

"And this is what's so weird, Eric. It's like they knew this was gonna happen. They got here before we did; hell, they were already set up. Filled up every bit of space in the buildings here. We couldn't get into any of them. There must be fifteen high-power radio transmitters set up in those buildings, and phone wires are running all over the place. Bad Bob [our squadron commander] has already had two severe set-tos with the chief of station this morning. Seems the guy thinks we work for him.

"Now get this. The hijacker is some old rube about sixty years old with a couple of boys in their late teens as his sidekicks. Says he doesn't have a political agenda—he just wants some money. And he's done this before—he took a plane, got the ransom, and went to Cuba about five years ago. Now he's back." Guy paused and took a thoughtful puff of his cigar before continuing.

"And there's more. There are five or six members of a network news crew on the plane and they're raising hell. The leader of the group gets on the radio at least twice an hour, screaming at the Hondurans that he's an important man so they should pay the ransom. A couple of other members of the TV crew who weren't on the flight are now running around town trying to raise money for the ransom. I guess they're taking up collections at the Hotel Maya and the other gringo-newsy hangouts. Knowing how well that crowd likes one another, they've probably raised thirty-five or forty cents already. I'm telling you, Cotton Mouth [my call sign], this is a real three-ring circus."

That's about the only thing that was obvious to me. "Guy, you got any ideas about what's really going on here?"

"Not yet," he replied as he shoved his cigar back in the corner of his mouth. "If I figure anything out, Eric, I'll let you know."

"Okay, Oso. See you at ringside."

"Sure," he said, tilting his head to blow an elongated cloud of smoke that looked like the spouting of a whale.

I found the boys and dropped my bag in the shade of a small grove of banana trees. As I got my equipment, Dan gathered the other team leaders so I could brief them on the DH-7. After the briefing was over, Dan told me what he knew.

"The commander is at the embassy duking it out with the chief of station. The ambassador is refereeing the fight. As things stand now, we're supposed to hit the plane tomorrow morning. But it doesn't look good—they've got explosives aboard. About an hour ago, the hijacker radioed the Hondurans for some lime. Said his dynamite was leaking and he wanted the lime to cover it with. We passed the word for him to just leave it alone and we'd send somebody out to help.

"Andres went out there with a load of sawdust. They let him aboard and sure enough, they had eight sticks of sweating dynamite rigged in two bombs. The old man knew enough about dynamite to know he had a problem on his hands so he let Andres put each bomb in a box and cover the dynamite with the sawdust. Then the old guy showed Andres how he's got the devices rigged to the main doors—just in case someone was thinking of assaulting the plane.

"Right now, we have the snipers deployed and are maintaining an emergency assault team. Feeney's team has it now; you relieve him at 1400.

"But the funny thing about it, Eric, is that no one's negotiating with the hijacker. Oh, they talk to him now and again sort of half-heartedly, but it's like they don't really want him to give up. Seems like they just want him dead."

"None of this makes any sense, Dan," I said. "We've got a cast of thousands running around here doing who knows what. There's enough radio frequencies flying out of here to smoke a low-flying bird. The Old Man and the chief of station are having a turf battle in the ambassador's office. Hell, I've been to a beheading in Saudi Arabia, six county fairs, and followed a syrup mill all over North Georgia, and I've never seen anything like this. What gives?"

Dan was an internal person and he seldom said more than was necessary. But he took in everything and he had an amazing ability to see through subterfuge and determine what lay at the heart of a matter. Dan was a long-range human polygraph.

"Eric, I believe the whole damn thing is a CIA operation gone wrong—probably a fund-raising mission for the Contras. But something happened and the Hondurans didn't pay off quick enough and no one counted on that news crew being on board. Before they knew what was happening, the cat was out of the bag and the last thing the Agency can afford is for the guy to give up and talk.

"So to protect their secret asses, the hijackers have to be killed and we're the ones who get to do it. And that's why the place is covered with those bastards—they've got to make sure it doesn't get any worse than it already is."

I mulled that over for a bit. It made sense. There wasn't another good reason for the overblown attention the Agency was focusing on this affair. Congress had recently put its foot down about funding the Contras, and rumors had been wafting about that the Agency was conducting some freelance work of its own to raise money for their pet Nicaraguans. So yes, this made sense. It was just a short step from running drugs to hijacking planes, but I was willing to bet the guy who dreamed this one up was sweating blood right now.

"Dan, that's a pretty shitty state of affairs," I said. "They get their ass in a crack and we get to be their hit men to cover it up. What kind of rat-bastards operate that way?"

"Thoroughly rotten ones, *mi amigo*," he said with a sigh. "Rotten to the center of their shriveled-up souls. But it's all just a theory, you know. I *believe* that's what's going on, but there will never be the slightest scrap of evidence to indicate what's really true."

I joined the rest of my mates and got into my assault gear. The rest of the day oozed by in the thick tropical heat. The guys were unnaturally quiet. There was very little of the normal joking and storytelling; mostly they seemed lost in their own thoughts, as if they were trying to transport themselves to a different time and place. I know that's what I was trying to do.

To break the fugue, every once in a while I'd walk over to the Honduran radio shack and listen to the latest talk from the airplane. It was always the same thing—the leader of the news group was asking about the progress of his friends who were trying to raise the ransom money. He had a whiny, condescending voice, and I could tell he had already managed to piss off the Honduran authorities. Ugly American—he wasn't helping his cause.

Just before dark, the squadron commander called us together. He had a surprise. "Guys, we're not going to make the hit. The Hondurans are going to do it. We'll provide sniper support for the assault; Eric, you and Andres will go with the Hondurans and hold their hands. The assault will take place at 0500 hours in the morning."

Everybody looked at us. I looked at Andres and lifted my eyebrows. Andres looked at the toes of his boots and shrugged.

"What are our instructions, jefe? Are we leaders or advisers?" I asked. "You know the Hondurans have never done a plane before— I don't think they've even practiced on a civilian aircraft. If they go in on their own, it will probably be a bloodbath. And don't forget about those dripping boxes of dynamite on board."

"You'll be leading the Hondurans. You're the assault leader, Eric; Andres, you're the two IC [second in command]. I'm counting on you two to keep it from becoming a bloodbath. We're all counting on you.

"The Hondurans are expecting you. When you've got your gear together and you're ready to leave, come and see me. I want to speak with you both in private."

This was getting worse and worse. The Hondurans weren't bad—but they weren't good either. They didn't have much experience and there wasn't much we could give them in the time we had left. Andres and I conferred before we reported back to Bad Bob. We were both worried about that dynamite. Andres said that while he was aboard, one of the passengers was able to tell him that the hijackers attached the bombs to the main doors only when something was going on that made them nervous. The rest of the time, the bombs stayed on the front row of seats under the direct control of the old man.

That was good information. At least the hijackers had the good sense not to keep active booby traps hooked up all the time. When you do that, you run the very real risk of accidentally setting them off yourself. And if they were hooking the devices to only the two main doors, maybe we could still get in without setting off those damn bombs.

We went over to join the boss. Larry Freedman also came over so we could coordinate with the snipers. Andres and I felt we had a plan and explored it with our guys.

"Larry, do y'all have a good clear shot at the hijacker when he's on the radio?"

"Yeah, Eric. He has to stand in the middle of the cockpit to handle the mike and we have a converging shot on him from each cockpit side window. The pilot and copilot are seated well below the angle of fire, so they're safe. It would be a righteous shot."

That's what I was hoping to hear. I turned to Bob. "We can get into the plane by way of the emergency exit hatches located on each side about midway down the fuselage. The hatches are spring-loaded; they pop to the outside. That gives us two breach points, one on either side, that can't be blocked or rigged with the explosive devices they have on board.

"If we can place the assault teams into position at those hatches just as daylight breaks, and then place a radio call to the plane, the snipers will be able to take out at least one of the hijackers. At the crack of the shots we can be inside immediately and, more than likely, will roll right over the other two before they're alert and have any idea what has happened.

"Andres will lead one assault team and I'll lead the other. That way, the Hondurans don't have to think about what they're doing. They just go where we go and do what we do—and they're pretty good at that."

"We'll give you a good shot," said Larry. "You want me to count it down or do you want to?"

"I'll count it down, Larry. That way, if something screws up I'll be able to stop the count if I need to. I'm not sure how easy it's going to go with the Hondurans once we get them out there and next to the plane. They may get excited and hard to control, or they may get hesitant. I don't expect any trouble with them—they're a good bunch of boys—but we need to be prepared for anything."

Larry nodded in agreement, and then Bob spoke.

"The priority here, guys, is clearing the plane and releasing the hostages unharmed. If you don't like the feel of it when you get out

there, back off and we'll wait—or we'll try something else. Some
people around here may think the attack time is set in stone, but
I'm not one of them. You do what you think is best. I don't want
you two taking any unnecessary chances."

Andres piped up with a grin on his face, "What chances are you
talking about, jefe? It's only an airplane with three terrorists inside,
armed with submachine guns and bombs. You'll know immediately
whether we've won or not."

"How's that, Andres?" Bob asked.

"Simple. If the plane doesn't blow up—we've won."

Bob laughed and said, "Then my advice to you two is: don't
blow up the friggin' plane! I want to see you both tomorrow, telling
me what a magnificent job you did, and trying to talk me into giving you a week off so you can recover from your ordeal."

"You can count on it, Bob," I said as we wrapped up our meeting. The atmosphere felt light and back to normal. We'd get the job
done in the morning and then everybody could go home. Whatever
was going on here would be sorted out before the earth completed
another revolution on its axis. It might be strange, but it was all part
of the great play of life, and I knew we had our part to play during
this act, just as the hijackers did.

We picked up some extra radio batteries, performed a radio
check, and had a last-second coordination conference with Larry.
Then we hitched a lift in the pickup for the ride to the other side of
the taxiway where the Honduran Cobra Force was set up. Andres
and I had worked with these guys before, so it was like old home
day when we joined the group.

The Hondurans were the best of all the Central American mili-
taries. The army had never been the repressive force in Honduras
that it had been in the other Central American countries. For the
campesinos, a tour in the army was viewed as a leg-up in society, so
the enlistees usually did their best. The Cobras didn't have a lot of
confidence in their abilities yet, but they were tough and they
wanted to do well.

The plan we outlined was a simple one. Once we talked them
through it, we drew a diagram of the plane on the hangar floor with
chalk and started rehearsals. It wasn't hard to understand. When the
snipers fired, we would assault the plane. Andres would lead his

team in through the left emergency exit and clear aft. At the same time, my boys and I would come in through the right exit and clear forward.

When we were satisfied that everyone knew what he was supposed to do, we tested their weapons. We filled a fifty-five-gallon drum half-full with sand, tilted it forty-five degrees, and had everyone test-fire his weapon into the drum's neck.

Then we made a radio check and put the guys down to sleep. We'd get them up at 0400, and the assault would follow quickly. I didn't want them to have a lot of time to think about things. Just enough to clear the sleep from their minds, make a last-minute equipment check, get a big drink of water, and move into position.

Andres and I spread our poncho liners on the ground in front of the hangar and got some rest. I fell asleep listening to the slow, rhythmic footsteps of the Honduran guard as he paced back and forth on the tarmac nearby.

I came wide awake at 0300 hours. This is the world's quiet time. The night animals have finished their endeavors and the day animals are resting silently. Nothing moves at that time of morning; even the insects are quiet. It's one of my favorite times, and to be awake at that hour always gives me a faintly self-satisfied feeling, like I'm in on a secret of some sort. I lay snug under my poncho liner for a few more minutes, hands linked under my head, just thinking and looking at the night sky.

From the vantage point of my warm, comfortable spot on Mother Earth, I could see off into infinite space and the eternity of time. *In just a few hours,* I thought, *some of us are going to make that leap into eternity. And I will be one of the instruments of that voyage. I may also be one of the travelers ... it's going to happen sooner or later. But if today is my day—I'm going to have a cup of coffee first.*

I rolled over and dug in my rucksack for the makings of a big canteen cup of MRE (Meal, Ready to Eat) coffee.

Andres stirred and turned over to look at me with alert eyes. He didn't say anything. He just reached into an outer pocket of his rucksack and tossed me an MRE bag filled with coffee, cocoa, cream and sugar packets, and heat tabs. Then he lay there watching me as I filled the canteen cup with water and set it on the tiny stove that held the blue flames of the burning heat tabs. When breakfast was in motion, Andres rose and we broke out our shaving kits and readied ourselves for the day.

I made a thick, strong brew of coffee and cocoa, one with plenty of sugar and powdered creamer. This would be our meal. When it was at the optimum temperature, just before the boiling point, Andres held out his canteen cup and I poured him half of the thick, aromatic liquid. He inhaled the sweet smell of the cup and lifted it to his lips. Just before he took a sip, he stopped short and said, "You know, Eric, I really don't want to kill that old man and those boys. I'll do it. But I don't want to."

I knew how he felt. That was the thought that had awakened me—and the same one that had worked at my mind while I slept. Hijackers are terrorists. Our job was to kill terrorists. But this hijacking had been remarkably short on terror. When the old man took the plane in the first place, he apologized for the inconvenience he was causing everyone. No one had been harmed at any step along the way. He had voluntarily released the women and children, and the sick and elderly. He had started with a full plane of about fifty passengers, but was now down to fewer than thirty hostages.

And he had never asked for an outrageous ransom—just five hundred thousand dollars and a continued flight to Cuba. But that was funny in itself because Cuba always turned over air pirates these days, and he had to know that. A lot of this just didn't make sense. I didn't know if I completely bought Dan's theory that the Agency was behind it all, but something was definitely unkosher at Toncontin Airport in the fair city of Tegucigalpa, Honduras.

While we sipped our coffee and chewed on our thoughts, I turned on my radio, plugged in the earpiece, and made a commo check with the sniper TOC. Nothing to report. It had been quiet on the plane all night and no movement had been spotted inside. That made sense: the hijackers and the hostages should be just about exhausted by now. I checked my watch.

I had finished my coffee and was rolling up my poncho liner when the radio spoke into my ear. "Cotton Mouth. Can you see the plane from your location?" The voice was animated.

"No. Not from here," I responded.

"Well, get to where you can. The hostages are escaping. A bunch of them have jumped out of R-2 [the emergency exit on the right side of the plane]. Otto's team is policing them up right now. Hang on a second, I've got more stuff coming in."

Andres had also heard the report, and he jumped up and slung his MP-5 around his neck. I grabbed mine and we sprinted to the end of the next hangar, where we could get a view of the plane. In the dim illumination of the airfield lights, we could see a gaggle of people being herded off the field and into a ditch by two black-clad figures. The radio barked again.

"Otto reports that about a dozen hostages were able to get out before the hijackers regained control. The Old Rooster [hijacker] is on the radio with the Hondurans right now. Your orders are to stand by. The assault is off. I say again, the assault is off for the time being. Acknowledge."

"Roger TOC," I answered. "The assault is off until I receive orders otherwise."

"Andres, go rouse the Cobras and stand by in emergency assault mode. Who knows what's liable to happen next? I'm gonna link up with Otto and see if I can make sense of this. Continue to monitor the command frequency, but you and I will talk on channel four. I'll call you when I know more."

"Okay, *hermano*. I'll get the boys and bring them to the back of this hangar. We'll be closer to the plane but still out of sight when daylight comes. I'll let you know when we're in position."

Andres trotted back to get the Cobras ready, and I headed in the opposite direction to see what the escapees had to say for themselves. I found the crowd in the ditch where I had seen them disappear. Rick Downing was giving first aid to one of them while the rest were huddled about Otto's feet like frightened chicks clustered around a mother hen. Otto was on the radio giving a report, so I went to see if Rick needed any help with the casualty.

The man had been given a chem-light and he was holding it near his uplifted face so Rick could see what he was doing. The poor guy had a broken nose—that much was certain—but other than a sore but unbroken wrist and a good case of road rash on his face, he seemed to be okay. None of the other escapees were injured, but they were all thirsty as hell and guzzled the canteens we gave them.

Otto and I conferred when he finished his report to the TOC. "Eric, the guy with the busted nose is the chief of the news group that was on the plane. You know—the guy who's been making all the noise. Here's what we've been able to piece together so far. I think it's pretty accurate.

"Just before midnight, the Old Rooster put the two boys in charge of the passengers and lay down to get some sleep. Once he was sawing logs, the two young dickheads got into the onboard liquor and had a little private party. When they fell asleep, our newsman here, who was leaning against the R-2 hatch, just reached up and pulled the handle. Little did he know the hatch was spring-loaded. So when she popped open and fell outboard, he went out with it—face first into the tarmac. As soon as he and the hatch disappeared, everyone close by started leaping out. If they'd been quiet about it, I'll bet everybody could have gotten out. But they started yelling and making such a racket that the Old Rooster woke up and put an end to the great escape."

He motioned to the passengers, who were still passing the canteens around and acting pretty perky. Nothing like escaping death to spice up life.

"If you'll take these guys up to the hangars, Larry will send a truck around to pick them up. Then Rick and me can get back into our position and see how this thing plays out. I understand the assault is on hold," he said, glancing in the direction of the plane.

"That's the way it stands right now. But who knows what could happen next," I replied.

"Yeah. Well. I hope it stays on hold, Bubba," Otto said grimly, his brow furrowed under the camouflage paint on his face. "There's no need to kill that old man."

Otto feels it too, I thought as I got the former hostages to their feet and started moving them to the hangars.

When the old man saw that half of his hostages had jumped ship, he got on the radio and told the Honduran authorities he was through dealing with them and demanded to speak with the airline station manager.

Once he had the airline representative on the radio, he laid out his new demands: fuel for the plane, food for himself, his accomplices, and the crew—and a cash payment of two hundred and fifty thousand dollars.

If all of that wasn't forthcoming by ten o'clock, he said he would release the remaining passengers and crew members—and set the airplane on fire. He suggested to the station manager that his company contact their insurer and see what those sensible people had to say about *that* idea—fork over a measly two hundred and fifty thousand dollars or buy a new airplane.

He got his way. The money was quickly delivered—along with air charts and approach plates for Cuba. The airplane's crew thought so much of the old man that they actually volunteered to make the flight themselves.

Otto, Andres, and I clustered on our little knoll near the taxiway and watched as the plane cranked up and took to the air. Within a few minutes, it was just a shiny speck in the distance and then it was gone.

I never heard anything about the Old Rooster or his two young apprentices again. I like to think that he invested his money wisely and was able to enjoy his remaining years in peace and quiet.

The newsman ran around for a while trying to interest someone in his story, but even his own network ignored him.

My mates and I returned home, pleased with the outcome of the affair. Sometimes it isn't the job you do that gives you the most satisfaction. It's the one you didn't have to do.

Master Sergeant Otto Clark died during Desert Storm trying to rescue his wounded comrade, Pat Hurley. Pat also died in the attempt.

We weren't home very long after that before something else called for our attention. We spent the better part of a year planning the invasion of a small tropical country that had managed to get itself on the U.S. government's shit list. I won't name the country. It would serve no purpose now and would just hurt their feelings.

The invasion was planned as quite a substantial operation. Along with Delta Force, participants were to include the 1st Ranger Battalion, a brigade-sized Marine amphibious unit, and fighters and bombers from the Navy and the Air Force. By the time we completed the final rehearsal for the attack, the cost of the preparations for this extravaganza had exceeded a billion dollars.

Now what, you might ask, could a little country do to get itself into such a notorious position that the greatest power in the world felt so threatened that it had no choice but to make war? Simple. It had decided to tax the largest corporate concern located within its borders. But this wasn't just any company. This was a huge and powerful American corporation. As the largest and wealthiest entity in this small country, this company was smugly accustomed to having its own way. And having its own way *did not* include *paying taxes* to its poor, third world host.

When the American corporation's efforts to stave off the implementation of that tax proved unsuccessful, the company took its concerns to Uncle Sam, where it found a sympathetic ear. It was quickly decided that such a tax rammed down the throat of one of America's largest, most respected companies was not only wrong— it was communist!

But the issue was eventually resolved another way. The CIA did one of the things it knows how to do and do well. A young man in that small nation's military, along with a number of his friends, was induced to revolt and commence a small-scale guerrilla war. And surprisingly, one of the central tenets of the guerrilla group's manifesto was a provision firmly opposed to the taxation of foreign corporations.

Before long, concordance was reached. The old president agreed to step down, the guerrillas came out of the forest, the obnoxious tax law was repealed, and everybody went back to the carefree and lighthearted ways of before.

There would be no invasion. At least not of that country. But we had a custom-tailored invasion plan sitting on the shelf—an expensive one—and it seemed a shame to let it go to waste.

I was on my way home from a trip to Korea. I had been working as an adviser to the South Korean military as they struggled to devise and build a counterterrorism force. Their objective was to have the outfit up and running before Korea hosted the upcoming Asian Games, and they would use those games as a dress rehearsal for their security forces in anticipation of Seoul hosting the summer Olympics.

It had been a long, tiring trip. The Koreans are a dynamic people and they approach every undertaking with unrelenting intensity. Just being around that much focused activity will wear you out. But there was another concern nagging at me on the long flight back from Seoul. At the airport just before boarding, I had seen a television news flash: An explosives-laden truck driven by a suicide bomber had attacked the U.S. Marine barracks in Beirut. Hundreds were dead and many more were wounded.

An attack like that wouldn't go unpunished—and we knew just where to strike. For months now, we'd been tracking several of the most active terrorist cells in Beirut and we were ready to make a clean sweep of them. It wouldn't put an end to the terrorist activity in the region, but it sure would put them out of action for a while. I fully expected a return engagement in Beirut.

It was late at night when we landed in Fayetteville, and as I walked into the terminal, one of the first people I saw was Don Feeney's wife, Judy. We were old and close friends, but I knew she wasn't here to meet me. After we said hello she told me she was meeting her cousin, who was attending the Special Forces Officers Course. Then she turned me to the side and spoke in a low voice. "Eric, Donny got called in less than an hour ago. It's a full alert. If you want to go straight to the unit, I'll stop by your house and let your family know where you are."

Damn, I'd gotten back just in time. This was moving faster than I had anticipated. I had no time to waste. "Thanks, Judy, that's very sweet of you. Just say I'll be home when I can."

"Sure, Eric. That's the one we hear all the time," she said. Then she gave me a hug and said, "You and Don be careful—all of you be careful."

"We always are, Judy," I said over my shoulder as I headed for the parking lot. Even then, Judy Feeney was one of the most capable, courageous women I'd ever known. In the years to come she'd prove a cool head and steady hand in the many dangerous child rescue missions she and Donny have undertaken around the world. In fact, the last two child rescues I've executed were with Judy.

One of the hardest things about responding to a Bowstring Alert is making yourself drive the speed limit as you make your way to the unit. Every fiber of your being is screaming, "Let's go! Get this damn thing moving!" But you have to resist the urge. You can't afford to draw attention to yourself—and the last thing you want to do is get a speeding ticket. But it was midnight on a Sunday, the traffic was light, and I made good time across Fayetteville and Fort Bragg to our Butner Street compound.

When I got there, the parking lot was as full as on a Monday morning. I went in through the side gate and down the long corridor to my troop bay. One of my squadron mates, Daryl Evans, was coming out of the Bowstring equipment storage area pulling a dolly loaded with crates of ammunition. I grabbed the handle and helped pull the load down the hallway.

"Ready to go to Beirut, Daryl?" I asked as we strained against the heavy load.

"Not going to Beirut, Eric. We're making an invasion," he said with his head down as he leaned against the weight of the heavy cart.

"So we're finally gonna do it, eh? We're gonna hit that place?"

"Nope. Not them either," he answered, without looking up. "We're invading Grenada."

Grenada? *Grenada?*

That didn't make any sense. I'd seen President Reagan on television about a month earlier, telling the nation about the airfield the Cubans were helping to build in Grenada, but everybody knew there was no threat in that. The Cuban military had no forces that could use the airfield, and the Soviets would never hang their asses out in such a remote and indefensible place. It was just a good propaganda mission—socialist goodwill at work, helping a brother third world nation.

I stuck my head in the squadron office to announce my return. Bad Bob was standing there looking at a map on the wall. He looked up as I walked in. "Grenada?" I asked.

"Yep, Grenada," he confirmed. "Don't happen to have a good map of the place, do you? All I have is a Xeroxed page from a travel guide, and it ain't worth a damn. We've got a request in to Defense Mapping and to the CIA. You know what that's worth. We won't get any maps but we'll get some damn interesting excuses," he said.

"When do we leave?" I asked.

"Tomorrow...er...today," he said, consulting his watch. "C-5As loaded with Task Force 160 helicopters to Barbados. When we land, the helicopters will be pulled out and get their rotors assembled. And then we launch. We fly to Barbados tonight and make a predawn assault into Grenada the next morning. B Squadron hits the Richmond Hill Prison to liberate any political prisoners being held there. We'll also try to take the heat off the

Rangers as they jump onto the airfield. Your troop has all the information. You team leaders sort it out and put your plan together."

"Sure thing, Bob. A mission is a mission. But doesn't this one seem just a little *flojo* to you? I mean, Grenada for Chrissakes. If this is supposed to be in response to the bombing in Beirut, it's like shooting the dog that didn't bite you. Like when the Nicaraguans finally threw Somoza out and the Carter administration put sanctions on Guatemala. We're not just missing the target here, Bob. Hell, we're not even shooting at it."

Bob held up a hand to tell me to hold my fire. "Eric, you know I don't make these decisions any more than you do. We just do the best job we can at what we're told to do and try to all come home alive."

"Of course, Bob, and please believe that I'm not going off on you—far from it. I'm just an old country boy trying to make it through this world the best I know how. But the path we're on gets a little hard to divine sometimes. Like right now."

"That's probably true, Eric," he said, clapping a hand on my shoulder. "And that's why we're counting on you old-timers to get us through this one."

Here is the plan we choreographed.

B Squadron would form the initial element of the assault. We would fly in a lift of seven Blackhawk helicopters from Barbados to the southernmost end of Grenada and make an airmobile assault on the hilltop fortress of Richmond Hill Prison.

Once that was accomplished, we would sweep the high ground overlooking the Point Salines airfield and attack any enemy positions that might be situated to impede the dawn parachute assault the Rangers would make to secure the runway.

When the Rangers secured the runway, A Squadron would land by C-141s laden with "Little Bird" helicopters and make an assault upon an installation known as Fort Rupert.

The Ready Brigade of the 82nd Airborne Division would then start landing and the Rangers would push inland, up a nearby valley, to capture the facilities of the Cubans who were on the island.

Meanwhile, the Marines would make an amphibious landing on the northern side of the island. Once they were safely ashore, they'd sweep to the south for an eventual link-up with the Rangers.

My expanded six-man team for the operation included one

brand-new team member. The latest OTC class had graduated while I was in Korea, but I had already gotten my bid in for the "draft" and it was my turn for a first-round pick. I snapped up Bart Preminger, a big, tall, good-looking guy from Kansas. We had over-lapped in the Ranger battalion, where he had risen from private to sergeant in the Fire Support section. Following his tour in the Rangers, Bart had gone on to Special Forces and served three years before making it through Selection.

The other team members for "Operation Urgent Fury," as it was called, were my old pals Smiley and Andres, plus Albert Maker, Stan Johnson, and Robert Wilson. Our task during the assault on the prison was to descend by fast rope into the prison courtyard, fight our way into the building, and release any political prisoners we found inside. From there we would move to the hill overlooking the Point Salines airfield and assist the Rangers.

All in all, not a daunting task. But we had absolutely no intelli-gence about what to expect or where to expect it. We had no idea if there were any prisoners in Richmond Hill. We didn't know if the place was guarded—and if it was, we didn't have any idea about the size and composition of the guard force. We didn't know how the Grenadans were organized, what kind of Cuban forces were on the island, or what type of weaponry either of them had.

We didn't even have a rumor of decent maps. We were able to get our hands on a Michelin guide to the Windward Islands with a somewhat usable chart of Grenada. This allowed us to get a basic feel for the layout of the island. We would make our approach from Barbados on a flight heading of 186 degrees. We would travel in seven helicopters, with my team in chopper number three. Our flight path would bring us down the length of the island and carry us just to the east of the capital city of St. Georges. As we neared Richmond Hill, Fort Frederick would be on the high ground, just 450 meters to our east.

Just a rifle shot away from Richmond Hill, I thought as I studied the Michelin guide. The maximum effective range of an M-16 is 465 meters. Which brought to mind another thought—we wouldn't carry submachine guns on this mission. I had no idea what we might eventually run into, so our assault weapons would be M-16s and CAR-15s.

By midafternoon the teams had thrashed out their individual plans and the team leaders had coordinated their actions on the objective. But the thought of Fort Frederick sitting unmolested on the next ridgeline continued to nag at me. That place was close enough to give us some serious problems, but nobody was dedicated to hitting it. The Air Force promised to pound the place if it gave us any trouble, so we left it at that.

We landed on Barbados at midnight. The C-5As were parked on the taxiway with their ramps wide open and their bellies full of folded-up Blackhawk helicopters, but the helicopter crews were nowhere in sight. I didn't know how long it took to drag a Blackhawk out of a C-5A, extend its rotors, and fold its tail into position, but I knew it had to take longer than it took us to prepare a "Little Bird" Covert Troop Carrier or a "Killer Egg" Attack Helicopter.

We'd been told that the Blackhawk crews didn't want our help. It was the responsibility of the maintenance teams to put the birds in flight configuration. That was all well and good, but the helicopters just continued to sit there in the bellies of those planes and we were running out of darkness.

By the time the helicopters were finally ready, we had little more than an hour before daylight. The flight time to the target was supposed to be one hour and twenty-one minutes. If we didn't make up some time en route, we'd get there just minutes before the Rangers jumped. We climbed aboard the minute the crews said they were ready, and finally we lifted off.

There's no feeling in the world more exciting than making a combat assault on an enemy target by helicopter. The doors of the chopper are taken off and you sit with your feet dangling outside— or at least you did riding the old Hueys. The Blackhawk was so fast that you had to keep your feet pulled inside until it started to slow down, just to keep from being yanked out.

But the roar of the engines, the whine of the rotors, the earth whipping below, and the pounding rush of air pouring over you and ripping at your clothes make you feel like a cavalryman of old. You blast toward the target like a relentless and implacable spear hurled by the god of war. It is a stirring, phenomenally exciting feeling—one *almost* worth the cost of your life.

We crossed the coast of Grenada on the backside of a rainstorm, just as the first light of dawn lit the eastern sky. The terrain was mountainous, with steep, jungle-covered ridges separated by deep, narrow valleys.

Get ready.

We slid our feet and legs over the edge of the Blackhawk's floor as we arrowed our way to the target. I was hanging my head out the doorway trying to see ahead when I heard the first rifle fire. The shots were scattered at first, but rapidly gathered impetus and volume. Then the machine guns found us and the air was thick with tracers—red, ugly fingers trying to claw us out of the sky.

The first round that hit us came from a 23-millimeter automatic cannon. It punched into the cockpit with a shower of Plexiglas and detonated a fire extinguisher, momentarily filling the bird with a thick white cloud before blowing away in the slipstream. It was the perfect mood setter.

Almost immediately the next round found the navigator—hit him high in the left shoulder, ranged through his neck, and exited his right shoulder. And this poor guy had been the only survivor of a fatal crash in Panama just the week before.

Then the fire became so thick and heavy it was impossible to keep up with what it was doing to us. From my view out the wide-open doorway, it was nothing but a storm of red searching for us. Slapping and stinging us, tearing the bird to pieces, and plowing furrows through human flesh.

The door gunner was hammering away with his machine gun while we all fired at the hated enemy guns on the ground—then he stopped firing and slumped over his gun. I pulled him back and yelled over the roar of the fight, "What's the matter?"

He yelled back, "I've been hit!"

Stan and I went down the front of his face and chest looking for a wound but couldn't find anything. If he was hit, it wasn't an immediately fatal wound.

"You're okay," I yelled in his ear, and at that reassurance, he grabbed his gun and went back to firing.

Parts of the helicopter were being blasted off. I could feel the heat of the rounds passing through the bird and near my face. On the other side of the chopper, Dan Bryers was gut-shot and, just seconds later, hit again in the thigh.

Bart took a wound to the right thigh that looked like he had been chopped with a machete. I saw his eyes go wide with the first flush of shock as he looked at his shredded leg. There wasn't much bleeding, but there was a lot of gashed flesh. I reached over and grabbed him by the arm, gave him a shake, and shouted, "Are you all right?" His eyes immediately regained their focus and he yelled, "Yeah! I'm okay."

I felt a sharp tug up on my left shoulder and a stinging slap across the left side of my face and neck. The strobe light I carried attached to the shoulder of my equipment harness had been hit by a round and exploded in a spray of plastic. I reached up to feel for my left eye. It was still there and working.

Then the door gunner slumped over his gun again.

"What's the matter now?" I yelled.

"I've been hit again," he whimpered as a look of self-pity flooded his face.

Once more I looked at his face and head, and checked down across his chest and abdomen—no wounds.

"You're okay," I yelled again. But he shook his head and called back, "No I'm not. I'm hit in the back, and it's bad."

Stan cut open the back of the gunner's flight suit and found two parallel ripping wounds, two inches apart and nearly a foot long, running from his right side to within a half inch of his spine. I pulled the gunner out of his seat and Stan climbed over him to take over his position behind the gun.

Then we took a blast of fire so severe it seemed as if a giant's angry hand grabbed us midflight and shook us like a dish towel. The bird shuddered and pitched so hard I thought we would go down, but soon she regained her composure and kept flying.

A heavy-caliber round scorched by my face and I took such a gasp of breath that my chest muscles cramped—for a second I thought I had been drilled through the lungs. Then Andres slapped a hand to his right thigh and turned to look me in the face. We were sitting jammed thigh to thigh, and now we both stopped firing and looked down as he slowly pulled his hand away from his leg and we saw that it was covered ... in a wad of white goo.

I believe I've seen everything that can possibly come from the insides of a human being, but I had never seen anything like this. And from the look on his face, neither had Andres. We looked at his gooey hand and then into each other's puzzled eyes and I yelled, "What the hell is that?"

The light of understanding clicked on in his face and he yelled back with a huge grin. "Toothpaste! They shot me through my tube of toothpaste!"

Andres was inordinately proud of his pearly whites and always carried a toothbrush, toothpaste, and floss with him wherever he went—even in combat. For this mission, he had stowed his dental necessities in the right cargo pocket of his pants. A bullet had ripped through the bottom of the chopper, through the tube of toothpaste in his pocket, and then through Andres's thigh. I was worried for a second that the round might have hit his femoral artery, but he showed no signs of shock. The bullet plowed completely through his leg, coming to rest just under the skin on the top of his thigh, missing both the artery and the femur.

But the firestorm wasn't over yet. We were still being pounded with gusto.

I hung out of the bird again to check on the rest of the helicopters. Most of the enemy guns were firing at bird number one, which gave them the perfect lead for hitting us. That's why our helo was taking such a pasting. Then something mule-kicked me from behind and almost threw me out of the chopper. My right hip went numb and I felt wetness slide down my ass and leg. *Oh hell, my ass has been shot off,* I thought as I shoved my hand behind me to find the wound. Instead, I found my canteen had been blown to bits. I happily looked at my hand, wet with water and not blood.

I looked behind me out the other side of the bird and saw things were just as bad on that side as they were on this one. Nothing but a sea of red tracers and wounded men. I turned back to hang outside again to try to see the target; we should have been almost there by now.

Just as we took some horrifically intense fire, I saw bird number five break formation and dive down a deep valley, ducking under the stream of fire from a 23-millimeter. They were trailing a thick gray plume and going down fast—but they were still flying, so they weren't out of control. I hoped they could make it to a safe place and put her on the ground.

Suddenly the target loomed ahead.

Albert was holding the coiled fast rope in his lap and he got up on his knees to give it a toss as I yelled, "Get ready!" to the team. As we came to a hover, Stan silenced a machine gun across the valley. We all looked down into—a derelict and empty compound. The damn place was abandoned! The main gate to the prison was wide open, and so were all the doors we could see. The windows were broken and the courtyard was overgrown with weeds and brush. The ground was littered with broken furniture and garbage. I could even smell the place from the chopper. It smelled like a urinal.

"Do not! Do not! Don't! Don't!" I yelled to Albert, shaking my head in the negative as he poised in position to throw the rope. Bob was shouting over the radio, "Let's get out of here," as he and the rest of the team leaders reached the conclusion I had: "Dry hole!"

The choppers tilted their noses downward to pick up forward momentum and find a place free of the terrible fire we were taking. Within seconds we were over the ocean and out of range of the guns. I looked out over the water, and what a sight—Navy ships everywhere. Great! Ships have doctors and we needed medical help badly. Don was going into shock from his abdominal wound and the navigator was failing rapidly.

Nobody was dead on our bird—yet—but from a quick head count, it looked like we had eight men wounded. Eight out of fifteen was a pretty high ratio, but I was frankly amazed that we were still alive. And even more amazed that the helicopter was still flying. If we had flown this mission in the old Hueys, we all would have been shot down. *These Blackhawks are some damn tough birds,* I thought as we skimmed over the surface of the ocean. But I had never, ever, seen ground fire so concentrated and effective. *It was like they knew when we were coming and where we were going.*

The whole ordeal had lasted no more than ten minutes, but it seemed like several lifetimes. Even now, I shudder on the inside just to think about it. How can I explain the sensation of being the focus of attention for twenty machine guns? It's worse than being under artillery fire. At least when the big guns are pounding you, there is the prospect of taking cover. Even if you're caught in the open, you can flatten out on the ground—and believe me, you'll try to hide behind a thick blade of grass if that's all you have.

But in the air, you just have to take it. You make yourself as small as possible. You even think small. You sink your head as deep as you can into your shoulders, draw all your muscles up into a knotted bundle, pull your limbs in just as tightly as you can, and take small shallow breaths. When you can see the tracer streams coming at you, the thought's always in your mind that between each tracer, there are four other bullets that you can't see.

We were landing on a small helicopter pad on the rear deck of a destroyer—the USS *Moosbrugger,* I found out later. We hit the deck and bounced to a stop. *Get the wounded out and inside* was all I could think as I lurched up to jump out. I had been sitting with my left leg tucked under me, unable to move since we left Barbados. The leg was numb and asleep but I didn't know it, and as I bounded out of the helicopter, it collapsed underneath me and I crashed to the deck. I rolled over and examined my leg for an unknown wound and was glad to find none.

I was struggling to my feet to help the Navy crewmen who were pulling the wounded out of the bird when the sailor who was running the flight pad helped me up and asked with a shocked look on his face, "Are you okay, buddy?"

"Yeah, I'm all right," I yelled over the roar of the helicopter. "My leg was asleep, that's all."

"Your face and head are covered with blood!" he yelled back.

I ran my hand across my skull and face and pulled it away—covered in blood. Then it hit me—it wasn't my blood. It was blood that had been blowing off the wounded navigator sitting just in front of me in the bird.

"It ain't mine," I yelled.

"Good," he yelled back at me. "Now help me make that pilot fly this damn thing off of here before we shove it over the side."

"Why?" I screamed over the roar of the chopper.

"Because it's so damn full of holes I could see through it as you flared to land. It's leaking fuel and hydraulic fluid like a sieve. It's a hazard to the safety of this ship."

"That's your problem," I shouted as I limped over to help with the wounded. But that was one tough bird. She flew and fought the whole rest of the day.

We hustled our wounded inside the small bay forward of the helicopter pad. The floor of the room was covered with the wounded from birds one and two, and the place stank with the coppery smell of their blood. Smiley was an SF medic and he was already at work with the Navy corpsmen and the doctor. I helped get IVs started and then moved around to talk to the guys.

I sat with Don before a chopper arrived to carry him to the operating room on the hospital ship, the *Iwo Jima*. He was gray and his eyes were dilating from blood loss and the resulting shock. But just before he was carried to the bird, Smiley came running up from below with a bottle of oxygen, plastered a mask across his face, and hit him with the O$_2$. Within seconds some of the pallor of death left his face and the size of his pupils started to decrease.

I shifted over to talk to one of our radio operators who was snarling and cursing in pain. He had been shot twice in the thigh, in almost the same spot. When the first round hit him, he clapped a hand to the wound—just in time for the second bullet to take the ends off two of his fingers. He was lying on his stomach with the back of his right thigh ripped to pieces. I asked him how he felt, and he said that his leg didn't bother him much, but his fingers hurt like hell!

Andres was sitting off to the side by himself with a thoughtful look on his face. I sat down beside him and asked him if he thought maybe he should see a medic. He just shook his head and said, "No."

I left him alone and moved over to Gregg Halligan, one of our new guys, who was also sitting by himself. Gregg had a sad, hangdog look on his face. I decided I'd lighten up his attitude.

"Hey, man, how's it going, you're not hurt, are you?" I asked him, clapping a hand on his back.

"Naw, I'm okay, I guess. But my foot hurts," he said, staring across the room full of wounded men. "I sat on it the whole way from Barbados and it went to sleep on me. Now it aches like hell."

"Well, let me just take a look at that foot," I said, trying to make a joke of it. "Maybe all it needs is a little massage to make it good as new again. Which one is it?"

He slid his left foot forward. I took one look at it and said, "My friend, that foot has a perfect reason to hurt. You've been shot just below the top of the boot. The bullet's gouged out a path from front to rear—about a half an inch deep."

He looked down at his foot, wiggled it a little bit, and said with wonder in his voice, "Well, goddamn. No wonder it hurts." His whole face brightened almost immediately. Nothing like knowing you're shot to perk a man up. We put a field dressing on his leg.

A chopper was coming back for us, so the unperforated and the walking wounded alike climbed aboard to return to the island and finish the job. The Rangers were just a few minutes out, and we had to help sweep the high ground overlooking the airfield where they would land. It was less than a mile to shore, so we flitted just barely over the surface of the water toward the seaward end of the airfield. Several of the other birds had already landed, and the guys had moved up into the brush-covered hills to flush out any riflemen or machine guns that could hamper the parachute drop.

Don Feeney's team joined mine, and together we shifted one ridgeline over, spread out in an open formation, and started moving up to the highest point of the hill. We had just gotten to the top when someone shouted, "There are the planes!"

I turned around just in time to see a line of C-130s coming in low from the east. But as they approached the leading edge of the airfield, the first two planes were plastered with automatic cannon fire. The lead plane broke away, but the others just kept coming, and then we could see the Rangers pouring out the jump doors and into the sky. They were jumping at such a low altitude that their parachutes opened only a few seconds before they hit the ground. Goddamn, what a stirring sight! This was the first combat parachute operation since the Second World War.

We quickly got out some air-ground signal panels to let them know we were friendly and fired over the next ridge toward those 23-millimeters to give the gunners a little something to worry about. The first pass of the planes had dumped about a company of Rangers and now the planes were circling and heading back for the second drop. Rangers were scattered down the length of the ten-thousand-foot runway, just getting out of their parachutes, when two armored vehicles rolled out onto the airfield and started firing their machine guns and heavy cannon.

"Oh hell! Not that!" I yelled in frustration. "The sons of bitches will cut our men to pieces." But almost as soon as the vehicles gained the center of the runway, the Rangers opened fire on them with two 90-millimeter recoilless rifles—abruptly ending the armor threat on Point Salines. Now the second pass was overhead, and the air was full of green parachutes dangling brave men.

So the automatic weapons shifted their focus from the airplanes to the men in the air and on the ground.

This is bad, this is bad, I thought, watching the fire rip across the far end of the runway. This is when a unit is the most vulnerable. Just as they land and their leaders are scattered and they haven't had the time to reorganize.

But then I saw an amazing sight. The Rangers rose from the ground as one organism, screaming their war cries, and assaulted straight across the airfield toward the enemy guns. Within ten minutes, the guns went silent. The third and last pass of Rangers jumped almost unmolested.

Later that day I learned that a corporal had led the spontaneous assault across the airfield. Somebody said the guy jumped up from the ground and shouted, "I've had enough of this shit!" and took off across the airfield toward the enemy positions. Every man near him jumped up to follow, and the attack spread like wildfire up and down the length of the airfield. Goddamn! What soldiers!

We moved over to the next hill mass to see if we could provide any support, but now it was a pure-ass infantry fight—and besides, we were in a fairly degraded state. Minutes later, planes started landing and disgorging troops and equipment. A Squadron arrived in their C-141s. They hauled out the "Little Birds" they were going to use, spread the rotors into position, cranked up, and took off to attack Fort Rupert. They were back in ten minutes. The aerial fire from the heavy guns around the fort was so heavy the pilots wouldn't fly into it—rightfully so, in my opinion.

About the time A Squadron returned, Steve Ansley's team came back. They'd headed out on a mission to rescue the guys who had crashed in bird five.

The bird had almost made it back to the coast before she went down. The pilot was able to fly her into the ground but she went in hard. All her hydraulic lines had been shot away, so the pilot had little control left as he put her into the trees. The impact was so severe that the tail broke completely off and the main rotor blades flew off in every direction. Then the bird rolled over twice. By the grace of God, only one man was thrown out in the roll, but the bird came to rest on top of him. He was pinned half underneath her just as they caught on fire. And just as a Cuban patrol attacked.

The men on board were in pretty bad shape from the trauma of the crash. The scalding hydraulic fluid spewing from the shot-out hydraulic lines had blinded more than half of them. Even blind and disoriented, Chris Cable managed to crawl uphill in the direction of the attacking Cubans. By listening to the gunfire and firing toward the sound, he was able to hold them at bay.

The fire had taken firm hold of the cockpit, and the pilot was caught in his seat, the flames lapping his body. Though badly wounded himself, Amos Horton ran around to the cockpit intending to kill him rather than let him burn to death, when he saw that the pilot had been shot though the head and was already dead.

John Ginniff was the operator trapped under the helicopter, and as the flames spread rapidly down the fuselage, he called out to his mates, "Don't let me burn!"

Three of his injured comrades wedged themselves under the burning helicopter and in an amazing display of desperate strength, straightened up and lifted the massive bird with their backs, allowing John to be dragged to safety.

Steve's team landed on the beach near the crash site and moved in to help. Following the sounds of firing, Steve moved uphill and found Chris behind a small tree, his magazines and grenades laid out in front of him so he could tell them apart by touch, single-handedly holding off the Cuban attackers. They fired off several magazines together and Steve threw a couple of hand grenades—enough to discourage the Cubans. The Cubans pulled back, and Steve was able to bring Chris down the hill unmolested.

Everyone on the bird was badly injured. The door gunner was wounded the worst; he'd been hit by a large-caliber round that all but amputated his foot. The foot was dangling by just a shred of skin and sinew as they moved him to the beach. Ginniff was also in rough shape. Before the crash he had been shot through the leg, and when the helicopter rolled over on him and pinned him to the ground, it crushed his pelvis. Both he and the door gunner would eventually be retired as a result of their wounds. The guys were flown out to the hospital ship, the *Iwo Jima,* and turned over to the Navy medical teams.

It was hot and dry on our hill, so Doc Smiley went in search of some water for us. When he returned, he sat down with Andres and asked to see his leg. By way of an answer, Andres asked for a scalpel.

Smiley headed out again, returning a little while later with a tube of Betadine, a fresh bandage, and a brand-new scalpel still in its paper cover.

Andres cut open his trousers with his field knife and exposed a fist-sized black bruise on the top of his thigh. Right in the center of the bruise underneath the skin was a small lump. Andres cleaned his hands and then smeared Betadine over the bruise. He pinched the lump in the bruise like he was squeezing a pimple and made a deft slice in the middle with the scalpel. Out popped the bullet. He set it aside while he cleaned both the entry wound and the site of the "operation," and then he bandaged his leg. I never saw him so much as flinch as he doctored himself. In fact, he hummed a tune the whole time.

When the unit surgeon examined the wound the next day, he declared he couldn't have done a better job himself. My friend Andres is one hell of an hombre.

And that pretty much wrapped up our day on the lovely island paradise of Grenada. We were home that night by ten o'clock. I returned a few days later on the off chance of doing a little sniping, but nothing came of it. The Rangers and the 82nd stayed for a few more weeks to finish mopping up, and then a multinational Caribbean police force was instituted to maintain order until Grenada organized herself once more.

America declared a great victory and felt good about herself again. In fact, military enlistments took such a jump that a third Ranger battalion was formed and the Ranger regiment of today came into being. And at the prodding of Congress, the U.S. military started to take a much closer look at enhancing the interoperability of the military services. This eventually resulted in the creation of the U.S. Special Operations Command (USSOCM), which has done wonders for the Special Operations capability of our nation.

Castro went into a snit and declared he didn't want his captive soldiers back. The Red Cross finally made arrangements to fly the poor guys home. Life went on in the rest of the world as though nothing much had happened. And that ten-thousand-foot runway brings in a few peaceful visitors to Grenada, now and then.

I T APPEARED, AS THE DECADE WORE ON, THAT NONE OF THE troubled spots of the world were improving. If anything, they were getting worse, and we were busier than ever. The surrogate wars sponsored by the United States and the Soviet Union seemed to boil at even higher temperatures. The Middle East continued to crackle with its everlasting problems. Kidnappings of westerners in Lebanon had become commonplace, and aircraft hijackings were now almost a summer sport.

Africa was a continent in torrid conflict from east to west and north to south. Ethiopia was in civil war, as was the Sudan. South Africa was in the throes of civil unrest, and its problems had spilled across its borders to all of its neighbors.

The southern tier of Asia crashed and careened from one problem area to another. India and Pakistan stayed at a state of low-level conflict, and the Tamil separatists of Sri Lanka had embraced the use of terrorism in their civil war.

In Italy, a few years before, an American, General James Dozier, had been kidnapped, and that country was having a very difficult time with its homegrown terrorists. Croatian separatists were causing trouble in the Balkans, and Turkish terrorists were assassinating Turkish diplomats around the world.

We had members scattered to every place of trouble to be found, but nowhere did things appear less hopeful than in Central America. By this time Honduras was little more than a vast U.S. military base. We had an impressive air base and staging area at Soto Cano

Field in the center of the country. And there was a large but almost unknown training facility on the Caribbean coast near the town of Trujillo where American Special Forces advisers trained Honduran, Salvadoran, and Guatemalan combat battalions. The Swan Islands offshore were a remote location used to support clandestine operations into Nicaragua.

U.S. Army and National Guard engineer units were all over the country, building airfields and roads and, most important, drilling wells. Honduras is a relatively dry country and is not well blessed with streams or rivers. So the military engineers had been tasked with drilling large-diameter wells in a number of strategically sited locations around the country.

Once the wells were tested and proven, they were capped off for later use, to prevent the locals from using them. The wells and other assets that had been constructed were sufficient to support an entire United States Army corps, just in case we ever decided to attack Nicaragua. It was all done in the interest of raising the stakes of the game.

But the opposition wasn't exactly sitting on its thumbs, either. The Soviets watched intently with their satellites and knew exactly what we were up to. And they shared the information with their clients in the region.

The Sandinistas, with help from the Cubans, kept a very active intelligence operation going inside Honduras. The effort was especially effective at the national university, as large numbers of students were in opposition to the American presence within the country and, as some said, dominance of the Honduran government. Friction continued to grow, and then one of those defining circumstances took place. The kind that sets unforeseen events in motion, and brings about undreamed-of results.

Within Honduras there were about a half dozen would-be guerrilla groups. Small and ineffective, they had made contact with both the Cubans and the Nicaraguans, asking for assistance. Cuba had the charter for providing that sort of thing in Latin America, but they also had a very sensible policy. They would provide no assistance whatsoever until the dissidents of a nation spoke with one voice. Cuba had no intention of dealing with fragmented and competing groups.

I had been following the situation closely for more than a year and a half, and expected nothing to come of it, when the unimaginable happened. The Honduran groups reached an accord among themselves, and the next thing we knew, more than three hundred Honduran rebels had transited Nicaragua and were en route to Cuba for extended combat training.

The situation was starting to look serious. For several months the Honduran military had been screaming that the Sandinistas were putting patrols across the Honduran border. But every time we recommended slipping some of our ground tracker teams into the crossing areas, the Honduran chief of staff, General Gustavo Alvarez, demurred. (A few years later Alvarez would approach Charlie Beckwith, seeking his help in executing a coup in Honduras. Beckwith promptly reported the affair to the FBI and Alvarez was subsequently arrested, tried, and convicted.)

I was pretty sure I knew what Alvarez was up to. He had learned rapidly and well how to pump money out of the gringos. Yell loudly about threats on the border, and the money fountain flowed. Already he was riding around Tegucigalpa in a huge armored Mercedes, and it was known that he had acquired several nice villas and an appropriate number of mistresses with which to occupy them. It was a given that he had several fat foreign bank accounts.

Maybe it was because the Honduran rebels were in Cuba for such a long time, or maybe it was because we had been distracted by an outbreak of plane hijackings in the Middle East, but whatever the cause, all of us, myself included, were caught off guard when the newly trained and fully operational guerrilla unit slipped across the Honduran border and back upon their native soil. We had planned for that eventuality, and although the notice had been short, we wasted no time in taking action. Once again, I was fed into the breach.

The running fight had been long and horrible. We had laid hold of the guerrilla unit eight days earlier and, after nearly continuous battle, had finally run them to ground on this desolate Honduran mountaintop.

The force I led was a mixed unit of Honduran Special Forces, Black Carib trackers, and two teams from my Delta Force troop. After the trackers had found the guerrillas' trail, I kept "hunter/

killer" teams after them night and day, and allowed them no rest. I continually sent small units ranging around and ahead of their formation, and hit them from long-range ambush at every turn. Snipers shot down stragglers and the unwary. Water was one of the keys to this operation, and I was determined that the guerrillas would have none. Every time they attempted to fill their canteens at some small muddy trickle of a stream, we were there, and machine-gunned them without mercy.

They fought back with determination and tried desperately to shake us. But as the guerrilla unit weakened from casualties, sickness, and desertions, they became dazed and less effective. And as their powers of resistance lessened, I purposefully shoved them away from the potential sanctuary of the border, and deeper into the most remote and inhospitable terrain on the map.

I had a destination for them in mind, and by making it look like the best of several bad options, they went for it. The way had deliberately been left open to this mountaintop, and when the guerrillas took final refuge there, I closed the noose that was already in place and slowly squeezed them into a small perimeter at the top.

Originally the guerrillas had crossed the border with a force of about three hundred men. With desertions and casualties from the unrelenting pace of the fight, I estimated they had no more than sixty men left in their defensive perimeter. And those men were weak and demoralized.

My own troops, too, were in rough shape. We had pushed hard, moved fast, slept little, and fought continually in terribly difficult, sun-scorched terrain. But at least we had water to drink, food to eat, plenty of ammunition, and pack animals to carry the heaviest loads. More important, we had the initiative, and we had hope.

The guerrillas had none of those things. They were desperately hoping for an aerial resupply drop from Nicaragua, but it was never going to materialize. The guerrilla leader would realize by now that his headquarters had written him off. And now that the end was near, he would either be frantic in his efforts to break the stranglehold that gripped his force so tightly, or he would be resigned to the finality of his fate. Either way, he was still a very dangerous foe.

Twice during the night the guerrillas had attempted to fight their way out of the trap, and twice we had thwarted them. It had been a noble effort on their part, but the attacks were weakly executed, and thus were a fatal waste of ammunition and manpower.

After we threw them back for the second time, I ordered my unit to ready themselves for a final attack at daylight. I had received orders at the start of the mission to corner this unit and kill them to the last man. It was standard procedure for the times. Too often, captives became cause for negotiation or future terrorist action. Martyrs were always much easier to deal with than live opponents.

As the hours and minutes until sunup crept by, I circled our positions, talking to each of my units and giving them some final instructions. I patted the backs of my dirt-caked, exhausted men, and praised each team, telling them, "Just one last push and we'll soon be finished with this wretched affair. Then we'll go back to base and drink beer until we can no longer walk, and I'll pay the tab."

The Hondurans liked that last part. These small, shy men were wicked fighters. They only needed fair treatment and decent leadership to perform like champions. And I was glad we were on the same side.

I told my unit leaders that when I gave the attack order I wanted them to move forward slowly and cautiously, there was no need to hurry. Shift their men from cover to cover, keeping low to the ground, and scorching everything in front of them. I didn't want to see anyone needlessly exposing himself—it was a sure way to get shot. Take no prisoners and take no unnecessary chances.

Then it was time. We unleashed the assault just as the eastern sky showed the first gray light of the new—and for some of us, final—day. The attack unfolded like a textbook example of fire and maneuver. One unit would slither forward like venomous serpents while the others held covered positions and poured out a fatal rain of lead. Then the first unit would go to ground as another group left the lair to stalk their prey.

Deadly, yet hypnotically beautiful, arcs of machine-gun fire crisscrossed the small mountaintop plateau at knee-high level, destroying everything and everyone they touched. The ground shook as hand grenades searched out the crevices and holes in the ground where men clung desperately to life. A dust cloud rose into the sky and then settled back to earth, covering friend and foe alike.

We drew our coils tighter and pressed the attack with savage ferocity. Gradually, relentlessly, we choked the remaining life from our foe. They could no longer run, and there was no place left to hide.

In another hour it was over. Throughout the fight I had been watching, waiting for the guerrilla leader to expose himself. Finally I spotted him. He was up and moving, his radioman at his side, making a last desperate attempt to organize his few remaining scattered troops. I pitched my rifle to my shoulder, saw the sight come to rest just under his ear, slapped the trigger, and shot him through the neck. When the bullet struck, he went down so fast that he seemed to disappear. Fire from two machine guns converged on the spot where he had just been seen.

Moments after the guerrilla leader fell, all resistance collapsed. But I ordered the machine guns to continue their fire for several more minutes and yelled for the men to continue throwing grenades into the low spots and dead ground. After several minutes had gone by with no further movement and no return fire, I called, "Cease fire."

When the last grenade exploded and the shooting abruptly came to an end, the survivors paused to take a breath and listen, and to marvel that they were alive. Warily, I got to my feet and surveyed the tortured earth and the scorched vegetation. My men lay in position and reloaded their weapons with full magazines. The machine gunners changed barrels and clipped on fresh belts of ammunition. There was no other movement to be seen anywhere. But we weren't finished yet.

I radioed the teams to stay alert, to hold their positions and re-consolidate, while Jimmy Masters took one platoon of Hondurans and swept across the guerrilla position. I would take consolidation reports after the objective had been completely cleared.

When Jimmy started his men forward, I took my radio operator and shifted over to join him in the heart of the guerrilla position. I wanted to get to the body of the rebel leader before anyone else found him.

I had information that he was an American citizen who had gone over to the Sandinistas. I was supposed to bring his body, and the bodies of any subordinate guerrilla leaders, back to Tegucigalpa for positive identification. The rest of the guerrillas would be buried where they fell.

A few single scattered shots broke the silence as the Hondurans dispatched any wounded guerrillas they found. Mr. Reagan's secret wars in Central America were always merciless affairs.

I found the body of the guerrilla commander lying next to his radioman. Neither of them was alive. The radioman had not died easily. The machine guns had found him. His left thigh was shredded to the bone and his glistening, purple-gray intestines had spilled from his torn abdomen. Coils of his entrails looped through his fingers and over his dirty hands onto the ground. He had died while trying to keep them from all falling out. He looked about sixteen, with the unwhiskered face of a boy.

The guerrilla commander had crashed to the ground with his left arm crumpled beneath his body and his head twisted to the right. A small, black, dented bruise on the right side of his neck marked where the bullet had found him. The shot had broken his neck, and death had been instantaneous. There was very little blood.

I looked at him awhile and then squatted in the dirt beside him. I felt a need to be near this man. I placed my left hand on his shoulder. Before turning him over and examining him more fully, I paused, to say a silent prayer for all of us here on this mountaintop, both the living and the dead.

It is an awful thing to handle the still-warm body of a man you've just killed. It feels like God has you under a powerful microscope, and is minutely examining the wrinkles and hidden recesses of your soul. It's a moment that is sad, solemn, and utterly lonely. And it clears away all differences among men.

This man was an enemy no longer. He was now my brother—as in reality, he had always been—and I was the instrument of his death. Whatever he had desired in life, whatever his hopes and dreams had been for the future, they were now over. His desires would go unfulfilled.

God almighty. I'm so tired. I was only in my early thirties but I felt like a man who carried the weight of ninety years.

I rolled the man onto his back and looked him over carefully before checking him for documents. He would have been a handsome man in life. Medium-sized and tightly muscled, with a deep chest and wide shoulders, he had the perfect build for a soldier. I gazed at his dirt- and gunpowder-covered face as I closed his glazed eyes.

Jimmy had finished sweeping the perimeter. After positioning his men, he came over to where I was kneeling in the dust. I held up a hand and stopped him before he could give his report.

"Jimmy, take a long look and tell me if you think you've ever seen this man before," I asked as I thumbed through the various papers I had found in the pockets of the corpse. I pulled out a Nicaraguan military ID.

"Jesus Christ, Eric. You know who that is? That's Keekee Saenz. You remember him, don't you? He was in my Special Forces class and he went to Selection with us. I thought I'd heard he went back to 3/7 Special Forces in Panama."

I turned the ID card over and read the name on the front: "Capitan Enrique Eduardo Saenz-Herrera."

Enrique Saenz-Herrera, staff sergeant in the United States Army Special Forces. I remembered him from Selection as a quiet, competent type. A professional. I didn't get the opportunity to know him very well, but I had enjoyed talking with him on several occasions. I remembered now—he had been cut from Selection on the Day of Disappearances. Now he was gone for good. Dead. On a godforsaken, nondescript mountaintop, in a remote and utterly worthless part of the world. And I had killed him.

Something about this was badly wrong, and I was beginning to feel dirty and used. Some of the nagging little oddities about this mission started to come together in my mind. Like why the CIA had pushed so hard for this operation, and why we had been denied other support.

As always when dealing with those people, it was a good chance I wouldn't receive any satisfactory answers, but I was sure as hell going to have a serious talk about this whole mission with the CIA's chief of station when I got back to Tegucigalpa. But I couldn't stop to dwell on my thoughts just now, for there was still much work to do.

I called my other leaders over and received their reports. We had several men seriously wounded but, thankfully, no dead. The medics were at work on the wounded, and Jimmy's team was already clearing a landing zone. I put a detail to work burying the dead guerrillas, and then instructed my radio operator to send the coded report that the mission was accomplished and a call for the helicopters to pick us up.

My eyes throbbed and my head pounded as I pulled my last canteen from its pouch and took a long drink of piss-warm water. I lifted my face skyward and slowly poured the remaining water over my head. Then I wiped the muddy liquid from my face and eyes as I felt the remnants trickle down my chest and soak into my filthy, sweat-soaked jungle shirt. I hadn't smoked in years, but I badly wished for a cigarette.

My knees creaked as I got to my feet and looked around that cratered, weirdly peaceful slice of the earth's surface. The only sound I heard, through ears still ringing from the roar of combat, was the steady clang of entrenching tools chipping away at the rocky ground as a grave was prepared to accept the dead.

Answers? No, I never got any answers to my questions about that mission, only orders to shut up. I did as I was told. In the private world of my own thoughts, I never stopped wondering what it was all really about, if Keekee had really gone over to the Sandinistas, or if he was just an expendable pawn in another incomprehensible game. I just kept my thoughts to myself as my own disillusion and distrust continued to grow. To this day I'm still not sure I have any real answers. I believe this to the core of my being: When he was killed, Keekee Saenz was still working for the United States.

But the world kept revolving, the passage of the seasons marked our circuit around the sun, and the assumption of Bowstring Force marked our own method of tracking the years. By midsummer 1986 I was serving in the Selection and Training Detachment, as the senior instructor for OTC. I had moved over to S&T earlier in the year after being injured on a mission with the British Special Air Service.

I had completely recovered from the physical damage, but truth be told, I was tired. I was slow to admit it to myself, but the last eight years had taken a toll. The life of a Delta Force operator was physically demanding, you had to keep the fitness level of a professional athlete, with no off-season. But more than that, it extracted a decided mental and emotional cost, and that, ultimately, was more draining than anything else.

For a few months I had been toying with the idea of finding another assignment. Overseas somewhere, or maybe back with one

316 ERIC L. HANEY

of the Ranger battalions. It was a hard decision to make, because from here, there was no such thing as up. Professionally any change from Delta Force would be a retrograde, and every time I started to give it some serious thought, I would be overcome with a sense of guilt.

We had lost a lot of men. With debilitating injuries, retirements, reassignments—and deaths—we were barely keeping up with attrition. It was all we could do to keep our personnel numbers at anything close to the unit requirement. And if I elected to leave now, I would be deserting the unit and just adding to the problem.

Then the decision was taken out of my hands. When the results of the recently concluded sergeant major's promotion board were released, I had been selected by the Department of the Army for promotion to the rank of sergeant major—but there was more.

A subsequent board had been conducted to select candidates for appointment to the rank of command sergeant major, the highest noncommissioned rank in the Army, and I was one of the handful of soldiers selected for that position.

It was unbelievable. At one month short of my thirty-fourth birthday, I was the youngest man ever selected for appointment to CSM. Now I would *have* to find a new home. There is only one command sergeant major in any organization. Dan Simpson was our current CSM, and as he jokingly told me, "Haney, I ain't leaving just because you're getting promoted."

That settled it. If the Army was good enough to honor me with promotion to the highest position an NCO could ever hope for, I would repay the honor the best way I knew how. I would return to the regular infantry, where the rubber really meets the road, and give back to the units who carry the brunt of warfare as much of what I had learned in the last sixteen years as I could. When I considered where I would like to serve, there was only one answer: Panáma.

Things were happening down there. I was always going in and out of Panama on missions to Central and South America, and occasionally I would bump into old friends who were stationed there with the 193rd Infantry Brigade. There was another attraction—one of these days, we were going to have to sort things out with the Noriega regime, and when it happened, I wanted to be in on the action.

I placed a call to the sergeant majors' assignment branch at the Army's Military Personnel Center. I was prepared for a long, arduous campaign of negotiation to wrangle the assignment, but when I told the man on the other end of the line that what I'd really like was a posting to Panama, the immediate reply was "Can you be there a week from now?"

I shook off my surprise and answered very quickly, "No, but I can be there in thirty days."

The response was just as rapid. "Okay. Orders for Permanent Change of Station are on the way. Call me back if you haven't received them by day after tomorrow."

That was it. I stopped by to let Dan know I'd start out-processing in a couple of days. The timing would work perfectly. We were constructing a new compound for the unit and it was just about ready. I made up my mind that I would never set foot in the new building as an operator. Instead, I would leave this place for the last time on our final day in the original facility. That way, I would forever be a "stockade man."

And that's exactly how it worked out.

When an operator leaves the unit, there is no sentimental display. No parties, no extended farewells, just a quiet handshake with friends and comrades. And that's the way it should be for an organization with a mission like ours.

On my last day in the unit, I had lunch in the mess hall with some of my old mates from the Selection and Training Detachment. The place was pretty quiet. B Squadron was off in the Middle East chasing an airplane, and A Squadron was out at the drop zone working on a new parachute infiltration technique. The OTC students were out at the range, so there was just a handful of us old-timers gathered around a large table.

I'm going to miss these guys, I thought, looking around the table at my friends. *We've gone through a lot together, these good men and I. And there are a lot of other good men who are no longer here with us, men who have fallen over the years.* But there was no need to be maudlin. The Army is a self-replicating organism, and so is Delta Force. People come and people go, but the unit, and what it stands for, will live forever.

Now it was the time of departure. I was sitting in my truck, in my old parking spot on the lane to the Shooting House, taking a last look around. I cranked the engine and headed out. I didn't want to become teary-eyed and embarrass myself at this late date.

I stopped at the gate to turn in my badge and say good-bye to the guards, then I drove outside the fence for the last time.

I glanced in the rearview mirror as I pulled onto Butner Road and turned right, coasting slowly downhill. The reflection of the concertina wire atop the screened fence was visible for just a moment longer, until I turned the first curve.

Then it was gone.

EPILOGUE

Panama heated up more rapidly than I had anticipated. By the summer of 1987 we were on a decided collision course with the Noriega regime, and tensions reached the point of political boil when the Panamanian strongman negated the results of the May 1988 presidential elections. War was inevitable, and by the time it occurred, it was a welcome relief.

I had been given a free hand to train our troops in the techniques of combat in cities and in the tactics of building clearing and room combat. Additionally I was able to form and train a twelve-man sniper section in each of the two battalions of our small brigade.

When the war came were we ready. Those regular infantry troops performed the most difficult of all military tasks—an unsupported night attack in a city—and they executed the mission with the skill and aplomb of old veterans. Our unit, the 193rd Infantry Brigade, broke the back of the Panamanian defense forces within the city of Panama. We suffered three men killed during the attack and another dozen men wounded. And after an additional three months of cleaning up little pockets of problems, we returned back to our garrisons.

But I was ready to retire. I knew what was in store for the post–Cold War Army, and it looked like a force I didn't want to be a part of. And I figured if I couldn't enthusiastically support the coming changes, it was time to go. I retired from active duty on 1 November 1990 and never looked back.

After returning to the States, I tried being a "normal citizen" but it just wasn't in my blood. A nine-to-five existence was something that felt like a life sentence of dull labor, so I hung out my shingle as a special operations man for hire, and it appeared to be the right thing at the right time.

In my post-military life I have negotiated the release of kidnap victims in Colombia and headed the protective details of a Saudi prince, a couple of emirs, and the CEO of the largest corporation of Mexico. In 1994 I was protective detail leader for President Bertrand Aristide on his return to Haiti.

In between those missions I have worked antiterrorist operations in Algeria, trained foreign Special Operations forces, foiled a coup attempt, and with my close friends, Don and Judy Feeney, have conducted the rescues of American children who had been kidnapped and carried overseas.

Sprinkled throughout those activities were a number of surveys, security audits, and planning crisis response actions for clients doing business in the more dangerous parts of the globe. As I once remarked to a question about why I work the rougher areas of the world, "No one has ever hired me to go to Club Med." And that's the way I like it.

Where has Delta Force been during those years after I departed? The unit moved into its new facility when I left for Panama and immediately worked toward forming a third squadron. That was finally realized as the 1980s came to a close.

Tactics and techniques have remained basically the same since our early days. The foundation we laid in the late seventies and early eighties was solid, but rest assured that the operators have found ways to improve even those thoroughly tested methods. And even minuscule improvements may mean the difference between failure and success, life and death.

As far as equipment, great strides have been made in electronic tools that allow the operators to survey a target and transmit real on-site intelligence back to the TOC. In the same vein, digital photography has sped things up tremendously, as has the use of new high-security radio gear. Some minimal improvement has been made in firearms, but that has been incremental at best. Individual protective equipment has seen great improvement, particularly in body armor and protective headgear.

However, high-speed gadgets are not the reason Delta Force operators are so capable and deadly. They could be armed with muzzle-loading rifles and tomahawks and would still be formidable warriors. No, it is their phenomenal willpower, resolve, and determination that make them the world's premier fighting men. That hasn't changed since the very first days of the unit's existence.

Operationally the unit never rests. In Panama the boys ran General Manuel Noriega to ground and also apprehended a number of his worst henchmen. Afterward they continued their normal activities around the world, with a particular emphasis on Africa. With the outbreak of conflict in the Persian Gulf came missions deep behind the Iraqi lines—missions of both reconnaissance and direct action, culminating with hunter/killer strikes on Scud missile positions in the western Iraqi desert, missiles that were targeted against Israel.

Somalia was a rough one. C Squadron and a company of Rangers were trapped in a Mogadishu neighborhood when their transportation was destroyed and they had to fight for their lives. I've heard a lot of second-guessing from people who have no idea what those men were up against, so I will tell you this: that unit fought against overwhelming odds, all afternoon and throughout the night, with no support and only the weapons they carried in their hands. And they fought that part of the city to complete and utter exhaustion. The next morning, when the relief unit still had not made its way to the location of the survivors, the men of Task Force Ranger walked out on their own power. *And the Somalis left them alone.* They had had enough of those American soldiers.

If there was a failure at all in Somalia, it was a failure of the senior commanders to ensure the men had adequate resources for the job they were given. After Somalia, the unit came home, buried its dead, rebuilt itself, and got on with life.

Since that time Delta Force has been busy in the Balkans and every other hot spot in the world. Now and again, when viewing a particular situation on the evening news, I will catch a glimpse of one of the guys. It's always in a bad place, and the Delta Force member is the man who looks like he's at home.

POST 11 SEPTEMBER 2001

I finished the last major edit of the manuscript of this book several weeks before the terrible attack on that sad Tuesday morning, and I feel compelled to give my thoughts on the situation we face.

There is nothing we can do about the past. We can't go back and fix anything, we can't turn back the clock and pay attention to things that were ignored, but we can work for the future. And the first thing we must do is realize something about ourselves: We are a good and moral people, and we form a nation that is the hope of mankind—quite possibly, the last hope of mankind.

Don't listen to our enemies or the weak sisters in our own ranks who accuse us of all sorts of purposeful atrocities around the world. If we were what our enemies said we were, Afghanistan would be a smoldering and uninhabited moonscape. Iraq would be the same, and quite possibly several other places on the map would be in similar shape.

No, our sins have been those of omission and inattention. At most we have been a selfish people, concentrating our attention on the creation of wealth and becoming fixated on the contemplation of our financial navel. And as you have gathered from this book, we as a nation were never really serious about the threat of terrorism in the past.

Our government did little more than apply Band-Aids to abrasions while ignoring the festering infection within. All we really did was to keep terrorism away from our own shores. Little real work was accomplished because the political leadership lacked the will to tackle the problem, and their lack of willpower was caused by the intuitive knowledge that the American people would not support the effort.

Our enemies became bolder while the nation and its agencies were focused almost exclusively on the petty problems of self-absorption, rampant careerism, and bureaucratic infighting—and then came September 11, 2001.

We now know what we are up against, and I am convinced that we, as a nation, finally have the resolve to protect ourselves and eradicate the scourge of terrorism. But make no mistake, it won't be easy and it won't be quick. The worst parts, the most threatening parts, of the terrorist menace will be eliminated rather rapidly, but that won't be the end of it.

The work will go on for years, if not generations, until the sources and causes that bring about terrorism are addressed and changed. Notice I said changed, and not defeated. For what must change is the attitude of a large part of the Muslim world. The attitude that the United States is responsible for the ills suffered by that segment of the world's population. We can't do the changing for them, but we must help bring it about.

But at the same time that we are working to help the Islamic populations of the globe find their place in the modern world, we must continue to seek out and eradicate terrorist threats wherever they exist. Delta Force will be one of the principal weapons in that fight. Just be grateful that such a force exists and is filled with nothing but dedicated, capable, and self-sacrificing men. Men who willingly put their lives on the line for all Americans.

So I say to you all: Maintain courage. Have hope. Be patient but at the same time be vigilant. And tonight, when you're comfortably in your bed, in those last few quiet moments before you go to sleep, give thanks to whatever deity you speak to that we have a group of men who readily go in the worst of harm's way, and are prepared to lay down their lives, if that's what it takes, so that you can live a life without fear.

Remember, we don't call ourselves "the land of the free and the home of the brave" for nothing.

Eric L. Haney,
American Citizen, Soldier

THEN, NOW, AND THE FUTURE

The world situation has changed in dramatic fashion since I wrote the first edition of this book. America is now committed to a struggle with radical Islam, and with the recognition of that struggle, the first battle has been won.

The infrastructure of Al-Qaeda has been wrecked. By the end of 2001, it lost its sanctuary in Afghanistan and has been on the defensive ever since. Bin Laden's ability to mount credible operations against the United States has been severely degraded. And the very fact that the intelligence organs of our nation are looking and listening (and that within those organizations, counterterrorist functions will now get you promoted) means that Al-Qaeda will have a tremendously more difficult task the next time it attempts to make a direct strike against the United States.

The role of Delta Force during the recent years has continued to be one of the most important elements in the campaign against terrorists. Its members have hunted down and killed most of the high-level operatives of Al-Qaeda and of the Saddam Hussein regime, but its effects have been even wider than that.

The tactics and equipment we developed in Delta have trickled down over the years to the rest of the Army and are paying great dividends today. Not only Army Special Forces and Rangers but the regular infantry units of the Army and Marine Corps are now employing the fruits of Delta Force's pioneering labors. Close Quarter Combat is now a training task for all infantrymen.

Improved body armor is finally (after what I consider a criminal delay) making its way down to the regular units. Even the body armor my troops had in Panama was insufficient to protect them from rifle fire, but the new body armor is working wonders in saving the lives of many of our soldiers.

Weaponry that we developed for our own use is now in the hands of all our combat forces, and it is getting even better. The Army and Marine Corps are in the opening stages of purchasing a completely new weapon to replace the M-16 family of rifles and carbines and the standard squad automatic weapon. The new rifle is much more reliable and easy to use. It has built-in optical sighting and laser designator systems. Its barrel can be quickly changed to reconfigure it from a carbine to a rifle to a light machine gun. Its magazines are plastic and practically unbreakable, and they are transparent so the soldier can tell at a glance how many rounds he still has.

Back in the field of Special Operations, Delta has been busy with new innovations. As I write these words, a new weapon is being adopted for the Special Operations Command. It is similar in some aspects to the new infantry assault rifle, but it has been designed for the peculiar needs of Special Operations soldiers. And the operators of Delta are the ones who drove those design requirements.

Probably one of the greatest benefits that Delta Force has provided has been the men who have served within the unit over the years. Former members, though still relatively few in number, can be found in just about every intelligence and law enforcement field in the nation. And their influence can be felt wherever they are and with whomever they work. Many of the operators have gone on to careers as protective specialists and as such are personally responsible for preserving the lives of dignitaries, business, and government officials around the world.

Delta has been in existence long enough that young men join the Army with the idea that one day they may be able, if they prove themselves, to make their way into the organization. The very fact that it is thus able to perpetuate itself should be comforting to us all.

Delta Force itself has continued to change and adapt to the times while still retaining its basic character. If anything, the wisdom of Colonel Charlie Beckwith in organizing the force around a tightly knit group of specially selected senior NCOs has paid off more than any other military concept in the last three decades.

The Delta Force operator is still the only fighter who can be sent out alone or in very small teams. He can operate under varying degrees of cover and can be trusted to perform extremely delicate missions under his own initiative and with minimal guidance. All he needs is a mission and the necessary resources to take on the threats we face.

Still, there remain many difficult challenges ahead.

Contrary to what some people say, the Bin Ladens of the world have no thought whatsoever of bringing down our government or destroying the American way of life or converting the West to Islam. Their objective is simple: they want things the way they were a thousand years ago. Their fervent desire is for a pan-Islamic government encompassing the entire Muslim world.

The terrorists' tactic is to inflict pain and suffering upon us, as they believe they suffer from our existence and at our hands. They believe that if we are made to suffer sufficiently, we will recoil in cowardice and leave them once again to their own devices. But the world is just too small for that to happen, and the good old days never were that good, either in the Middle East or in the West. That brings us now to the War on Terror and our invasion and occupation of Iraq.

Islamic terror has morphed over the last thirty years. When I first entered into the fray, terrorism against America was the province of the Palestinians, but since the mid-1980s the Palestinian factions have renounced the use of terror against America and concentrated their energies directly against Israel.

About the time the Palestinians dropped that cudgel, the Islamic Revolutionary government of Iran adopted it wholesale, and for the next decade or so it and its surrogates committed a drumroll of attacks against American targets and interests.

Then along came the Iraqi invasion of Kuwait, and the American-led war to push Saddam's forces back inside their own border (principally to protect the Saudis or more particularly the Saudi oil fields). The outcome was this: a boiling, rolling hatred within Saudi Arabia for the United States.

The original manifesto of Bin Laden and Al-Qaeda centered on the presence of the Western infidel on the sacred soil of Saudi Arabia. To say that this idea found fertile soil in the populace is a sublime understatement. The Saudis have a fear and loathing of foreigners, and not just Westerners, that is astounding to anyone who has never been witness to it.

The Saudis are "the Pure Ones." In their eyes, the strain of religion they practice is the only pure strain, and almost no one else measures up. They are rabid in their practice of religion, and they have worked diligently to spread their particular view and version throughout the Muslim world.

Know this if you know nothing else: Islamic terrorism in its current form is a creation of the Saudis. It has its ideological source in Saudi Arabia. It has been funded from Saudi Arabia. It has been exported by Saudi Arabia. Fifteen of the nineteen hijackers of 9/11 were from Saudi Arabia. Al-Qaeda was conceived and developed by a Saudi. Most of its members are Saudis, and the bulk of Al-Qaeda prisoners held at Guantánamo Bay are also Saudis. The fundamentalist *madrassas*, the religious schools that preach such intolerance and hatred around the Muslim world, are principally funded by Saudis.

The Saudi monarchy expelled Bin Laden because his first pronouncement was to replace the monarchy with his own movement. And that message has found traction with the people of Saudi Arabia because the royal family is so notoriously and publicly corrupt. But the Saudi government, at all levels, has been complicit with Al-Qaeda and other extremist groups both before and since 9/11. So why the attack against Iraq and not a full-court press against the Saudis, demanding that they change their ways?

The Saudi monarchy, the vast house of Al-Saud, wants one thing above all others: maintenance of its own power. This is an extended family that in essence owns a country, and a mighty rich country at that.

It was not always so. Saudi Arabia was created in 1932 when the patriarch of the family, Abdulaziz, had by war and treaty unified the tribes of the current state, pronounced himself king, and announced the creation of Saudi Arabia, which means "Arabia of the Saud family." Almost immediately after the creation of the kingdom, vast oil deposits were found and the U. S. government, in order to forestall the British, moved in and cuddled up to the king. The result was Aramco (the Arabian/American Oil Company), a consortium of the big American petroleum outfits that carved up the pie for the benefit of all. The pie stayed principally in American hands, with the Saudi ruling house receiving its royalties, until the early 1970s, when the host government took over the operation. At that point the Americans became clients and dependents. And since that time the Saudis have wielded their incalculable wealth and vast oil reserves as an invisible yet terribly powerful weapon.

The political upper class of the United States (and that includes members of both political parties down to third-level appointees) have kowtowed to the house of Al-Saud for decades. As consultants and board members of companies doing business with the Saudis, they have been well paid for their obeisance, which brings us to the current situation.

The ruling regent of Saudi Arabia, Prince Abdullah, and the rest of the ruling faction sit very precariously on the throne. I can tell you from first-hand experience, as one who has lived in the kingdom and worked in the house of Al-Saud, that the people hate the members of the monarchy with a quiet passion, and the monarchy knows it.

The CIA has predicted that the monarchy, in its current state, will probably not survive another five years. So again, if this is true, why attack Iraq and not Saudi Arabia? The reason is that the only thing that could possibly replace the Saudi monarchy is an Islamic extremist government the likes of which the world has not yet seen. There is no other internal possibility. In fact, that government is waiting in the wings.

The Ulema, the court of senior Islamic scholars, is the group that interprets Muslim law and advises the Crown on how the law should be enforced. Saudi Arabia is the only nation in the world where the Sharia, Muslim law, is the law of the land, and the Ulema is the entity that wields the power of that law. Its major function is to tell the people that the house of Al-Saud rules by divine right and at the will of Allah. When a similar theocracy existed in Europe, it resulted in the Inquisition.

The Ulema is a group of religious extremists and fundamentalists who would put the rest of the world to the sword if that world did not follow their edicts. They do so within their own country, and they have exported their extreme views to the poorest and most desperate areas of the Muslim world.

The attack into Iraq, the overthrow of the regime of Saddam

Hussein, and the imposition of a friendly (or at least complaisant) government in that country was conceived as a means of corralling Saudi Arabia. Iraqi oil would be a counterbalance to the Saudi oil reserves. Iraq would provide a base of operations from which to seize the Saudi oil fields, because there is no way an American government could allow that massive wealth to be used by the worst possible form of an extremist government.

Even with limited wealth, a radical Saudi regime would be a thing of sheer terror. The excesses of the Islamic Revolutionary government of Iran would seem like child's play by comparison. And if that isn't bad enough, another nightmare scenario is to be found farther east.

What would be your response if a radical Islamic nation possessed not only nuclear weapons but also the ballistic missiles necessary to deliver them? The world is only one coup away from such a reality, and that reality is Pakistan.

Pakistan was created as a Muslim nation. It was the largest recipient of Saudi money used to fund the *madrassas*. Within Pakistan there were, and still are, hundreds of these schools teaching the virulent Saudi-inspired strain of Islam and espousing hatred of all things Western.

Pakistan's government was one of the few to recognize the Taliban regime of Afghanistan. Pakistan changes government by coup. The current Pakistani president, General Pervez Musharraf, seized power in a military coup. Large segments of the Pakistani government, especially within the army and the secret intelligence services, were very sympathetic to Al-Qaeda and the Taliban. Musharraf has been the target of at least three close assassination attempts within the last year.

Were an Islamic extremist government, one sympathetic to the aims of Al-Qaeda, to seize power in Pakistan, India would have no choice but to attack with nuclear weapons. There is a long and deadly history of violence between the Hindus of India and the Muslims of Pakistan. At the partition of India and Pakistan, Muslims and Hindus waged a vicious campaign of violence against each other, and they continue to do so to this day.

In the teachings of Islam, Christians and Jews are known as

"People of the Book," fellow monotheists who worship the same God as that of the Muslims. According to the Quran, Christians and Jews are to be well treated and even protected by Muslims. Hindus, as polytheists, receive no such consideration and are regarded as veritable enemies of God, worthy only of extermination.

Just a few years ago India and Pakistan rattled their nuclear sabers at each other. In a surreal war of words, otherwise intelligent people on each side of the border clamored for the final showdown between their two nations. In Nevil Shute's classic and chilling novel *On the Beach,* the war that destroys mankind starts in a similar manner—as a nuclear exchange initiated, not by the major nations of the world, but by the smaller ones, the "Irresponsibles."

So what do we do? First, we need an American administration that will come clean with the American public about its true aims in the Middle East. Next we must support, to the hilt, the objective of achieving an equitable peace between the Israelis and the Palestinians. If such a peace can be achieved, it will take away a major propaganda tool of the Islamic extremists. We must help the Islamic world develop to its maximum economic potential, and I'm not speaking here of oil production alone.

A country whose principal source of wealth is oil is a politically corrupt country, and that's just the way it is. A quick look around the world will reveal the truth of that statement. In countries that have a lot of oil, wealth is held in too few hands. There are not enough jobs to go around. Idle men in their twenties (the prime recruiting age for militants) are always ripe for trouble. But those who have a meaningful job and a young family to support are too decisively engaged in the business of life to be lured into jihad by the hateful rhetoric of mad mullahs.

Next, we must all realize that military action cannot cure social ills (and terrorism is a symptom of those ills). It is possible to confront enemy combatants by force and at least put them on the defensive and thereby lessen their ability to attack. But military force alone will never bring about a cure.

The only answer is a long-term and mature approach to helping the people of the Middle East, and the greater Islamic world, develop the ability to create popularly elected governments that promote individual liberty. In essence, we must help them create what we enjoy here in the United States.

If we are patient, and if we are smart, we can help that ideal come about. It will take time and effort and a genuine concern for human rights. If we focus solely on gaining access to oil riches in that part of the world, we, and its inhabitants, are doomed to a perpetual cycle of murderous violence.

The good side of all this is that those things are starting to poke their heads above ground like the first lilies of spring. The current administration is starting to speak about the requirement for democratic development in the region, even among the despotic regimes that the United States has long supported. Perhaps we are on the threshold of change that may usher in a whole new era for the Middle East and the world.

I, for one, believe that it is about to happen. I saw that sort of change take place in Latin America. By the start of the 1990s, the Latin American dictator was an extinct species, and fledgling democracies were building throughout the region. Now, let's help the Muslim world achieve those same results. It's a much better idea than killing one another.

Eric L. Haney
8 March 2005

ACKNOWLEDGMENTS

I have many people to thank for the assistance I received in writing this book. And although I'm sure I'll miss a few, here are those I wish to publicly thank.

My deepest thanks to Katie Hall of Random House for believing in the project and giving it life. To Fred Willard for his advice, companionship, and conversation about writing. To my great friend, Gene Hanratty, for being my honest broker and keeping me straight. To my brother, Lowell Haney, for the electronic storage of the manuscript and his keen insight. To Frank Weimann, the Delta Force of agents. To Irwyn Applebaum and Nita Taublib of Bantam Dell for their consideration and vision. To my editor and fellow paratrooper, John Flicker, for his invaluable eye and professional abilities. To the people of the United States of America for allowing me to serve in their Army. But most especially I thank my wife, Dianna, without whom this would have all been an empty gesture, void of meaning or personal value.